Hope Betrayed
A
Stripping
of
Trust

HOPE
BETRAYED
A
STRIPPING
OF
TRUST

CHARLES R. KUHN

Copyright © 2023 by Charles R. Kuhn

All rights reserved. No part of this publication may be reproduced, distributed, or transmitted in any form or by any means, including photocopying, recording, or other electronic or mechanical methods, without the prior written permission of the copyright owner and the publisher, except in the case of brief quotations embodied in critical reviews and certain other noncommercial uses permitted by copyright law. For permission requests, write to the publisher, addressed "Attention: Permissions Coordinator," at the address below.

ARPress
45 Dan Road Suite 5
Canton MA 02021

Hotline: 1(888) 821-0229
Fax: 1(508) 545-7580

Ordering Information:

Quantity sales. Special discounts are available on quantity purchases by corporations, associations, and others. For details, contact the publisher at the address above.

Printed in the United States of America.

ISBN-13:   Paperback   979-8-89330-684-2
            eBook   979-8-89330-685-9
            Harback   979-8-89389-138-6

Library of Congress Control Number: 2024902690

TABLE OF CONTENTS

CHAPTER 1 1
CHAPTER 2 6
CHAPTER 3 12
CHAPTER 4 14
CHAPTER 5 17
CHAPTER 6 20
CHAPTER 7 23
CHAPTER 8 29
CHAPTER 9 37
CHAPTER 10 40
CHAPTER 11 43
CHAPTER 12 48
CHAPTER 13 58
CHAPTER 14 67
CHAPTER 15 76
CHAPTER 16 80
CHAPTER 17 88
CHAPTER 18 100
CHAPTER 19 106
CHAPTER 20 114
CHAPTER 21 124
CHAPTER 21 134
CHAPTER 22 138

CHAPTER 23	142
CHAPTER 24	149
CHAPTER 25	166
CHAPTER 26	177
CHAPTER 27	197
CHAPTER 28	207
CHAPTER 29	214
CHAPTER 30	230
CHAPTER 31	237
CHAPTER 32	249
CHAPTER 33	271
CHAPTER 34	282
CHAPTER 35	297
CHAPTER 36	303
CHAPTER 37	307
EPILOGUE	320

CHAPTER 1

The first attempt on my life came one fall morning. It came from nowhere. Though terrified by the event, I was not surprised, nor without forethought that it might happen.

Months before I had been diagnosed with a disease. It slowly robbed me of certain skills abilities. The disease would not take me, but it did lay out a dim future. My ability to walk on two strong legs was stolen. Though confined to a wheelchair, my ability to think, to reason, to understand and to predict were not lost. I knew why the death threats had been sent and now, an assassination attempt came for me. The only question answered that morning, was when.

As I wheeled my chair, no more than two blocks from my apartment I suddenly heard the noise of impending doom and snapped my head to the right to absorb the sound of tortured tires squealing across asphalt. The smell of burnt rubber and the rising smoke pushed me into a flight instinct even as I realized escape in my wheelchair was useless.

I witnessed the reality of the moment as death rushed toward me. In an automatic reflex, I tightened my weakened body and bent at the waist into a ball of muscle and bone at the anticipated compression. In a split second I tried to prepare for the shock that would end my life. This was the moment they came for me. This was the moment I knew would come.

Terror enveloped me at the impact that would throw me from my wheelchair against some immobile object. My mind screamed out, but the expected blow to my handicapped body did not come. *What happened? Where was it?*

The instrument of my death struck the curb and sailed airborne. The car rotated to the driver's side with violent abruptness from the moment of impact against the high curb, the front wheels still turned from the violent change in direction the car had taken in the street. The curb, the violent turn, the shift in the center of gravity of the careening vehicle, were just enough to send it into an unbalanced rotation away from me in a contorted twist of speeding metal.

A tremendous rush of heat scorched my back as it missed me by inches. The car nearly tore a woman to pieces just starting to step by me, who began to scream, "My God!" over and over again. I heard the noise of the hurtling vehicle, the woman screaming, and knew I would never forget the terror of that moment. Someone's world had been rocked, but whom?

Flight was paramount in my mind. It would be useless to fight against a hidden adversary, so the flight instinct kicked into high gear. I crouched in the chair, and reached for the wheels, gripping them with adrenaline charged strength and pushed to rotate the wheels so hard that I began to flip backwards in the air. I grasped the chair in a white knuckled grip and flung my weight forward to reverse gravity, and avoid being thrown to the sidewalk. The front wheels of the chair lifted and now settled to earth, not with a slam onto the pavement as expected, but as a gentle caress back to reality.

The pace of time slowed as I anticipated would occur when the psyche experienced sudden, unexpected moments of horror. Books had told me events would slow as if the gates to eternity opened and sucked the very air of existence from the world and then with a great rush, the gates would slam back into their rightful position, as the true pace of life roared back.

I immediately pushed hard to escape the chaos. The thunderous explosion of the vehicle against the building alongside the sidewalk shook the ground. My attention jerked to the wall. The vehicle had smashed into the brick structure I had been rolling parallel to. The windshield blew out and became a mass of flying glass shards. The front end of the car transformed into a compressed chunk of crumbled metal.

The wall seemed to shudder. Red brick dust filled the air, as if a fine mist of blood circulated around me. But, this was the injured blood of the building, now damaged but not fatally maimed by its injury. A thin layer of broken brick particles and mortar crumbled into ash by the crushing impact floated in the air, as an eerie darkness crept into the daylight, signaling mourning could begin.

Screams raised in terrified commotion were swallowed up by the gasps of the dying vehicle. Hot steam blasted from the fractured radiator. The damaged fan blade shrieked against metal as it ground to a final stop. The screams of the woman standing near me echoed against my ears. Death and injury cried for ritual assistance. Neither succumbed and neither was successful in their gasps.

Though stunned, I continued my escape. Perhaps fear, or adrenaline, or an instinct to survive drove me, yet I knew I must head in the opposite direction. Flight remained my mantra. Escape was paramount. My chair accelerated as I pushed harder in a desperate getaway from the horrific scene.

My adrenaline pumped and heart pounded. I couldn't believe the attempt had actually happened. Whoever did this would now live with the consequences of their actions. I would survive. Right then and there, I swore to complete my investigation and I renewed my commitment.

As I reached the next corner, I hesitated a moment and looked back at the carnage. Debris splayed onto the street. People scrambled around the scene. The airbag in the crippled car had deflated and rested against the slumped driver. The passenger door had been crumpled and ripped from its hinges. I could see the driver's head slumped atop the steering wheel, eyes fixed in a dead glassy stare. Blood stained his face. Although I could see the mustache and brown hair, I didn't recognize his features, but I did see metal rods that had come up through the floor of the car impaling him in place. The proposed instrument of my death had become another's.

Sirens wailed. Though the sound of the impact had ended, horror still swirled near the tragedy. The fall chill that surrounded me seemed colder than moments before. People began to emerge from nearby buildings drawn by the horrific sounds.

Many exited their office doors with shouts of shock at the horror that unfolded on their street. A typical American city thoroughfare had turned into the bleachers of the neighborhood tragedy.

I had no way to prove it at that moment, yet I intuitively knew the accident was an attempt to extinguish my life and silence my voice forever, most likely by one of the many hate mongers casting their aspersions at me through their vitriol laced nasty-grams. The attempt had failed. My efforts to help myself, no matter the political correctness of my pursuits would not be stopped.

The importance of my survival intensified. I grappled with the thought that some people would resort to any action to silence the truth that would change their existence. Whether the hate-mongers or, industrial power brokers, or both, I had stumbled on during my newfound intensive research, their secrets threatened to bare to the world a tale of deception, so deep and dark that those who hated me, or wanted to protect their secrets, would resort to murder. I came to the hard realization the ramifications of my research were no longer just about me. This was much bigger. I now had to deal with the reality that my own life might be sacrificed in pursuit of a greater truth.

Chapter 2

My life changed the moment I heard that heartless expression of death tossed at me. It originally came from a physician. It came callously, with little sympathy. Turmoil enveloped me. I saw no way to escape the uninvited guest at my table. There were snippets throughout the day where I found respite from the horror, but the stench of death couldn't be scrubbed from my skin.

Peace of mind of any kind was found only in the hope that I might one day escape this nightmare. Only through my search for answers to the unexplainable dimension I found myself trapped within could I immerse myself in a cleansing tub of hopeful suds to attempt to wash the stench of death and illness from my body and watch gleefully as it swirled down the drain at the end of each day. I became addicted to scrubbing the odor away.

When I now look back on that life altering moment, I recognize the doctor's prognosis had not been uttered in in thoughtless hate, just represented an incredible insensitivity, near cruelty I now tried to wipe from my mind.

Previous to my diagnosis, I experienced physical changes that first led me to seek medical help culminating in the doomsday forecast.

The initial changes started quietly, and escalated to rob me of one of my senses. I lost eyesight in my left eye. Daylight turned to darkness. My nerves were on edge. I neared panic, plagued by dire thoughts and questions I couldn't answer.

Fear of blindness filled each moment. Time taken to read the paper became a moment of the past. Simple tasks, long taken for granted, took on new difficulty. Normality vanished from my life.

When I could no longer deny the inevitable, I scheduled a doctor's appointment and diagnosis began. Then two new words entered my world. Multiple sclerosis, or more simply represented by the acronym MS.

I simply asked the doctor to define MS for me. I was a newbie, a neophyte. This was as all new to me. "Will you define MS for me?" I asked the ophthalmologist I visited that day life changed for me. His reply tagged him irreversibly in my mind with the label Dr. Frankenstein, and will never be forgotten, or forgiven.

He answered precisely, with a cold and cruel directness.

"MS is a disease that affects the central nervous system, and results in death."

Wait a second! I'm 37 years old! This could not be true! My health had always been good. I was always active, very much alive, employed, played to win, drank a beer on weekends, every once in a while the occasional cocktail. *How could my life take such a dramatic turn?*

The weight of the unknown wore on me. I dug into research to learn of the illness I had been saddled with. I found there was no known cure or cause. It was a mystery, one of unacceptable ramifications.

I found I could lose the use of my limbs, cognitive function and a laundry list of other potential heart breaks. Such was the legacy of MS.

But, I refused to be so callously tossed into that barrel, defined so simply by the acronym MS. I vowed to fight back against this invisible monster. MS might try to take a seat at my table, but it wasn't welcome. No invitation had been extended and no courtesy was to be offered. I would fight back. I would research. I would study. I would find a way to toss this unwelcome guest from my presence. MS didn't define me. I refused to succumb to its curse.

I studied. I learned. And most of all, I moved towards an understanding of shedding the scarlet acronym, MS.

Slowly, my mobility was taken. It did not stop me. A wheelchair became a necessary tool to maintain normal tasks. They were accomplished at a slower speed, but they were still accomplished.

During the early stages of diagnosis and treatment, in my restless moments of quiet, I considered the uninvited guest that had showed up without announcement. It displayed no manners, possessed stinky breath, foul body odor, and ate with smacks, drools and burps with no regard for others. My goal was to find a way to eradicate it, to kill it to kick it from my life for good.

But, I found no immediate cure to accomplish this goal. My eyesight returned, though I knew the monster lurked waiting to throw my life into chaos at its first opportunity. Before it could strike again, I continued my research to find a way to deal with the beast, before it devoured my heart and soul. I knew a cure was under development. It had to be. I refused to accept any other possibility.

I had always reacted to the world in a very workman like manner. When faced with a dilemma, the answer must be found. It had worked for me before. Questions raised more questions. Logic demanded an answer. There was no reason to change my formula now.

The need to understand pushed me onward. I was determined to prove Dr. Frankenstein wrong. Death did not wait at my door.

In my new existence, life changed. I spent hours with my

nose buried in medical texts, in the review of MS research from around the world, and soon I knew more than I ever wanted to know about auto-immune disease. My passion to learn of the illness that infected me turned me into an encyclopedia of the illness.

The long term prognosis was poor. There were no treatment options. The term 'management' drugs entered my world, and I learned the beast could be controlled, but not thrown out the door. Still, my pursuit did not waiver. To accept the unacceptable was simply unacceptable. I clung to hope for improvement, yet existed in a dismal state of malcontent.

Finally, I found a beacon of light that could help illuminate the darkness I traveled through. The use of stem cells for medical regeneration of diseased or damaged tissues ignited a spark of hope, a means to tame the untamable. My crusade took on an even greater part of my life.

I wrote letters, made telephone calls, and sent e-mails to those in positions of power to gain whatever foothold of influence I could find. The use of stem cells to cure disease took on a new life for me. My contact list grew.

Time to lobby the State legislature for increased research funds into the cause and cure of MS was etched into my schedule.

I soon developed a reputation not only as a passionate spokesperson on living with MS, but for the advancement of stem cell utilization. I was relentless in my pursuit, and as my tenacity began to be recognized, my opponents began to emerge.

My name appeared in newspaper articles, I was invited as a guest speaker on radio talk shows, I began a blog and posted about my success and failures, and even a national news program did a story on me. My personal information no longer stayed private, my identity no longer secret.

Then, the hate letters began. I read them all. *Why?* I asked myself that many times each evening. I needed to learn it all, including their opinions, perhaps for comic relief, maybe to know each side of the argument.

The nasty-grams mostly repeated the same vile anger. After a quick scan of a half dozen one night, the seventh grabbed my attention. 'You will die soon. You won't know how, or when, yet you will know why. You cannot expect your blasphemous actions to go un-punished.'

The attempt on my life by the car accident came shortly thereafter.

The anger in the hate letters manifested a new fear in me. I had been exposed to unkind words before in my life, even suffered the cruel backlash of their tortuous meaning, but nothing like this had ever been thrown at me.

These words took on a revulsion that scared me, made me shake at night, double check to make sure the door locks had been secured, and forced me to watch over my shoulder. Hate filled rhetoric from people like these indoctrinated me into their callous beliefs, changed my thoughts and actions, my very world.

By and large the letters mostly carried the same message. That was a message of fierce hatred that burdened me daily. A hatred that stemmed from their beliefs I was advocating against the rights of the unborn.

Compassion had always been a part of my life. I had a strong love for my daughter and at one time, my ex-wife. I loved my childhood dog, family members, success at my job, and winning, whether at the stock market, or the weekend softball game. To win exhilarated me, and now victory at the biggest challenge of my life, became essential.

The debate over stem cell utilization in the use of medical procedures was a hotly contested subject that filled each vile letter I received. *Did no one have any compassion? Why couldn't they understand?* It seemed so simple. My goal was not to be a killer of life unborn, but a survivor bent on improvement. To better my existence, and return to normality, to be able to perform simple tasks was my only goal. *Was this so hard to understand?* Compassion and empathy of any kind took on a new meaning for me.

I wondered where the venomous hatred in the letters I received came from. How could these people I had never met have such contemptuous regard for me? I began to gain a better understanding when I found this was more than the argument of the use of life for the betterment of life. This involved the use of money and power, used to stoke the incredible hatred towards me. This elaborate web had been spun to maintain strength, money and solitude. My simple effort to help myself threatened to bring it crashing down.

Chapter 3

My supervisor, William Blane called me into his office. I made my way with mixed anticipation. It surprised me to find a corporate manager also present.

Mr. Blane blurted out, "You're fired." He complained my research deviated from tech companies I had been assigned to track and leaned towards the medical industry. The company already employed specialists in that area. The corporate manager stayed silent and listened. Mr. Blane offered me continued company medical insurance, termination pay and payment of accrued vacation with obvious reluctance.

The intricacies of the moment were lost on me. I had toyed with the thought of unemployment, but now the reality set in.

As I rose and left shaken, *it had ended,* circulated through my head. After eight years, my employment with Northern Brokerage had come to an end.

Unbeknownst to me, after I departed the office, the corporate manager returned to his upstairs suite, and picked up his phone to make a call. He couldn't wait to make his report.

"Good afternoon, Ashton Pharmaceuticals. How may I direct your call?"

"To Steven Drake, please. This is Robert Samuels."

After the transfer, Robert started. "Steven, Robert from Northern here."

"Did you complete the task?" asked Steven.

"Mr. Armstrong no longer can be considered an employee here."

"Good. Have you scanned his hard drive yet?"

"It will happen tomorrow. I'll let you know if you show up anywhere."

"We can't afford that, Robert. Let me know as soon as possible, and Robert," Steven said in a threatening tone, "Keep this private."

Steven Drake peered over his eye-glasses at the award certificate on the wall received last year, and hung up the handset. 'For Ten Years of Admirable Service as Vice President of Communications' the certificate read. Steven hoped the minor blip on the radar screen would now disappear.

CHAPTER 4

Previous to my dismissal, the research into my diagnosis and search for a potential cure or treatment continued to be my obsession. Help might arrive someday, though much too slow in my opinion. I would not, could not sit idly by and wait. I wasn't built that way.

Following my diagnosis, I listened to the same old diatribe from doctors, friends, or support groups. It became obvious my destiny lie up to me to find a way to keep the snarls, snaps, and sharp teeth of the beast at bay. My future lay in my hands.

It was easy for me to become disenchanted in my search for hope to beat the beast back. During this emotionally trying time, to find that one glimmer became my quest. Others looked for it. They researched, studied, and wrote. *Except, did the professionals understand the urgency? After all, this diagnosis belonged to me, not to them. How many of those who looked for an answer, also have the illness?*

For me, the personal side resonated. For others, their job performance mattered. I researched. My job suffered, which would come back to haunt me, however my new task kept me enthralled and drove me on.

I was given latitude at work for quite a while, due to my rising star achieved in the rise of the technology sector that afforded me certain privileges allowing my indiscretions to be over looked, at least initially. My success during the dot com era had not gone unnoticed. The company made money, as did its clients and enough by me was set aside for a rainy day that would help fund my future endeavors.

The work tasks assigned me, I still performed with diligence, but knew my divergence into my personal quest drew attention, and could result in the outcome I so dreaded.

The bio-technology and medical industry became my new playground. As anticipated, my direction gained notice from my co-workers and my supervisor, culminating in my termination.

Prior to my dismissal, a cohort, Amber, offered her assistance in what she saw as my new found passion. She was close to my age, attractive, and smart. She offered to help in my research endeavor, an offer I could not refuse. Her participation seemed to be from compassion for her work, perhaps flirtation, or so I thought. However, a deeper secret lie tucked away, one based on her philosophical belief. It stayed hidden as a dangerous secret fueled by her passion and her indoctrination into the teaching of the moral right, received throughout her life.

My own life became consumed by research into my disease. Amber's cute remarks, tight sweaters, short skirts, baby blues, and flirtatious comments failed to distract me.

I lived alone, had divorced some years back, and found time to throw myself into research without other personal commitments holding me back.

My divorce moved forward in as amicable a manner as possible. We married after college, in a rush to tackle the world. The passion of our relationship became buried in our desire to advance our careers, without acknowledgement of the attention needed to keep the domestic fires alive.

The marriage produced a baby girl we loved, although she threw a curve into the job success both of us desired. The failure to meet our professional goals led to disappointment, which led to the collapse of our marriage.

We made the decision to move on alone, and share joint custody of our beautiful baby girl, Brenda. Our co-parenting arrangement allowed Brenda to grow into my pride and joy. She recently turned sixteen, a vivacious, intelligent, athletic young lady who could do no wrong in my eyes. My presence at her soccer games, school plays, and numerous other events soon became a ritual.

When not with my daughter, my weekends were devoted to my computer, or trips to libraries, in pursuit of additional applicable research data. My letter and telephone campaign continued unabated.

My commitment soon made me an unofficial spokesperson for living with MS and the search for a beneficial treatment program.

The grid of interested onlookers in the bio-technology and medical treatment industry soon lit up. My activities took on new importance to those in the shadows. No one could generate such energy on such a controversial topic and not draw attention. My activities attracted interest. Quiet surveillance was soon initiated to track my endeavors.

My education curve into MS grew. My multi-task chores of balancing work and a new research direction continued for over two years. I recognized it would only be a matter of time before my employers called me on it. And, then one day they did, though I had no idea of the involvement of others in that decision making process.

CHAPTER 5

My return to my apartment the night after my termination found me shaken. It seemed my world had collapsed. My research work must continue. Except now, I wondered, *how?* Economic stability was required. I had savings, but how long before I exhausted that supply?

The next day started off slowly, but then I leapt into my research more determined than ever. To give up, or in could not be considered.

That day, I spent hours in the pursuit of undiscovered information. In between time, I printed resumes and addressed them to prospective employers.

My research tactics changed from a study of the disease to a review of treatments and stem cell regeneration techniques. Hope seemed dim.

How could this be? I lived as a citizen of the 21st century. A man had landed on the moon. Vaccines had been developed. How could illnesses have no cure, no treatment and no defined cause? The enormity of this reality made me dizzy. *How could it be?* It enraged me. There must be a way. My search continued with even greater drive to uncover answers.

Thousands of people every day received the news the medical affliction they carried might have ties to genetic inheritance. This presented me another scare, and a sad curse of my heritage.

At first diagnosis, the illness affected me alone. Now I learned the sunshine of my life, my daughter, could suffer the same. The leg massages given at bedtime as a child stood out clearly in my mind. Those originally had been blamed on growth pains. Now there was the potential they may have been the start of more ominous developments.

At age seventeen, she began to walk off-balance. Her future became cloudy. She could no longer play soccer, or run long distances.

Together with my ex-wife, we scheduled the doctor appointments. A full regiment of tests ensued. They poked and prodded, took pictures, put her through diagnosis hell. The neurologist sat before me, my ex-wife and daughter weeks after my job loss.

"I'm sorry to tell you this," the doctor started. "Brenda's symptoms indicate the early onset stage of MS." I erupted like a volcano.

"How could that be?" I shouted. "She's a teenager! Onset stage of MS was defined as hitting in the twenty or thirty year old age group. Not during teenager years!"

"Don't shoot the messenger, James," the doctor pleaded with his hands thrown up. "We have found MS can be contracted at much earlier ages than we knew in the past. The first stage of MS as you know is called relapsing remitting. It comes and it goes. It can even impact infants these days." It did no good. I sat stone faced, lost in my depression.

We left that day transfixed on the disease. The continuous injections, the potential loss of mobility, and the many challenges she faced weighed on us all. My worst nightmare had materialized. My illness no longer mattered. Hers meant everything.

My hope had always been to shield her from this potential. Now failure squarely faced me in my greatest mission in life.

My search took on new importance and intensity. I threw myself with greater aggressiveness into the unknown. The ultimate answer became bigger than me. The message changed. My own anxieties must be buried for the betterment of my daughter. Crisis mode arrived. All the rules changed.

At the moment of her diagnosis, she became my only concern. My own predicament and loss of job was irrelevant. My daughter's diagnosis changed the formula.

Super charged by this cataclysmic news, my efforts were amplified to find success. It seemed a problem with no answer, but that finality, I would not accept.

My letters to medical companies, pharmaceutical manufacturers, politicians and doctors continued. I targeted those that seemed most connected to the disease. I continued to make phone calls. My relentlessness continued. Any potential relevant information on the planet was pursued. Hope of any kind developed into the greatest endeavor of my life. To hope for anything less was simply unacceptable.

CHAPTER 6

As my activity picked up, so did that of my monitors. Then it happened. The moment I had worked so tirelessly for.

The call came from Ashton Pharmaceuticals, a company I contacted earlier that had been on my list. They invited me to form a relationship. *I wondered what that meant. Did it mean a new high level trial?* I made travel plans.

Our get together started with nervous apprehension on my part. I was ushered into a luxurious board room filled with an array of professionals. These people did not make up the public relations staff or laboratory technicians. They included upper managers, legal professionals and higher echelon personnel.

I determined to listen and offer little information about myself, or current direction. They did not speak of medical trials, but asked me to participate in a partnership. My diligent efforts had attracted their attention, and they believed my drive and knowledge could uncover information they themselves would not. They asked for a communal use of skills to mine data.

It thrilled me. The offer came with a small stipend that would help me through my period of unemployment. This had become an agreement to move forward. If we enjoyed success together, my daughter and I would be the recipient of that success through preferential treatment.

The agreement allowed me to perform my work in whatever manner I deemed appropriate. The one caveat called for me to write and submit status reports every two weeks to note any new information uncovered.

The question arose in my mind, *Why me? A firm as big as their own could muster the resources to do their own work.* I asked the question.

Excellent point they noted. However, as big as they appeared, they did not have the same personal tie to treatment as I did. The arrangement made sense and acceptance of their offer sealed the agreement. My role had taken on that of a contributor. I had taken a position of strength in my own destiny.

As I departed, various players within the boardroom stayed behind. Their conversation stayed subdued.

Later I learned, Steven Drake, the Vice President of Communications arrived. Mr. Drake started the conversation.

"Did he buy it?" he asked.

One of the senior members of their legal team replied affirmatively.

Drake reminded everyone in the room of the implication of the direction they pursued. He then had asked of one of their prominent, yet secretive supporters.

Legal staff suggested they not be brought in at that point. Other members in the board room agreed.

Mr. Drake was shown an updated conglomerated balance sheet.

All parties except Sheldon Medical had made their contributions for the month.

Drake addressed Frederick Todd, head of security for the corporation regarding the ongoing surveillance of Mr. Armstrong. Mr. Todd assured Mr. Drake resources were in place.

Drake rose and left the room and the remainder of the assembled members agreed their silent partner would not be pleased, but concluded the meeting satisfied their goal.

During my trip back home, I enjoyed a moment of quiet fulfillment.

That weekend, I shared a takeout pizza and beer with Amber, and told her of the agreement forged with the pharmaceuticals. The pizza and beer relaxed my mood and lips. She listened, sure to recall words that described with whom and what the agreement meant to all parties, comfortable she understood before her departure that night.

Amber relayed her message the next day at services. It passed like an electrical charge from the pastor of her church to the management of his clergy.

Conference calls burned up phone lines. Dismay developed as the shocked expression of the day. Quick calculations determined revenue decline. Various people met at different points across the country. Strategic plans sprang forth to evaluate options. Entry into the fray became of paramount importance. Hesitancy could be fatal. They had been betrayed.

The relationship bonded between medical groups such as Ashton and Sheldon and faith-based groups seemed positive when first begun. Religious organizations remained devoted to their role as vocal antagonists. Revenue they received funded the supposed grass roots protests, mostly vocal, a few overly aggressive and menacing. The medical firms had agreed to finance this outcry of social outrage, while they hid quietly in the background. Both stayed well served. Now, that would change.

Chapter 7

My gaze turned across the aisle to the other side of the plane, and stared out the portal window unable to see much through the darkness of the cabin, or through the opaqueness of the dark sky. Turmoil roiled my emotions.

My journey had started with innocent unawareness of the events that would unfold, and now I found myself destined across the globe to pursue aid, and a continuation of hope. I had little conception of the forces that aligned against me, though hints of their strength had begun to emerge from the shadows.

The day not long ago, when that knock on my door had come flashed through my mind. Two detectives from the New York City police department stood there. They showed me a picture of a battered and bloodied man, and asked if I could identify him. The man had no familiarity to me, and I asked why they ended up at my door.

They explained the man carried letters in his briefcase with my name and address upon them. The man now lay unconscious from a suspected mugging attempt in a local hospital, carried no identification, and possessed a letter written in Italian with my name on it.

I asked if the letter bore any description of intent. The detectives replied that information could not be released, but did divulge the letter came from a pharmaceutical company by the name of Alpha Drugs near Rome, signed by Tony Mirastani. I didn't know the company, or the signatory, but wondered what role an international pharmaceutical firm might have in my life.

The darkness within the plane enveloped me. My heart ached, as I clenched my hands until the pain brought attention to my repetitive behavior. Headaches plagued me and the furrows on my brow grew deeper each day. Sleep did not come easily. My eyes darted from left to right, as if my brain worked with high speed film to record each moment. A close observer would wonder of my sanity. An even closer observer would wonder of my freedom from chemical stimulants.

When had it become so crazy? I tried to remember.

Fear of the unknown churned my stomach. The consequences of failure remained unacceptable. I forced the thought from my mind with a realization there could be no good served to dwell there.

For the hundredth time, I wondered of my capability. My father had always told me of my insignificance. Words like underachiever, loser, failure, were thrown at me. The words cut my soul like jagged glass. The wound never healed.

A pity parade could not be afforded at this time. The verbal assaults of my youth hung over me like a cold fog. That dark shroud lingered and I must find a way to cast it off. To this day, I wondered of my strength to do so.

To carry this disease with no cure or treatment could not be accepted. Now my daughter had the same illness, and my desperation grew. I became mad as hell. My past failures seemed insignificant.

Acceptance of my daughter's condition could not be allowed to take root. There must be a way to battle back. This trip served as a means to begin that fight.

Shivers ran up my spine as I remembered the words used to cut me down from my childhood. Perhaps the dominance of my grandfather could be blamed. A strict disciplinarian, no hugs at holidays, birthdays, or words of congratulations ever passed from him.

Love did not exist in his unemotional realm. In my grandfather's mind, success must be achieved at any cost. Exceptions to the rule did not exist. That same mettle had been passed to my father, but had skipped me. Cold and uncompassionate, were chiseled into his being.

Yet that drive he tried to instill in me did not build me to overcome, or make me stronger, but quashed any hope that tried to grow there. It did not motivate me to succeed. It made me question my desire to live.

That terrible moment of long ago that led to one of the most painful moments of my life I lived again. I shivered and remembered. *Would I never forget?*

The crowd of several hundred stared at me. Sweat condensed on my upper lip. Cotton balls sucked every drop of moisture from my mouth. My chest rose and fell beneath my sweatshirt. My palms were damp, my arms and legs weak. Relax. These people could all be counted as friends or acquaintances. Don't be nervous.

Then I had seen him. Like a demon hovering near my soul, ready to snatch it from my chest and run laughing manically into the wilderness. He leaned against the door jamb of the rear exit of the gym. *Damn! Came for the failure, no doubt? Murmurs quieted. Heavy footsteps echoed on the stage.*

"Quiet please," rang from the speakers. "We have assembled today to hear our candidates for Student Body offices." Silence enveloped the gym. "You all know me. I'm Principal Sorenfeld. We have assembled here to hear our first guest speaker, senior classman James Armstrong. Mr. Armstrong, your turn." I didn't move. My muscles had refused to budge, as I stared at the audience. Principal Sorenfeld stepped back to the microphone. "James. James, you are up."

I pushed myself to a standing position. The microphone sat on a podium at the middle of the stage. It looked a hundred miles away. As if in a dream, I remembered my first step forward and the walk as if weights had been slung on my ankles. I slid towards the center of the stage, touched the podium, placed my hands on the sides of the stand, and reached for the microphone. Eager faces stared at me as I held the microphone close. My hands remained damp.

"My name is James Armstrong." I remembered the looks. The moment stayed memorized, and then with deliberateness I reached out and placed the microphone back, and began to shuffle to my seat. A low murmur had oscillated through the crowd. I reached my chair, lowered myself down, leaned back and stared straight ahead. Principal Sorenfeld then introduced the next speaker.

"Our next speaker is, Annie Peters. Annie, it is now time for your turn."

I didn't hear the rest of the speeches. My father disappeared.

My mind flipped back to those terrible memories of twenty years past before my classmates and worst of all, my father. The same dread swallowed me now. Not the embarrassment, just the fear. It shook me. The fear of the unknown terrified me.

My doubt grew with age. My father and brothers told me, I would never be an achiever. They rebuked and ridiculed me. I questioned my own legitimacy.

My grandfather started this sad legacy on the backs of so many. The son of immigrants, he developed into a power broker who earned a small fortune. The same confidence, cruel attitude and dominance passed to my father did not take hold in me. My wires did not connect the same way. Perhaps my genetics had been tweaked. Maybe my mother's compassion over-wrote genes attributed to harshness passed on by my grandfather to my father. I would never know. In my case, the apple had indeed fallen further from the tree than expected.

My early development had been torture, led by my father and brothers that mocked me without mercy. Doubt grew in me, not trust. Encouragement never materialized. My father and brothers, chastised and demoralized me, never built my spirit, or offered encouragement. My father tried to spark my rage, to get me to fight back, to prove myself, yet I failed the test. The thirst to succeed, to prove myself never grew in me. The spark did not ignite, and even now in adult hood languished.

My father disowned me, considered me a failure. My mother cried, and my brothers disdained me. Supposed allies mocked me. I squirmed away to find my own identity.

The fire within me now at last sparked, though the flame just smoldered. Fear held on. I wanted to succeed, though questions still burdened me.

My new found anger aroused the flame brought on by the potential of my premature death and that same consequence for my daughter simply being unacceptable. When told I faced death, anger ignited that ember. I needed to believe, now more than ever, but worried that hope had died long ago, and wondered of my courage to breathe life onto that ember.

MS represented a large speed bump on my life path, but now, I pledged to myself to not let it derail mine, or my daughter's life.

Then my world truly changed. Hope experienced a rebirth, with the advent of stem cell regeneration as a real potential. It offered me hope, a new beginning.

The ember inside finally burned brighter. Excitement filled me. I turned into an optimist. Though doubt still lived there, my determination surged. This new found burst of energy did not go unnoticed and in fact led to my invitation for a meeting at Ashton.

Mr. Drake had been informed of my new born energy. He considered his options. There was a wide consensus developed among the conglomeration to stop me.

Secrets lay hidden they wished to keep buried. Steven Drake at first resisted, though he then succumbed to the pressures. He contacted their silent partner. An agreement was negotiated to escalate surveillance. Phone taps took effect. Electronic bugs quickly became operational, installed under the auspices of maintenance workers. Physical tails began their task.

Unknown to me at the time, I continued my research, unaware of how close the watchers came, or the extent to which I had become a threat. I balanced on the edge of discovery and termination.

Drake was the judge and the one to give the execution order. His partners grew more nervous with each new day. At last, Drake gave in and ordered their silent partner to take action.

Wheels began to roll. Additional spies were hired. The risk of discovery grew, and then a cease order came down from the very top. They needed to know what had been found, and if indeed that most critical information of all had been uncovered.

They waited to issue the ultimate order, though they waited with little patience.

Chapter 8

My research continued, driven on by what I hoped would be a critical moment in the world of stem cell therapy. I needed to find out. My daughter needed me to succeed.

Research indicated who the power players might be. They began to emerge, slowly at first, then clearer in the bright light of discovery. I realized the author of the road map must be known. *Who called the shots?*

They must be powerful. I needed to know. I guessed they were leaders in their respective worlds and those with the most to lose. Giants of capitalism and self-anointed champions of morality emerged.

My direction began to wander to the political world. The world stage changed on a continual basis. Introduction of a bill to fund new stem cell lines and escalate private research grabbed my attention. It thrilled me, but the powers from the fringe became more vocal and opposed, and the bill soon died.

My curiosity with these developments kept me dialed in on trips to Washington D.C. to take in Congressional testimony. I identified proponents and opponents of the bill. I soon had a desire to meet with the strongest opponent.

My arrival to meet at the Congressional offices occurred without fanfare. After the clock ticked past the appointed time by an hour, an aide approached.

"I serve as Congressman Belfay's campaign manager and chief aide. Congressman Belfay will not be able to meet with you today. Please accept his apologies."

After my trip to Washington, I set a goal of no more than

four months to find a treatment to stop my daughters' and my own progression. Day sixty of my schedule now approached. Pushed on by my need for discovery and the arrangement made with the pharmaceutical company, I proceeded with haste. My efforts became more critical.

Unemployment provided me the luxury of additional free time. I spent hours at the library, hidden deep within the stacks of research manuals. It became routine for me to arise, leave my apartment, hit a coffee shop and roll my way to the library. My route grew predictable and my schedule near synchronous. That all changed at the start of a new week.

The same people were spotted behind me the last few days. That coincidence in a city as large as New York seemed peculiar. I changed my route, than altered my schedule. The same two faces still appeared nearby. They looked to be muscular, clean shaven and well dressed.

Confrontation with one of the men became necessary. I spun my chair on the sidewalk that early morning and rolled towards my closest follower. He changed direction and merged into the throng of pedestrians. My followers had shown themselves. The question than grew into why? I considered my agreement with Ashton.

My routes soon became changed more often. Unbeknownst to me at the time, this change could not have occurred at a more favorable time. The order had come down to orchestrate an accident. The powers that be had become much too nervous about discovery.

One Monday, I left my apartment, after a long weekend of work with Amber. As I moved down the busy sidewalk surrounded by the throng, a follower closed in. He worked through the crowd. I continued past the usual coffee shop stop as a safety precaution.

As I passed, I peered inside the shop and saw the second familiar face scramble to his feet and rush to the door. I turned briefly and saw the first follower give a circular hand signal for his partner to go around the block. *They wanted to box me in!* I grew nervous with this development. *Why? What did they want?*

My respiration increased, sweat broke out on my brow, and the wheels of my chair propelled me forward even faster. My primary follower moved up to thirty yards behind. I pushed through the front door of a large retail store and headed towards the elevator lobby. Apparel stands cluttered the floor, between which I disappeared.

My primary tail entered the store. I pushed harder across the last distance to the elevators. As I emerged from the apparel racks an elevator door slid open. A polite Samaritan stepped aside to let me enter.

Someone on the elevator pushed the button for the sixth floor. I turned my chair, and saw the primary tail sprint across the last few yards towards me, one hand outstretched. The door slid closed and blocked further view of him.

On the seventh floor, I exited from an empty elevator with a realization my routine must change.

For the remainder of the morning, I stayed hidden behind a counter of electronic equipment on the seventh floor. Near the lunch hour, a floor attendant asked if she could assist me to the foyer in a freight elevator. The attendant escorted me to the bottom floor where I exited with no further signs of my tails.

When at home, I fired off a fax to Ashton Pharmaceutical and received word back they did not follow me. I considered their response and moved ahead with my travel plans.

In my mind, darkness lurked. I peered into the murkiness

of the plane.

Thoughts of the moment this nightmare began, of the doctor's office, the dispassionate words, the emptiness, filtered through my mind. I remembered the emptiness, despair, and panic. It all flooded back.

Most of all, my need to act returned. Though not deemed a success by my family, I possessed the need to act, with the desire to learn and know the how and why.

The most joy of my four years of higher education had been spent on my senior project. Now, a new reason to pursue an answer to a complex problem presented itself.

Dimness surrounded me. The plane continued through the dusky air. My hands clenched into fists against my eye orbits so hard, my eyes began to hurt until I pulled my hands away and extended my fingers into the darkness.

In exhaustion my head tilted forward until my forehead bumped into the back of the seat in front of me. My head snapped back with an uneasy awareness as I wiped my hands on my shirt, wet from the dampness of tears against my cheeks. *Why me? Why her?*

This disease will result in death. The words echoed like thunder in my head as I jerked alert with thoughts of that moment fresh in my mind.

When the words had first been said to me, I gasped as blackness enveloped my world. There had been a desperate, uncanny desire to strangle the bearer of the news, yet I recognized he served as the simple, though in-compassionate messenger. *Who could I strike at?* To attack the messenger at the time seemed legitimate. Now other parties emerged as the enemy. They hid in the dimness.

Cold shivers shook my spine. Streaks of light flashed before me as I recalled the original moment of announcement as if a nightmare began. Gnarled fingers with yellowed elongated finger nails reached out, the silence broken by a cackle that did not come close to laughter. *Could death itself be a celebratory participant?* My life had tumbled into a chasm of darkness.

With a reflexive jerk, my head hit the back rest of the seat. Present day seeped back into my consciousness, and once again the dark place that crept into my soul vanished. Goosebumps rose on my arms. I folded them across my chest, and swung my head from side to side to erase the memory.

The perfect storm had crashed on me. The monster rose and reached the pinnacle of its height, teeth snarled, saliva bubbling from its mouth. It rose into my life without invite and must be thrown out.

The time to do what I did best arrived. Think. A good head graced my shoulders. My fear must be suffocated. It was no longer time for flight. I must fight.

Thoughts of my diagnosis needed to be squashed into oblivion. I recalled the doctor in my imagination as no more than a tiny caricature at the end of the room, his back turned, a white smock draped over his tiny form. He sat on a small black stool and scribbled notes into a file. Loneliness filled me. I had been left alone to grapple with the unwelcome guest. This bizarre experience had turned into a Greek tragedy, one I had no desire to star in. Now, I simply wanted to destroy this unwelcome memory and wipe Dr. Frankenstein away.

"Are you sure?" my voice had croaked past parched lips.

"Yes" he replied. "That all?" the ophthalmologist snapped as he swung back to the chart. My blood boiled and emotions exploded in my memory.

"No you little prick! You just told me I could die! Now tell me how!" I shouted.

His response came back to me as a cold and dispassionate subtitle on life. The good doctor, without doubt flunked his God 101 class in medical school. "MS impacts the central nervous system and results in death. Your disease may progress, it may not. It cannot be cured and it cannot be stopped."

It cannot be cured and it cannot be stopped. The words rang in my ears.

The moment stayed so focused in my thoughts. Now, the words echoed through my sub-consciousness, never forgotten. The time had come to banish those words from my existence, once and for all.

Death soon became an imagined part of my life. Sleep did not come without the hideous crush of its weight on my soul.

The airplane cabin shuddered, followed by a voice that penetrated my consciousness as if it arose from faraway. Reality ratcheted back.

"Ladies and Gentlemen, please secure your seatbelts until further notice. We can expect some bumpy air ahead."

A soft bell followed the captain's voice that fully woke me. The cabin shuddered. Eerie shadows danced on the walls. Passengers murmured. The time neared dawn. The plane sliced the air somewhere over the Atlantic.

Three rows behind James, Arturo Salsado sat, eyes glued to the back of James' head. Arturo filled the seat he sat in, his arms pressed into passenger space on each side of him.

Arturo hailed from Italy, and now called Boston home. The call came late at night. Word passed to him reported that tails on the subject discovered the withdrawal of a considerable sum of cash in traveler's checks. Quick research found he flew to Italy. An airline ticket had been purchased, and an appointment set to see a doctor near Milan.

Arturo worked for this client before. He recognized the southern accent and proper use of the English language. Negotiation of terms had been simple. The plane ticket arrived via courier the next day.

The plane lurched forward, an involuntary gasp elicited from passengers. The flight continued on with occasional shudders.

Sound sleep did not come to me, though I did manage to put my head back and slip into a haunted consciousness. Dark places guarded by faceless sentries of unimaginable horror lived there. My lips moved silently in quiet rage.

A clock tower pounded in my head. I shook myself awake, put my hands to my face, sat back, and looked to the side. I pushed the service button to call the flight attendant. She appeared with promptness.

I requested a glass of water and blanket. Both quickly appeared, the water rapidly consumed. The clock tower echoes subsided.

Try as I might to put the thoughts from my mind, the events that led to my start on this trip tumbled through my head. I recalled my anger, denial, and trembled with a remembrance of my charge forward into the world of investigation, with no knowledge of the disease, just a simple determination to understand.

Anger filled me. The lesson my father worked to impart on me smoldered deep within.

The thought of the article I found helped to moderate my anger and drove me forward to find answers. More needed to be uncovered. I had stumbled on the first piece of the puzzle. *Would there be others?* I believed there would be.

The discovered information I kept as my own. After the

experiences on the streets of New York, my arrangement with Sheldon could not be trusted. They had become a question mark of suspicion, unknowns and danger.

Now my travel took me to another part of the world to pursue a potential treatment for MS through stem cell therapy. Perhaps I was finally on a path of discovery.

The doctor and her procedure had been identified in an article published in the National Multiple Sclerosis newsletter. The article referenced a technique performed by the doctor at her office in Italy through stem cell regenerative procedure.

I communicated with the doctor via electronic mail and now traveled to take part in her program. The article indicated the doctor found a way to target stem cells that would differentiate into adipose tissue, the fatty material used to encapsulate neural pathways in an insulating layer referred to as myelin. For some unknown reason, MS resulted in the immune system attacking the myelin surrounding neural pathways generating scar tissue that reduced neural transmission. The doctor's technique resulted in increased adipose deposition over the scar tissue, bridging a blocked neural pathway, making MS induced immune attacks less impactful on the nervous system.

Her process could be described as revolutionary. I initiated contact, and scheduled an appointment after several of my questions could be addressed. Perhaps, I had found that most valuable of gems in the rough.

CHAPTER 9

While in Italy, I also hoped to look up Alpha Drugs. *Could they be defined as friend or foe? What could they be interested in me for? Where did the association start?*

My plan involved getting answers, first from the doctor, and second from Alpha. My flight to Milan involved the discovery of information and pursuit of a successful stem cell regeneration technique. At last maybe, my path would take a turn for mine and daughter's betterment.

Though the doctor's program excited me, the idea of the obstacles that would be thrown up before me could not be imagined. At times this path seemed so contorted.

My heel touched the briefcase wedged beneath my seat for reassurance. Confidence welled within me.

The document lay sealed within an envelope lettered in bold capitals, 'OPEN IN CASE OF DEATH OF HOLDER.' The outside of the envelope carried a date of two weeks previous, September 22. An identical copy sat locked away in a safe deposit box, the key to the box, sent to my attorney.

A letter of last rites rested, folded in my wallet in case of the worst of events. The instructions stayed simple. Upon my death the larger envelope lettered in caps, would be sent to Mr. Benjamin Lancaster, Esquire. My personal attorney would read the instructions for actions to be taken. Comfort swelled through me with the arrangements made.

A flight attendant's voice broke the relative quiet of the cabin as we landed. The attendant made the announcement in Italian, followed by English. My attention stayed riveted on each word. My passport pressed against my chest in the breast pocket of my shirt.

Passengers began to stir. The cabin vibrated. My gaze shifted to a portal window. Light of a new day stared back.

Cabin lights flickered on. I did not feel the cold gaze centered on me. Milan beckoned.

Though worn out, excitement filled me, yet fear of the unknown increased my heart rate and respiration. Cautious optimism nipped at me as the plane taxied to the terminal for disembarkment.

The back of the chair in front of me became the tool to pull myself up. I reached for the handle of the overhead baggage compartment and maneuvered other bags out of the way, until I found my carry-on and cane.

My carry-on and cane secured, I dropped back into my seat, with the bag in my lap, scooted back further, and balanced my cane between my knees.

A flight attendant passed by. She leaned to me and let me know my wheelchair would take a few minutes to bring up from the cargo hold, but it would be waiting at the gate with an attendant as I departed. I would wait for other passengers to disembark before starting my arduous track from the plane.

Arturo knew it would be easier at the airport. Once they left the terminal, a whole new jurisdiction would enter the picture. He would follow the wheelchair and approach from the rear, stumble onto the back of the chair with a fake fall onto the shoulders of the occupant. A quick, yet violent choke hold would render the man unconscious.

Arturo would grab the briefcase and walk away from the chair with never a look back. The occupant would be left for discovery by his chair attendant or curious passerby later. It could be minutes, or sooner. Regardless, he would be gone from the scene, his job completed.

He had no reason to ask why. He chuckled to himself. A religious organization, and yet they solved problems with the use of barbaric means. They used him as a tool. To ask why went beyond his job description.

The plane came to a stop. Passengers stood and moved towards the exit. It seemed the line of passengers would continue forever. Passengers from my aisle squeezed past. At last the flight attendant who spoke to me appeared. "All ready?"

"Ready, set, go," I replied.

She took the carry-on bag from me while I held my briefcase with the critical article in my grasp. The briefcase would not leave my possession. I pulled myself upright.

"Go ahead," I said to the flight attendant. "I'll use the seat backs. I'm a little slower."

"OK" she said. "If you need any assistance, please ask."

She turned and started up the aisle. I followed, and moved one hand from one chair seat back to the next and made my way after her. I used my cane to steady my balance as I shuffled forward.

Arturo stood and started toward the exit. Other passengers followed and entered the aisle, a space of several feet now between James and Arturo.

My arrival marked a momentous occasion. A new chapter in this Greek tragedy now opened. I had a strong urge to head to Dr. Giovantti's, the specialist that would see me, though I laughed that off, as my scheduled appointment had been made for the next day. Perhaps, she could also enlighten me on Alpha Drugs.

Chapter 10

The wheelchair assistant waited at the exit door. She offered her arm, which I accepted to make my way towards the chair, briefcase clutched in one hand, my cane in the other.

She stood tall, about twenty-two, or twenty-three years old, I guessed. I arrived at the chair, settled in and readied myself for the next part of the journey.

The attendant pushed me towards the terminal after the airline attendant delivered my small carry-on bag to me. We reached the top of the ramp and entered a new world. My chair assistant steered me towards an elevator to take us to the first floor.

As the attendant pushed towards the elevator, I spied an open store. I pointed in that direction. We arrived at the entrance. I reached into my trousers pocket for miscellaneous American currency carried there. The attendant shook her head. She pointed to a currency exchange counter nearby that stirred with activity, but had not yet opened.

The attendant chewed gum. I pointed to her mouth and made a chew impression. She waved her hand and pointed to herself. She would get the gum.

She left me parked outside the store entrance.

The opportunity Arturo waited for arrived. His pace quickened. He glanced for any witnesses, or a stray security guard.

As he advanced, he pulled his right arm across his chest for the anticipated fake fall. He gauged the distance to the target, feigned a stubbed toe and began to fall forward.

The wheelchair attendant appeared at that very moment. She stepped into the path of the lunge. Arturo struck her hard and pushed her into me. She fell against me, with a sharp push and rolled to the floor. The push and sudden body impact on my back took me by surprise.

Though I had set the brakes on my chair, it heaved forward. I threw my hands at the wheels to stop the forward roll.

But, the attendant's fall had struck me with suddenness. My grasp for the wheels left me off-balance. My carry-on and briefcase slid to the floor. Then with slowness, I teetered and tipped over.

My fall occurred with remarkable slowness. The wheelchair attendant fell on me. With a quickness that belied my handicap, I rolled and caught the chair attendant to lower her to the floor, and lied prone on top of my briefcase.

Arturo reached to pull the attendant up, his physical attempt at harm and document retrieval interrupted.

As he pulled the attendant from the floor, Arturo looked at the briefcase under James. He could not retrieve it.

Arturo lifted the chair attendant to her feet while they talked rapidly. The conversation meant nothing to me.

He left without a word, or look at me. The attendant apologized time and again. I asked of her condition, to which she replied she was fine.

She retrieved my chair and managed to pull me back onto the seat. She handed me my briefcase, carry-on bag, cane and gum. With that, she resumed her position and headed towards the currency exchange counter. Neither of us appeared worse for wear.

As Arturo left the terminal, he dialed the number stored to memory on his cell phone. The call receiver answered on the second call tone.

"Briefcase is still with subject. Interrupted," he reported.

The voice came back cold, devoid of emotion. "Any sign of the document?"

"No time to look, or take the briefcase."

"Follow him tomorrow. Get the document."

The phone went dead.

When my chair attendant and I made our way to the exchange counter, I pulled several travelers checks from my wallet and exchanged them for Euros. We left the counter and headed to reclaim my luggage.

As we rolled into the luggage claim area, I noticed that many of my co-passengers from the flight had departed. The man who knocked into us upstairs could not be seen.

My bag rotated towards me on the carriage. I placed my carry-on on the floor and leaned my cane on the bag. I set the brakes on the chair, as I waited for my big bag to pass again.

As it came by I reached out, grabbed it by the handle and heaved it from the carriage with the help of my attendant. I lifted my large bag onto my lap, reached for my smaller bag and briefcase, placed them on top of the large piece of luggage, balanced my cane on top and prepared to exit from the terminal.

Though burdened with luggage, a burst of energy threatened to overwhelm me, the incident upstairs already forgotten. The attendant pushed me from the terminal into the fresh air of the day. I took note of my arrival as a huge life changing moment.

Chapter 11

Outside the terminal, I turned, thanked my chair attendant, and tipped her with no knowledge of what she had done for me.

Cabs circled the terminal. With bags and chair loaded, I worked my way to the rear door, and folded into the back seat. My journey began on the beautiful streets of Milan.

My driver spoke broken English. He drove me past some of the more notable attractions of the city on the way to the motel. Street lights dimmed as the sun began to rise and cast a glow over the landmarks of the city. We passed the La Scala Opera house with its gorgeous old architectural look from ages past. The Cenacolo Vinciano displayed its ancient columns. At one time it housed Da Vinci's Last Supper, per what the driver explained, and there stood the great Duomo, known as the fourth largest church in the world. *How did it survive World War II?* I became lost in the wonder of it all and marveled at its beauty.

The city cast a spell on me, a historical place filled with treasures of the past, and the beautiful clothes and models of the present. Both drew my attention, as I resolved to make time to explore its beauties.

The cab pulled into my motel, a modern structure adorned with mystical characters that allowed it to fit into place within the courtyard. The cabbie brought my chair and bags. After I arranged the load on my lap, the roll into the lobby became an exercise filled with palatable excitement.

My ecstasy at the beauty of the plaza and arrival took my attention away from the sedan that parked and the large gentleman from the airport that slipped out. Arturo stared, as I entered the motel and mopped a large club-like hand across his forehead.

The weather of the new day arrived as a gorgeous respite from the bitter cold left behind. It could have poured rain. My mood could not be spoiled. The temperature was warm, not brought on by concrete and glass structures that trapped heat within their tall edifices, or the emissions of hundreds of vehicles, but by the pure clean morning air that crept into the city. The sun crested the horizon. The full light of the day would soon grace the sights around me.

By my watch, the time stood at almost six-fifteen in the morning. There would be plenty of time to rest and explore before my appointment the next day.

The front desk clerk directed me to the lift that whisked me to my floor.

Arturo entered the lobby, found a chair and watched from an obscured location. I wheeled from the counter towards the elevator. Arturo watched as I disappeared into the lift.

Arturo pulled a cell phone from his inner pocket and dialed.

"He arrived at hotel. Observation continues. I will report at next sight."

My entrance into my room came as the act played out below. While I awaited my luggage, I took time to navigate the room, as my cane counted out the beats between furniture. Soon, I had drawn a visual map in my mind of the room's dimensions and furniture placement. The less my shins knocked the furniture, the happier I would be.

The courtyard below my window glowed in the sunlight. I gazed at the foot traffic. Colors shined from the sunrise, and took my breath away. A fountain played its magical tune. Water jets shot cascades from spigots atop its design.

My revelry in the moment left me happy my eyesight had been restored from my earlier bout with optic neuritis. To imagine life without the beauties I now looked upon was a nightmare.

A knock echoed at the door to interrupt my thoughts. My luggage arrived.

The bell man brought the large bag and small carry-on into the room. My briefcase and cane had stayed with me. After tipping the bellman as he passed, I sat and opened my briefcase.

The envelope so important to my presentation to the doctor the next day stared back at me. Tomorrow it would be delivered to Dr. Giovantti.

The article weighed on me from the day of discovery at the Library of Congress. My eyebrows rose in genuine surprise with the discovery of the document, and that it missed detection by some protective watch dog group under the Freedom of Information Act.

A doctor with a Ph.D. in biochemistry, and former board member of the FDA wrote it. The author left the Board when he saw it politicized, and dominated by conservative appointments that carried pre-ordained agendas.

When he resigned, he wrote a paper that attacked the contamination of the scientific community for presentation at a convention of medical scientists to combat untreatable illnesses that could arise in a terrorist-prone world. The document, though submitted, and accepted, never made it to the light of day. The author had been killed days before the presentation when struck by a hit and run driver. The coincidence could not be ignored.

Though never introduced, the paper found its way into the archives of the Library of Congress hidden away under the category of new world medicine. There it sat, and collected dust, until I stumbled upon its existence.

My hope had always been the document would become the first of many instruments I would use to shed truth on the parties that opposed me. The shock value alone would reverberate far and wide. The paper unnerved me, but it must be revealed. I would not share it with the drug company.

My thoughts turned to Dr. Giovantti. My knowledge of her did not go deep, except the little gathered from my research online. My trust must start soon, and she seemed a viable candidate.

The next day two huge events would unfold for me. The stem cell procedure practiced by the doctor would be explained and implemented, and I would release the article to Dr. Giovantti. I anticipated each with excitement.

The full energy of the sun brightened the day. I ordered breakfast from the room service menu, printed in English and Italian. My meal consumed, I gazed in silence at the plaza below. After my meal, I pulled a pleasure book from my bag, to enjoy in the soft lounge chair next to the open window.

My mood had grown so exuberant there seemed no need to bring it down with any negative arguments found at the heart of stem cell articles brought along with me. The time to relax now arrived, not to become incensed. The arguments on the start of life represented a debate I cared not enter into at that moment.

As I read my pleasure book, the hours ticked by, and soon the heaviness of my eyelids won. It seemed weeks since my last good sleep. My need for rest won out. I rose, made my way to the bed, stumbled onto it, and fell into a slumber.

My thoughts of the next day never disappeared from my

mind. Thoughts of the moment exhilarated me, though not enough to beat back the encompassing sleep that won out.

Twilight broke outside. Disappointment filled me with the realization my first full day in Milan had been lost. Relaxation crept through me, yet I grew sorrowful to think I sacrificed my first day in this beautiful place for sleep. As I washed my face, the thought of dinner entered my mind. I again reviewed the room service menu. After a second perusal, my decision had been made to head downstairs to find a restaurant to enjoy dinner. A fresh shirt came out to wear, I twirled my wheelchair to the door, and soon I headed out.

As I had entered earlier that day, an eatery on the other side of the foyer grabbed my attention. A divine aroma now crept though its open entrance as I departed the lift. My decision came fast. The spot tantalized my palate, and I entered the restaurant. My selections made, my taste buds awoke with ecstatic anticipation. I over ordered and selected a bottle of local Chianti to wash down the anticipated tasteful delights to come. The waitress returned with the bottle, and my preparation for a good rest with my first glass of robust wine began.

After my meal, the time to retire arrived. My stomach full, I knew a comfortable night sleep would find me soon. The trip to my room came fast where blankets buried me deep within the comfortable confines of the bed. The next day waited and with it all its adventures.

CHAPTER 12

After a restful night sleep, the new day arrived. I arose as the sun did, unusual for the change in a different time zone. My excitement woke me, and pushed me to the lobby. I received directions to the nearest bakery at the front desk, and my journey commenced to a recommended cafe across the plaza.

My excursion across the cobble stoned street began. Though my journey was slow, I made good time, and arrived all in one piece. My biggest problem had been to keep my cane wedged between my knees as I bounced across the cobblestone street.

The interior of the café held onto its darkness as sunrise began to light the windows that stared at the plaza. The interior had already become filled with smoke. My intuition told me the customers visited on a regular basis, even at this early time of day.

My wheelchair just squeezed through the entryway, and to a nearby unoccupied table adorned with a cheeky tablecloth of red and green. I placed an order with a lot of points of fingers and nods of the heads with my server. The cappuccino and sweet roll arrived. The coffee smelled fresh as steam flowed around the brim of the cup.

Patrons passed the time of day with the exchange of snippets of news from the local newspaper, not that much different from papers in the States. The enjoyment of the camaraderie of patrons surrounded me. Time spent here seemed a tradition.

This activity passed as if these people sat at the local

chapel, or cathedral with their prayers offered to their God. A barrage of foreign languages from the crowd surrounded me. I understood none of the conversations, but sat back and relaxed with the new flavor of my environment.

With my coffee, and sweet roll finished, the time came to begin the drive to the doctor's clinic. My breakfast paid, I placed my cane between my knees, balanced the briefcase on my lap, and headed outside to flag a cab.

My long held dreams of this moment began to materialize. The hopes I held for myself and daughter were becoming reality.

The clinic sat on the outskirts of Milan. My travel took me past several downtown plazas. The cab at last pulled into what must have been the suburbs of the city. Workers hurried to their appointed places of employment. Perhaps, I would be able to do that again someday.

The outskirts of Milan carried a unique beauty. The area breathed life. Greenery filled my senses. Hillsides rolled by covered with thick pastures, and olive trees. After several turns, and small hill climbs the road began to narrow. The destination neared.

The cab rounded a final corner, and pulled into a gravel lot. There stood a low, single story structure, very quaint, with a sign attached to an outside wall, the name of the doctor displayed with prominence. White paint adorned the walls. A shake roof covered the top of the structure, like a well-worn bonnet subjected to years of exposure to the elements. Green moss grew on the wooden shingles.

A fairy tale look surrounded the structure. Olive trees dotted the yard. Green shrubs stood pruned.

Yet at this hour the scene that appeared before me looked like some horrible unhealed wound. It appeared as if a great master piece sat distorted. My mind convulsed with the horror before me. My heart pounded. Police cars surrounded the clinic, blue lights on the top of their cars left on to rotate. This could not be right!

A woman, I assumed must be Dr. Giovantti stood before several officers on the front steps of the clinic her hands and mouth working overtime. She looked irate at their presence.

The echo of her rapid volley of angry dialogue could he heard from inside the cab. An officer of obvious authority stood at the head of the group, and took her verbal assault. The woman's barrage did not seem to have an impact. The officer appeared stoic, and uninterested, arms crossed on his chest with an expression of someone intent and unchangeable on his face.

Panic swept through me. Sweat rose on my forehead, my respiration grew erratic, and my heart pounded in my ribs. *What could this be about?* After a struggle, I pulled my wallet from my back pocket. The driver flung open the door, currency exchanged, and the transaction was completed. The driver moved to retrieve my chair. The woman's voice rose clearly, her rapid fire vocabulary directed at the officer. I understood none of it, yet I needed to get through the circle of officers, and reach her. The anger of her voice could not be mistaken except for an exasperated exclamation of dismay.

My roll towards the gathered crowd commenced. An officer separated from the crowd, and blocked me from further advancement. I brought my chair to a stop. The woman stepped forward past the officer in front of her, and fired a rapid volley of words at the police officer who blocked my way. The officer stepped aside in a hurry.

She extended her hand, and stated in plain English with an Italian dialect, "Doctor Giovantti. I have a problem to resolve. Please wait."

She shook hands in a firm shake, her hand diminutive compared to mine. Her cheeks had flushed. Her eyes flashed brilliance. Dark hair spilled onto her forehead. She spun back to the officer that led the crew to continue her diatribe.

The barrage went on for several minutes. At last the officer pulled a folded paper from his jacket, handed it to her, turned on his heel, and headed towards the nearest car. He motioned his men to follow as he walked past me. He didn't utter a word, and dared not steal a look in my direction.

Engines started, and the officers left. Dr. Giovantti stood on the porch, her hands on her hips, brow furrowed, her jaw set as she stared after the officers. I didn't watch the officers leave, and dared not move my stare from the doctor.

As the officers left the premises she realized I sat alone. She descended from the porch in a hurry, and approached her hand outstretched.

"I'm so sorry. I must correct some sort of mix-up. I own the clinic."

"I'm James Armstrong from New York. We exchanged e-mails a few days ago about your procedure of stem cell rejuvenation, and how it might be applied to my situation."

She looked at me in sadness. "You have traveled here too late."

My mouth fell open as if struck by a punch.

"I apologize, Mr. Armstrong. The government order they delivered restricts me from performance of the procedure any longer," she said as she shook the paper she held.

My blood froze and feet began to turn cold. *So, they reached to the other side of the ocean to stop it?* Their audacity over whelmed me.

"Can you walk?" she asked. The doctor's voice broke my

shock.

"Yes" stammered from my mouth. I placed the end of the cane on the side walk, and pushed up from the chair, briefcase in hand. She reached to grab my arm, and helped me to the porch.

We entered the front room of her clinic. My wheelchair sat abandoned on the walkway. Neither of us spoke.

The room smelled of antiseptic. Plastic chairs lined the walls. A coffee table sat covered with piles of local magazines. A front desk for check-in stood at one end of the room. Pictures of the snow-capped Italian Alps adorned the walls.

She walked to a door located on the other end of the room, and offered an apology to me again. "Can you make it without help? I didn't mean to abandon you."

"I'll be just a moment. I don't walk as fast anymore." She exited the front room into what must have been her office, the door left open behind her. With the help of the backs of the chairs aligned along the wall to balance against, I made my way to the other end of the room, and entered her small, organized office.

She began to speak on her phone. I spied an easy chair, and made my way to it, and fell into it, my briefcase placed on the floor next to the chair, leaned my cane back into my lap, arranged my position, waiting for her to end her call. She hung up, and looked at me.

"I spoke with my attorney. I need to call my staff now. Would you care for some coffee? I need to make those calls," she stated.

"No, thank you. I'm fine for now."

"If you want to wait, I have several calls to make," she let me know. Her fingers raced on the keypad of the phone. Her voice traveled the line to her staff, and others unimagined.

She gestured as she relayed her message to a list of employees. I exited her office, briefcase in hand, with a last glance at her as she talked in anger on the phone.

As I exited the office, her rapid fire dialogue in Italian could be heard clearly. Several minutes later, the calls stopped. The desk chair squeaked as she must have leaned back to catch her breath. A moment later she entered the front room with a sad expression on her face.

"Mr. Armstrong, I can no longer perform the procedure. I have been shut down. I apologize," she said in a dejected tone.

"Doctor, can you tell me what happened?" She exhaled as she sat.

"Well, they yanked my certificate. The Policia Lieutenant carried an order issued by the Italian Department of the Interior that revoked my license to practice. He advised me that if I performed any further stem cell transplant procedures, I faced prison for many years, and could be hit with a substantial fine." She sat back on the plastic chair.

"Who signed the order?"

"The Chief of the Department of the Interior," she said.

"May I see it?"

"Of course," she replied as she handed me the document. It did me little good to stare at the foreign language, but then I found the critical line that told me so much more.

There, by the Director's signature I found it. Next to the signature appeared a date line and there on the date line the truth of the order hit me. Printed by day first, followed by month, and year had been written yesterday's date. *They reached the top level of the government the day ahead of my arrival.*

"Did you notice the date of execution?" I said as I handed

the letter back. She looked at me with inquisitiveness and lifted the paper to eye level. She lowered the document with a perplexed look on her face.

"I have performed stem cell transplantation routines for the past seven months. Why now?" she stammered.

"They wanted to stop you so you couldn't perform the procedure on me."

"Why?" she uttered.

"How many transplant procedures did you have scheduled today?"

"Just you," she answered.

"The people behind this reached to the top to get their way. They needed to stop you. I'm afraid that based on the information I have uncovered, they want to keep your stem cell transplant success as quiet as possible, as long as possible." It came time to drop the bomb. I extracted the document from the envelope and handed it to her.

"May I make that coffee, while you read the document?" She never looked up. She pointed towards her office.

"Go through the door behind my desk."

I struggled to my feet, and headed to her office. A small kitchen space sat behind her desk. The coffee bag stood next to the pot, a stack of filters nearby.

The aroma of fresh perked coffee soon filled the room. I waited to begin my venture back to give her time. Several minutes later, I entered the front room.

She never turned to look at me as I returned. She held the document as her hand hung over the edge of the chair.

"Are you all right?"

"Where did you get this?" she asked. She seemed lost. I fell back into a chair next to her. Dr. Giovantti waited. I watched her with a blank face. She stared back. It appeared she neared my age. Dark hair crept down to her shoulders. Her eyes showed a deep brown, and an expressive, yet beautiful inquisitiveness. A white smock covered a curvaceous figure that could be made out beneath. Her complexion held an olive tone to it, as did most Mediterranean cultures, though now her face appeared pale.

"I found that document at the Library of Congress within the archives. I have kept it with me ever since."

"Have you verified its authenticity?" she asked.

"Yes. I did as carefully as possible. The process must not have been that quiet though, because I have been followed for some time now. The people behind this have become more aggressive to assure the procedure never occurred." She looked at me with a doubtful stare.

"How do you know you have been followed?"

"I have noticed small things that began to add up. To see the same person, at different locations, day after day, at different times makes no sense. The same man on a number of occasions appeared behind me. One time, I pulled some evasive maneuvers to escape him and one of his friends. The same person on the subway at different times, on various lines, becomes much more than a coincidence." She looked hard at me.

"On my return home one day, I found my documents disturbed. I'm sure of it. I always leave my documents with one extended from the pile to mark my end position. It's a bookmark. One afternoon after work, I found my documents stacked straight. None protruded from the pile. They had been restacked. Whoever searched them did not realize I knew. At that point, I began to pay more attention to the foot falls behind me.

It's possible they have been into my e-mails, or my phone calls, or both, and found my plans. I have brought a terrible mess on you. I'm sorry." I finished with a look of disappointment on my face.

"Answer me" she demanded. "Why?"

"That's the million dollar question." To not be one hundred percent honest with her did not please me, although I did not know all the answers myself.

"You think they followed you here?" she asked. My smile was not laced with any humor.

"Without doubt they did. I wanted to warn you, but figured you might think I'd hit my head a little too hard." *And you wouldn't be incorrect* she thought as she sat and considered the words she heard and the document in her hand.

"I appreciate your discretion, though it doesn't seem to have worked."

I nodded in agreement with a heavy heart, and the realization that my hopes may have been dashed. "Not at this very moment. They must have known of the order from the Interior Department, if they didn't push for it themselves. However, they may have followed me since my arrival, or even on the aircraft, or someone picked me up at the airport." The doctor's face went even paler.

"Why?" she asked again. "What do they want with you? What have you done?" she queried.

"Now wait a second." I held both my hands up in mock surrender. "My actions haven't broken the law." She sighed with resignation.

"I'm sorry. You show up with an article not seen for years and a rather incredible story. It's all quite a surprise. We must talk more." She extended her hand, and offered to help me up. "Please call me Isabelle, not Doctor." I agreed whole heartedly as I looked at the pretty face and curvaceous body.

"Can I take you back to town? I assume your cab left?"

Isabelle asked.

"Yes, we could talk on the way."

"Actually, there's a small cafe a few kilometers up the road. They have good coffee and even better croissants. Want to try it out before we head back?" she asked.

"Deal," my response came still anxious to talk of the paper.

"Give me a few minutes to make some calls, and we'll go," she stated.

"Take your time. I don't have any place to go."

Her tone became sad as she said, "Perhaps we can find another path."

"We'll work on it. Though, first let's get to basics. Call me James, and could I get the article back please?" She responded with slight embarrassment as she handed the document back.

"Yes, of course. Give me a few moments."

She returned to work the phone. She didn't seem that surprised by the document. Surprised to see it though, not astonished by its' content. That observation would be explored later.

After more than a few moments, Isabelle finished with her messages. She slammed the receiver back. The chair creaked as she leaned back.

She tried to make sense of it all. It happened so fast. Her attorney could get no answers. No one at the Department of the Interior would return calls. The Police Department offered no hope. It became a moment filled with madness.

With a loud sigh, she headed into the front room to find me.

"Let's go," she announced. "No one will return my calls. I need a stiff coffee or a good glass of wine if this does not get better fast," she exclaimed. "I'll grab my car, and meet you in front."

CHAPTER 13

My exercise to stand began. My rickety walk along the backs of the chairs against the wall for support commenced. I moved with a depressed heart, and shook my head at the turn of events. All hope seemed dashed. At least I would have the opportunity to quiz Isabelle as to what to pursue next.

She pulled her mud splattered burgundy Peugeot up at the end of the sidewalk. She had pushed my wheelchair onto the lawn by the front of the porch. My briefcase stayed locked inside her office. The letter to my attorney still rested inside. I carried the extra copy of the primary article folded and squeezed into my breast pocket. It had become habitual for me to have my briefcase. To not have it left me naked, though now, there seemed no need to have it with me.

As I eased into the car, settled into the seat, and placed my cane by my side, she hit the accelerator, and the car sped off with gravel spinning from under the rear wheels. She approached the pavement with a slight tap to the brakes, turned abruptly, and headed away from Milan. We carried on a rapid conversation.

We drove into a small village a few kilometers away. She pointed to an older structure, pulled up, and let me know she would meet me inside. My struggle from the passenger seat seemed more than clumsy. I turned and stared at the old structure with a look of admiration on my face as I left the car.

It looked like a former farm house. Shutters stood attached to well-oiled hinges I could envision drawn over the windows at night, or in case of serious weather conditions.

The old house had been painted white with a cheerful light green trim. Large potted plants stood guard on either side of the doorway. The scene reminded me of some quaint picture from a tour book that touted the charms of the Mediterranean.

My shuffle to the steps of the porch was accomplished with little grace, my weight on the cane. I reached the steps and studied them with care. A wooden hand rail had been secured to either side of the steps. I took hold of the right hand rail, and began my ascent. I pulled my weight forward on the rail as each foot lifted to take the next step. Those cautious steps gave me the confidence to approach the door with care.

Footsteps bounded to me, as Isabelle arrived. She had shed her smock at the car, and appeared vivacious.

She wore a plaid skirt, a long sleeve white blouse open at the neck, black flat shoes, a gold wrist watch, and no other jewelry, except ear hoops that appeared acquired from a local craft fair, not an expensive jewelry store. I stretched a hand towards the door, and held it open for her as we stepped into a scene imagined, yet never experienced.

It seemed as if I walked onto a movie set. Tables had been packed close together. A rotund woman stood at the counter. As we entered, she began to fire questions. Isabelle pointed to a table close to the front window. I headed in that direction. The smell of the interior filled my senses with fresh baked goods, coffee, and so many more delicious tidbits.

My maneuvers took me past other tables with care, until I reached a chair at the designated table. No other guests sat in the cafe at that hour. Isabelle made her way to the counter where she spoke in rapid Italian to the woman that waited there. I admired the goods beneath the glass counter the curator stood behind. Packages of smoked meats, jars of olives, delicious salads, and numerous pastries waited. On top of the counter sat several bottles of wine, and behind the counter an old stove, porcelain white, stood with pride atop four round feet anchored to the floor. Charm screamed at me.

As Isabelle finished her rapid hand movements and chatter with the woman, she turned with a smile, and made her way to the table. She sat, and offered her apologies.

"She wanted to know about all the excitement earlier. I told her some government confusion."

The woman showed up at our table with a tray that carried two hot cappuccinos, and two croissants. We sipped with caution on the hot coffee.

"So, can we discuss the paper and our next steps?" Isabelle asked. My surprise must have shown in my face. She chuckled.

"How did 'I' become 'we'?"

"Well, that's what I thought. I figured I would gain your trust, anesthetize you, and steal your organs. Didn't you know?" She laughed. "You should have seen your face. I thought you would pass out." She chuckled with no mercy.

"Nice. Next time I want a whacko doctor to scare the wits out of me, you will certainly make the list."

"All right, James. I just wanted to ease it up here. Let's talk business," she said. "I happen to know a fellow stem cell practioner across the channel by the name of Thomas Hopkins. I've come to know Thomas well. He asked me several times to visit and check on his research."

Did more than professional interest rest here? If so I couldn't help but be envious of Thomas Hopkins.

"We might be able to replicate my work at his clinic with

the right equipment and supplies. Now might be a good opportunity to take him up on his offer to visit."

"Am I still the butt of your joke?" I stammered.

"No, I have come to know him from attendance at many presentations. It would be nice to hear more of his work." My mood changed.

"You mean you will take me to meet Dr. Hopkins?"

"Si, of course," she stated.

It seemed the day started anew. My hopes had been dashed earlier, and with Isabelle's revelation, they rose again. The pieces could yet fall together.

"Isabelle, my return to Milan can no longer be an option for me. It would make sense that if they tailed me on the plane, or picked me up at the airport, I should stay away."

"That's fine" she replied. "Let's go back to my clinic. I will pick up some overnight items kept there. You can buy some clothes and toiletries when we arrive." It became a plan and she could keep an eye on his successes, or failures.

"Isabelle, I need to know what the article means. Can you help me?"

She looked across the table at me. *He deserved to know. How would he accept it*, she wondered?

"Let's start where all stories should start." she said. I settled into my chair, and took another sip of coffee. Isabelle began. "You know by the late nineties the potential medicinal use of the first line of human embryonic stem cells became a reality. This started a series of debates. Some viewed the advancement as momentous. Others viewed it as disastrous." I knew the history.

"At the time of discovery, I studied at the University of Wisconsin. We sat on the cutting edge of stem cell research. At graduation I took a position with Beechum Pharmaceuticals.

They hired me to work for their R&D department on stem cell therapies. We made good progress, until politics stopped further federal fund utilization for research on new lines.

The company put millions, if not billions into the program so they made the decision to continue R&D anyway. The Administration grew unhappy with that decision, and moved to block it at the FDA level, the regulatory approval Board, with handpicked allies that the Administration knew would hold true to their beliefs, and kill any stem cell procedures that came before them."

The puzzle materialized further.

Isabelle continued. "Our procedures never came close to approval, even though we showed significant progress on some illnesses such as diabetes and various neurological disorders. When the program neared termination, I left the R&D department, and headed for medical school. After graduation and my internship in southern California, I came back to Italy to open my clinic.

The former program director of the R&D department at Beechum wrote the article you found. I'm sure they pooh-poohed him as a mal-content, with a grudge towards the government, though he spoke the truth. Our procedure did have a very good chance of success if we could have gotten approval."

The news took my breath away. The conclusions I arrived at had been correct. Stem cell therapy had become a reality for release to the world at a much earlier date than reported. Energy drained from me. I couldn't speak. *I, we, all of us had been betrayed.* I understood why the pharmaceuticals wanted to make a partnership agreement with me. The research would be performed by me, and they would know if I got too close. They used me to spy on my own work. They could fly beneath the radar.

Isabelle continued. "The ex-Director tried time and again to get approval, though they refused at every turn. He convinced the company to look into the background of the people appointed to the board. The news supported his suspicions. The FDA was stacked with religious conservatives. Their first priority would always be to protect the ideals of the moral right and the sanctity of life. They provided opposition to stem cell medicinal development at every turn.

We found that each and every appointee to the board, had either held positions at or been strongly supported by the Coalition for Life, a very conservative, evangelical based group opposed to stem cell utilization. The former Director where I worked tried to secure the lobby power of an outside firm to Beechum to push for less stringent requirements, or even new appointees, without any luck. In his frustration, my former boss wrote the article and stood ready to take it public. Then he suffered the accident that took his life.

When the article materialized, the Coalition for Life attacked him with viciousness, and labeled him as a vindictive personality denied so many times, he must attack the FDA. Beechum dropped their pursuit. The conservatives seemed too strong. I thought the last of these article reprints lost, re-called, or destroyed long ago."

Isabelle stared at me. Sadness threatened to overwhelm her. They warned her she might be approached. It seemed easy enough. Play along, and keep quiet. She would be rewarded. She desired a return to R&D. Private practice offered its rewards, though being back within the think tank excited her, and the perks appealed to her even more. Now she didn't feel so sure.

The call to her had come out of nowhere. They did not

bother to contact her for years. They used the words, a 'just in case' stopgap to entice her back in and they went on to describe the potential contact as erratic, emotional, and out of control. She found James the opposite. The call originated from a local firm in Italy, by the name of Alpha Pharmaceuticals.

"So a treatment may have been available years ago? There could have been a cure? My legs could be useful today? Life without MS may have been a reality? My daughter could live without it now?" My head hung low.

"Yes, you might have been treated years ago, along with millions of others", Isabelle said.

"My thoughts don't include the millions of others," I shouted. "This concerns my daughter." Weariness overcame me. "I'm so scared."

The verbal attacks from my childhood crept over me. Fear of failure threatened to suffocate me. Tears welled in my eyes. *How can I do it?*

Isabelle reached towards me.

"You can do it," she uttered. "You can help so many others. Together we can do it." *They count on me,* she thought.

The ember inside of me roared to life. "Yes, damn it, we can do it!" My rage ignited. I struggled to my feet standing close to Isabelle. "A physician told me I would die from this disease. I have lost the ability to walk any farther than five feet. My eye sight disappeared in one eye on three different occasions from optic neuritis.

When I fall down, people don't stop to help me because they think I'm drunk, and then my daughter was diagnosed with it. Will she bear children? Will she work? Will she be able to walk on a beach? Will her life ever be normal? She can't drive like her friends! Am I mad? Of course! There can be no forgiveness."

My rage burned. All the years of anger, my very disgust at the way my grandfather and father pursued their successes welled up inside. My empathy for others disappeared. A feeling of betrayal is all that remained.

Weakness suddenly overcame me. The adrenaline rush passed.

"Isabelle, you don't understand. So many hopes have been chased. I met with a pharmaceutical company to solicit a partnership with them. We agreed we would keep each other appraised of our progress. Not more than that."

She watched him. He stared at the table unable to look at her. "Since childhood, my mentors have told me, success cannot be attained. They chided me, and now the greatest challenge of my life faces me. My daughter means the world to me. I do this for her."

Isabelle didn't say a word. She thought of the hundreds, thousands, or more she might be able to help. She'd been offered the chance to do just that. She would never be able to do it on her own. The financial cost soared past her means. *Think*. Should she tell him? She didn't.

"I can't believe it. Isabelle, do you mean to tell me that stem cell therapy could have been successful at a much earlier date?" I asked my anger rising again. "How do you know this?" It made sense. Evidence I discovered indicated this to be the case.

She considered her response, and chose to ignore replying.

"I have a plan," she at last offered. "We need to go to London to see Dr. Hopkins," she said. "I do not know his exact work right now, though perhaps we might get lucky, or he can refer us to someone else."

"What of your practice Isabelle? What of your pursuits?"

She waved as if to brush away any questions. She needed to pursue all options.

"My practice has been closed. We cannot make progress here. At least if we see Hopkins, we move forward."

I stared at her emotionless. "Are you sure?"

"Si," she said. "We must keep this hope alive. Our responsibility to others must not be ignored." I wanted to reach to her and hug her.

Chapter 14

We left the cafe in a hurry. As we headed for the door, Isabelle turned and shouted "Ciao" over her shoulder to the woman at the counter. At the top of the steps, Isabelle offered her hand, which I accepted not for stability, but because a longtime had passed since an attractive woman gave me her hand. As we cleared the last step, she released my hand and jogged towards the car.

"Can you make it on your own the rest of the way?" she called.

"Yes."

With the use of my cane, I shuffled along the edge of the trimmed border of the lawn. She pulled the car to me. I clambered in, placed my cane next to me, and settled into the seat for the short ride.

"It will not take me long at the clinic. I keep a bag packed for emergencies. I'll check for any returned messages, and call Dr. Hopkins to let him know our plans and then we can head for the airport." I hesitated.

"Can we fly out of another airport and not Milan?" She glanced at me as she wheeled her vehicle on the narrow country road.

"Oh, come on James. Let's get off the cloak and dagger stuff. We can go to Milan, or if it concerns you that much we can go to Pavia, although if we buy our tickets at the Milan Airport it is a direct flight. If we travel from Pavia, the route will go through Rome, and then on to London." She already had made a huge commitment and I didn't want to seem ungrateful, but knew I must ask.

She roared into the open area of the clinic where dust and rock rose. *Did everyone in this country drive like this? Maybe fast drivers remained a tradition.* After all, the country had given birth to Fiat, Ferrari, Maserati, and the Alfa Romeo.

"Give me a few minutes to gather my bag, and then we can head off."

"Excuse me, Isabelle. Could I wander the grounds?"

"Of course," she replied. "Help yourself. I'll be back soon." She displayed life and energy.

A stone walkway led to the garden. There I found ferns, blooms on azaleas, and miscellaneous plants un-recognizable to me. After several minutes spent in admiration, the front porch called me. There a large rattan chair awaited me. As I pulled myself onto the porch, and eased into the chair, my legs knew I made the right choice.

The new direction we pursued crossed my mind. The UK had become our destination. A well-known and respected place of research on stem cells, *yet would they be as advanced as Dr. Giovantti? Would they conduct her procedure now that the Italian government had closed her down?* These questions and more rolled in my mind as the silence on the front porch became silent no longer.

Her scream pierced the air. The hair on the nape of my neck stood on end. *No, you bastards! Not here! Leave her alone!* I struggled from the chair as fast as possible. My cane clattered to the wood boards of the deck. Her footsteps raced across the floor, and then there came the sound of torn material and another gargled shout. More footsteps raced towards me. Her steps raced closer and faster.

As I leaned forward my cane came within reach. I grasped it, and leaned back into the front wall with hope she gained at least one step, and maybe more on her pursuer.

My grip tightened close to the bottom half of the cane, the handled part of the stick held high over my shoulder. The screen door burst open. She raced past me like the wind. I braced myself and lifted the cane higher like a baseball bat.

My cane served me well, yet it held no long-term sentiment. It had been purchased from a shoe store. It carried a thin, sturdy look to it with a standard curve on the top for a hand grip. It served as a good tool. Now, it would be more.

After one, maybe two seconds the screen door burst open. With all my strength I heaved away from the wall and swung the cane. The cane struck the shins of the pursuer with a heavy crack. The pursuer yelled in surprise and pain. The cane splintered against the attacker's lower legs. Wood debris flew about. I lost my balance and fell forward. I'd given up on swings like that long ago.

The assailant fell first. He fell hard to the ground. His head smashed into the brick path. I fell forward on top of the man as he struck the walkway, and wrapped my arm around the man's neck without the realization that the fall knocked the assailant unconscious. I began to yell in the man's ear.

"Who sent you? What do you want?" The words fell on deaf ears. Isabelle appeared at the scene. She began to strike me on the arm.

"James, can you hear me? James, look at me. James he's unconscious. Can you hear me?" At last the words began to break through. "He's knocked out, James. Let him go," Isabelle pleaded with me while she pulled at my arm wrapped around the man's neck.

Her words at last broke my rush. I looked up at Isabelle, and released the man's neck. His head slapped hard against the brick.

My attention turned to Isabelle. The sleeve of her pretty

blouse lay torn from her shoulder. Blood trickled from her mouth.

"Are you alright?" She wiped her mouth with the back of her hand.

"Yes, I'll be fine. Not any worse than what my brother used to do to me."

Clarity began to return. I rolled off the man's back onto the lawn next to the walkway and continued my roll to my hands and knees.

"Let's see if we know this joker." I reached into the man's back pocket, and found it empty.

With a heavy grunt I rolled him to the grass and faced him. A gasp escaped me as I settled back on my haunches. Isabelle grabbed me by my shoulder to stop my fall.

A nasty gash on his head dripped blood onto the ground. I recognized him in an instant. Arturo Salsado, the man who knocked my chair attendant down the night before at the airport stared back at me with sightless eyes.

Isabelle asked, "Do you recognize him?"

"He followed me from the States on the plane yesterday." Isabelle's face blanched.

"Are you sure?"

"Yes. He knocked my chair attendant to the ground at the airport." This now had become a nightmare. The man groaned, though didn't move.

My actions began. I patted the assailants' front pockets, then the breast pocket of his shirt. Nothing had been left there.

"We need to go. If he doesn't call in soon, they may send someone to check on him." I pushed myself up. Isabelle grabbed me by the arm and helped me to stand, my elbow held close to her.

"Let me go grab another cane and my bag. Ouch, his shins have got to hurt," she said as she looked at the broken pieces of wood cane that lay spread on the ground.

"I hope for a long time," I uttered. "Leave me here. Will you find some good material to tie his wrists and ankles? We won't make life easy for him. Not so long this time." She turned and smiled back at me.

"Fast as I can," she called.

This guy won't be about to move I thought as I lowered myself to the grass, and then turned and sat on the man's back. She returned in just a few moments. She locked the door as she left with a new cane in hand. She laughed to see me on the man's back, and handed me a roll of duct tape.

"This will keep him still," she said with smugness. She'd taken the time to clean up, put a fresh blouse on, and looked her radiant self, though pale from the recent attack. I pulled the man's wrists together to bind them, laid one ankle on top of the other and wrapped them together with duct tape.

"Where can we put him?"

"On the side of the house," said Isabelle. The idea sounded good. I stood, made it to the man's bound ankles, bent down, grabbed a hold, and gave a mighty tug. The man's inert weight dragged on the lawn. I pulled with great exertion to move the big man. After several pulls, I dragged the man into the garden.

My breath came back as I stood, stepped over the prone man, and bent to turn his face from the dirt to make sure he could breathe.

Isabelle waited with the car at the end of walkway. I piled into the seat with my new cane, and we began our rapid departure.

As we reached the pavement, she turned away from the

direction that would take us back to Milan.

"We can't go to Milan. We will go to Pavia, and take a puddle jumper to Rome. It should be easy to get a direct flight to London from Rome." The knock around she endured must have shook her up.

"He heard me on the phone to Dr. Hopkin's office." Frustration welled in me, though I couldn't blame her. "I called him to make the arrangements. I just finished the conversation, and he jumped me from the kitchen." This new development circled through my mind. *How much did he hear? Should they try to meet with Dr. Hopkins?*

"What will we accomplish with Hopkins?"

"The doctor wanted to share some research data with me."

"Do you know what kind of information?"

"No. Perhaps we can use his lab."

"Isabelle," I murmured.

"Si?" she replied.

"Can we drive to Paris?" She turned her head to give me a confused look.

"What?" she asked.

"We shouldn't go by plane. These people may find us. They have lots of contacts. Whether Milan, or Pavia, or Rome, or Heathrow, they will find us. We should head to Paris, and take the train. We can get into London by the Chunnel. Isabelle, we should avoid planes."

As she drove the road she displayed remarkable skills with control of the car. She threw the vehicle into a sharp right hand turn at the next intersection without a drop in speed.

After a moment of silence she said, "I agree. We'll go to Paris. The drive is almost eight hours, though you will get to see Geneva." I settled back, and began to think of the long ride, and our appointment with Dr. Hopkins. I couldn't have asked for a more desirous travel companion.

The landscape zoomed past. Little traffic approached as we flew around the stiff curves. I relaxed and dozed.

Isabelle drove without a stop. I woke from my nap, and checked if I could take over. She answered no, though a rest stop would be appreciated, and with my concurrence we pulled into the next petrol station. We paid cash for our purchases, aware we could not afford to leave a credit card trail. As we passed through the outskirts of Geneva, I looked at the modern sky line and homes perched on hillsides.

As she sped through the City, I asked of a possible transplant elsewhere.

"Might we be able to find a clinic that could loan you their facilities?"

She considered her response with care, and then answered. "James, it doesn't seem possible. The UK is our best bet. If that doesn't work, we might be able to investigate Finland, or Sweden. As long as we have gone that far north, we may as well continue."

"Though with the progressive programs of the UK, wouldn't that be easier?" I asked.

"It would be easier, though you need to consider that my work and results have just been introduced. We might find some researchers who would allow us to utilize their facility, although their liability insurance carriers will have a fit."

"Of course, the litigators will be upset. Do you think we can find a way to beat that?"

Isabelle bit her lip, careful not to draw blood from her previous injury. "No, I don't. Many people support regenerative procedures, though few will put their names on it."

It seemed as if the whole mess boiled over into an

international debacle. I considered the amount of money spent to propel people into a happy and healthy old age, and the monies spent to protect that investment.

The U.S. National Institute of Health served as the single largest investor to advance technologies for drugs, therapies, and medical devices to move the industry forward. Yet, the insurance companies that underwrote the preposterous liability policies to protect the drug makers turned out to be the true winners.

The losers included patients who experienced delays due to political or philosophical opposition. I didn't like the reality, though recognized it as the truth.

How ironic. Lives could be changed. Hundreds of millions of dollars spent on Research and Development projects could be redirected. Stem cell research made up just one of many potential new pursuits.

Isabelle considered the procedure she had developed in silence. *Would she have a chance to pursue her procedure again?* The advances she could make defied current practices. Her efforts set a new direction for other medical professionals.

She didn't see herself as a trend setter. Yet she knew she set her career on a path that few traveled. The journey excited her, but also filled her with intimidation to carry that kind of responsibility. She relished the task. The reward of hope offered to patients like James lightened the burden.

As we drove, I asked out of the blue, if Isabelle knew of Alpha Drugs near Rome. She about lost her grip on the wheel.

"Si" she replied. "Why?"

"How much do you know?"

"Not much. Big organization, aligned with government thinkers, conservative and powerful."

"They sent a representative of some sort to the States to find me. He ended up in a hospital from a mugging. The police found a letter on Alpha letter head with my name on it."

She stayed silent. Her first contact began with Alpha. She knew them well. They offered a lot of money to take over her research. She turned them down due to their known close ties to the Vatican and her fear her research would be buried amongst their huge bureaucracy. *Why would they be interested in James?*

We continued into Paris comfortable our antagonists had been left behind. Our pursuers now knew we needed to get to Dr. Hopkins' lab. What would come next, neither of us imagined.

Isabelle spun onto a small side street, and brought the car to an abrupt stop.

"We're here," she announced with almost a gleeful tone to her voice.

My bent frame took time to extract from the seat.

My luggage, briefcase, and wheelchair had been left behind. I missed my briefcase, though the critical data stored there, now rested with me. My new cane and the documents I carried represented my most important possessions.

"The station is right there," Isabelle said as she pointed at a low structure on the other side of the street. She reached for my hand. I enjoyed the pressure of her hand in mine. I had no desire to pull away as long as she held me. We entered the station hand in hand.

Chapter 15

We made it into the station with no problems. Isabelle ordered two one-way tickets to London in impeccable French. My gaze settled on her in further admiration.

As she took the tickets I asked, "How many languages do you speak?"

She chuckled. "English of course, Italian, French, and I can get by pretty well in German" she answered.

"Great. We're covered."

"Give me your hand. Let's get a glass of wine," said Isabelle.

"How about a good beer," I said as we headed towards the eateries.

"Suit yourself. There's a little cafe I enjoy here. They have both."

Isabelle led me to a small French cafe. Once inside, I grew more comfortable. We found a table hidden away near the back. Isabelle ordered a glass of burgundy and me a beer. We both exhaled, and leaned back. Twilight approached. Our drinks arrived. Isabelle offered a toast in French.

"What does that mean?" She laughed and answered with a smile.

"Down with the assholes and up with the healthy." We both drank and laughed together as much from the relief of the moment as from relaxation.

As we talked, a phone call started by a young Frenchman in the front hallway rang on the other side of the Atlantic.

The young man worked as a baggage courier at the station. They had passed him as they left the ticket counter.

The young Frenchman received the broadcast fax earlier. It carried a picture of a man and woman that should be reported, if seen, and a telephone number in bold and upper case italics emblazoned on the page.

The facsimile sign off said, 'Your brothers and sisters with God', a common sign-off between the members and teachers of the organization.

Members had been taught in their indoctrination to share words of trust and belief.

The young man responded to the fax in excitement, his call routed from one international node to another until it ended at a cell antenna in New York. The answer came on the first ring.

"Yes" came the response.

"I've got them at a train station just outside Paris. They have purchased two tickets for London," and ended his report. The young man folded the fax paper with the fuzzy, though distinguishable pictures on it and placed it away.

The recipient list grew long, and varied, sent to most Mediterranean countries, and the UK. A hit faced long odds, yet the network served a wide area, and the sender could hope.

The sender of the facsimile was elated and reviewed the names of various soldiers overseas. He found two he could depend on. They served with dedication.

He knew who James Armstrong ventured to see. The call from Italy came in earlier. One of their independent agents suffered two broken legs, and a severe concussion, yet passed on the information to their first contact on the scene.

A search of the briefcase led to the envelope addressed to the attorney in New York. The enclosed letter told it all. He knew.

That document, and their secret alliance forged with the pharmaceutical conglomerate now threatened not just their beliefs, but the entire organization.

No choice remained. Both travelers must be stopped. A more complicated and messier solution existed, though options were minimized on a daily basis.

When first revealed by one of James' co-workers under the auspices of assistance with the research he conducted that the document existed, and of the relationship he put in place with the pharmacological industry, the plan became more complicated.

Fear stirred. As an agent of the Coalition for Life, the ramifications terrified him. Simon grew up in a strict foster home, blessed by the words of religious empowerment.

He always practiced and maintained a devoted belief in the words. These philosophies were integrated into his life from his earliest days as a young man to a career in the military and his professional pursuit. Those words had now become threatened by the blasphemous use of life for life. He would not allow it to occur. He pledged in the most devout fashion, to stop it.

The luck of Mr. Armstrong's research partner as a devout believer played into his hands. *How much more luck could he count on?*

Finding the article in Armstrong's briefcase now served as the valuable instrument that kept him alive. They must silence any potential leaks.

Simon discussed the potential with superiors in the order. The conversations centered on James' demise, yet that action had been vetoed without the assurance that the article could be recovered.

The go ahead for the attack in Italy came with cautious

urgency, and hope the article would be found. Yet the article remained at large, a copy in Armstrong's strong box as reported in the letter taken from the captured briefcase, an agent lay crippled, and Armstrong and the doctor had been alerted to their attempts to stop them. Top level managers became incensed. All their resources must now be called upon.

The organization prided itself on resourcefulness, financial austerity, adequate staff, and support from believers everywhere in the world. The alert went out and now it paid dividends.

"Good. Go to London on the same train," he said and hung up.

Simon considered available options. They had lost their trail, now enjoyed the good luck to pick it back up. He issued the orders for their team to move into place. Their luck stayed good. The time came to capitalize on that luck.

Now he must make the call he most dreaded. The phone rang twice.

"This is Simon calling. I have news," he stated. "They're headed to London from Paris by train. They have set up an appointment with Dr. Hopkins." Silence returned on the line.

"What time do they see Hopkins?"

"Tomorrow at eight-thirty, London time," Simon answered. The voice came back with a heavy sigh.

"Make sure the appointment does not happen." The line went dead. Simon knew what that meant. He called London, and issued new orders.

CHAPTER 16

James and Isabelle made it downstairs, and onto the platform for the scheduled departure. Several bullet trains entered the station, loaded passengers, unloaded arrivals, and departed for their next destination. The trains operated with smoothness and efficiency.

At the appointed time, the train entered the station, and stopped near us. A small crowd gathered on the platform. With practiced patience, I scanned the other passengers. No one paid any undue attention to us. The young man stood at the back of the crowd, content to remain ambiguous.

We boarded the train, and found seats with little difficulty. Isabelle offered her hand to me to board the train, which I accepted with graciousness.

Empty seats waited near the front of the car. As Isabelle moved ahead, the train jerked forward. I fell forward, my hands outstretched. My right hand fell and stayed grasped to Isabelle's right hip. I righted myself, my hand still against her hip. She turned and lifted my hand with a small smile on her face.

"James, you can be seated," she giggled at me.

I slumped into a seat. The train slid from the station, and began its rapid acceleration toward two hundred miles per hour. We would travel across parts of Germany, Belgium, and arrive at the London station close to eleven that night. With luck we would catch some sleep on the train, settle into a clean, quiet place when we arrived, and rise rested for the new day.

Isabelle dozed first as we accelerated from station to

station. It turned to dusk outside. Little could be seen from the window as scenes sped by, or as we coasted to stops. I rested my head back, and ordered a beer as the waiter passed. Isabelle stirred her head against my shoulder. A long time had passed since any woman exhibited such ease with me. I enjoyed the moment and the pressure on my shoulder. It made me feel respected and comfortable.

As darkness settled upon the night, I glanced at my watch, and guessed we traveled through Germany. Isabelle's language fluency would be handy here, if needed. The small towns that flew past lit by shadowed lights appeared like darkened pictures from my childhood fantasy books. Small and compact communities established around an old church steeple that rose in the center of town.

The dark countryside sped by. Gauges at the front of the car showed the speed we traveled. The speed registered both in kilometers and miles per hour.

As darkness enveloped the train, I nodded off still bothered by goblins of the darkness and my own capability.

The announcement startled me back to reality.

"Ladies, and Gentlemen," the voice began. "We will be entering the Chunnel in a few moments. The train will run underground for about thirty minutes and be near London on the other side. Thank you."

The conductor could have kept that information to himself and let me sleep. The intercom raised Isabelle as well. She stretched and looked at me.

"Thanks for the pillow," she said with a sleepy chuckle.

"Sure, any time you need a warm place to drop your head I'm available." She smiled up at me and stretched her arms.

"So, what's the plan?" she asked.

"Well, how far to Dr. Hopkins' clinic?"

"It's on the north side of the city."

"Let's grab a taxi and head to a motel in that direction. Do you have an address for Dr. Hopkins?"

"Of course," she answered.

"On our way, we need to grab a few toiletries for me. If you can stand my same clothes for another day, so can, I."

So with our thoughts laid out, we slid back into silence. The plan came together with simple directness and we hoped it would be successful. We would travel near Dr. Hopkin's clinic, find a place to stay, a store to grab a toothbrush, a razor, deodorant, and sleep until the sun rose, and of course, the most important unsaid part meet with Dr. Hopkins the next day.

We slipped back into unconsciousness. The young man stirred with eyes trained on the two he had been ordered to follow. The trip had been uneventful, his presence undetected, the cell phone he carried set to vibrate. It now became active. He reached deep to pull it from a coat pocket, and found the cold cover with his fingertips. He flipped it open, and looked at the new text message.

"Have you arrived? Do you have a status on subjects?"

"Arrive soon. Subjects visual," he typed and snapped the phone closed. The texts had been received and sent just before entering the Chunnel.

I sat upright. Isabelle regained clarity.

"Isabelle, what do you expect Dr. Hopkins to add?" Isabelle stifled a yawn as she answered.

"Even though he said he didn't, I want to know if Doctor Hopkins might have the equipment I need to perform my procedure," she answered. "We don't always know what we have hidden away until we do a thorough search."

"Would you proceed if Dr. Hopkins' clinic might have

the equipment to support your procedure?"

"Well, of course," she answered. "You didn't think I came all the way to London just to see Big Ben did you? Close your mouth," she laughed at me as she reached with her index finger, and placed it beneath my chin, to push up. "James, you don't know me that well, but I don't quit. If we can use the proper equipment and have access to frozen embryos, we can proceed. We can move ahead, as long as he doesn't object due to the insurance liability issue."

With that, I bent to her cheek and planted a kiss on her. She laughed and tossed her head back, "You didn't think I would send you home without a ticket to the ride, did you? James, I need to ask you more. Back at the cafe you said you didn't care what happened to others, just yourself and daughter. That bothers me as a professional practitioner. You need to explain yourself in more detail."

"Isabelle, it's a long story. My journey began in search of a treatment for me. I want to walk again. This disease carries so much hate. There exist so many unanswered questions. The unknown remains despicable.

When my daughter – the light of my life – received the same diagnosis, it broke my heart. When she was young, my desperation to convince myself, that the un-comfort she experienced couldn't be more than simple growth pains in her legs failed. I always knew better. Then a study I uncovered showed a direct genetic link to MS and my death from guilt came nearer. The disease came from me. Her own father corrupted her existence.

The reality overwhelmed me. My search took on new urgency. It no longer just involved me. It involved her as well."

"That can be understood James, but what of other parents

who face the same potential?"

"Their problem does not concern me. My daughter remains my only concern."

Isabelle wanted to scream. She understood James' own pain, though not to the exclusion of others. They grew silent.

Isabelle thought of the offer made to her. Not to keep her research private, but to take it back to the R&D environment she came from. She would be absorbed back into the corporate world. She knew the financial support would be huge. She grew tired of the burden on her own. The rewards would be great. The current cost of pursuing her success nearly crippled her, and now she had been offered the opportunity to help so many, not just the few. She battled these thoughts on a regular basis, not sure of her direction, and given the events of the last day, a well-paid position that she excelled appealed to her.

Isabelle rationalized she wouldn't turn her back on James and his daughter. She would opt to help the greater good, not just on the individualized basis James desired.

My goal remained fixed. My daughter remained my priority. My own condition no longer mattered.

"Ladies and Gentlemen, could I have your attention please. We have exited the Chunnel, and approach the London Station." I looked at Isabelle.

"Let's get a cab, and head north. How far away is Dr. Hopkins' neighborhood?" Isabelle thought of her last trip to London.

"About forty-five minutes. At this hour we should make good time."

Though we now approached a mere possibility, I couldn't afford any fall into unfettered excitement. *Would Dr. Hopkins' clinic have the necessary equipment? Would he allow Isabelle to perform the procedure? Could the procedure be successful under different international law? Would their pursuers give up the chase and let them continue on their path?* I had a thousand questions to answer.

My thoughts turned to our pursuers. *Had they ended their chase?* The chances seemed slim. They wouldn't let us continue unhindered. The risk to our pursuers had obviously grown to a level that dismissed my optimism as just that. Optimistic thoughts alone did not have a good chance of survival.

My pursuers followed me all the way to Italy. If Isabelle's conversation had been overheard, they now knew our destination. To give up was not a viable option for them. They would continue to fight to keep their secret just that.

My nervousness grew. Isabelle took notice of the grim look on my face. She patted my hand.

"James, don't give them too much credit."

She watched me, aware of how much weight I placed on her assumptions. I hoped to undergo the procedure. She knew it meant the world to me. I flattered her, yet that didn't stop her uncertainty and concern.

We arrived at the London Station. Isabelle gathered her bag. We departed the train car and began to make our way to the taxi cab area. I made slow time. The escape to Paris, and now the train ride cramped my legs, and left me with a desire to rest and let my legs recover.

An evil of multiple sclerosis remained a great fatigue. Many didn't understand. Strength drained, so that the simplest of tasks turned difficult. If I burned too much energy, or stayed immobile for long periods of time, my mobility disappeared. Such a moment now occurred.

Isabelle held onto my left arm. I used the cane with my

right and moved at a very slow pace.

The young man left the train well back. He placed a call on his cell phone as we walked, to provide a description of the direction we moved. A car waited outside for him, job completed.

We hailed a cab, and I leaned forward to ask our driver to stop at a convenience store on the way to our desired destination. Neither of us spoke exhausted by our travels with a simple knowledge that we wanted to head to the northern part of the city. Our travel time at this hour on the expressway went fast.

The cabbie saw a convenience store sign at a ramp off the expressway. He took the turn, and pulled into a spot at the store. I looked to the other side of the street, and identified what we needed.

"We'll stay here tonight." A motel stood there.

My struggle from the side door began. I reached through the open window of the driver's door, paid, and patted the driver on the shoulder.

"Can you grab the lady's bag from the back, and then you can go." The driver removed her bag, dropped it on the sidewalk and accelerated away. We stood alone. Isabelle picked up her bag.

"I'll head inside. Want to wait here or come in?" She pointed at a bench next to the doors.

After a few moments, I exited with my new essentials in a plastic bag.

"Let's go." Isabelle didn't say a word. She neared exhaustion. Her face had gone blank, her color pale, sleep waited to claim her.

We made our way across the street. She made no attempt to take my hand, and seemed oblivious to her environment.

Given the hour, no traffic moved on the street. Isabelle walked with her arms folded against her chest, head down. She walked at my tempo with no realization of the slowness with which she moved. We reached the motel door and entered. A remote control buzzer must have sounded as a blurry-eyed night attendant revealed herself at the front desk.

"We need two rooms, close to the back. Are there alarm clocks in the rooms?"

"Yes," the night attendant said. "I can also set a wakeup call for you."

"We'll use our alarms." I handed her cash for the rooms. The attendant made change, passed Isabelle's room key to her and handed the second key to me. As we left, I told Isabelle that we should depart by seven in the morning.

"We can have breakfast at the coffee shop there." We walked along the outside of the rooms to the rear, and turned to find the back entrance. I unlocked the door and we entered a long hallway. I guided Isabelle, our roles reversed. Our journey would continue again when we woke.

Chapter 17

I lay fully awake in the early morning hours. Given the little rest snuck on the train, it surprised me sleep was so hard to find. Isabelle's exhaustion the night before crossed my mind. Her conversation in her office gave our adversaries the necessary ammunition to keep abreast of us.

They appeared to have organization and money behind them. Their intentions and network could not be under estimated. Though it made no difference, I wondered, *who could it be?*

We must make atypical plans. Our opponents displayed greater power and capitalization. Of course, my motivation outweighed theirs. I wanted to see the research continue unencumbered by outside pressures, but a new found cure at this point seemed remote. I would provide what assistance I could to advance research, *but, could more be done?*

If the procedure worked for me, I would be overjoyed, yet the realist in me, understood the risks. If I sat in on part of a board room discussion, my own business scrutiny based on a risk/reward analysis would be negative.

My hope had always been to help move the process forward. With that hope, I understood that help could come closer to reality.

Our moves the next day circulated through my head. I remained worried about what extremes the people who wanted to stop us would go. My feelings for Isabelle had grown. I had begun to be very protective of her.

Our opposition walked a path to stop discoveries that could rewrite history. They appeared unafraid. I needed to think with care of our next steps.

The journey to see Dr. Hopkins must proceed though not by a direct approach. We must acquiesce to the realization we would be watched. Isolation would be desirable, though could not be a luxury to be expected.

We would take a cab. The driver would be part of the solution. Obscurity had become our best friend. Police involvement could not be considered. What could be reported? Besides, for all I knew, we had become wanted felons for assault and battery in a different foreign jurisdiction.

If we could get to the clinic, then we night be able to go back to work on Isabelle's program. We must find a creative means to enter the clinic. *Sure my handicap slowed us, yet how could we use it to our benefit?* With those thoughts, sleep found me.

At five-fifteen my alarm went off. The time arrived to start the day. A new direction would unfold for us. I showered, and called Isabelle's room at six. She answered right away.

"Good day. I'm up. Shower on the way. Give me a moment."

"You sound better."

"A little sleep does a body good. Give me time to shower, dress, and we can go. Thirty minutes," she said and hung up. *Good*, I thought. She seemed back on track. I needed her strong, not filled with fear and indecision.

Thirty minutes later a knock came at the door. I made it to the door, a bit rickety, and opened it to a fresh dressed, bathed, and wide awake Isabelle.

"Let's go," she said. "I'm hungry, not sure of where to go and ready to knock the next person that messes with us in the head with your cane!" *Now this attitude I could deal with!*

"Easy does it, slugger. I'm the one who gets to break

canes, not you." We both laughed and headed out to begin our adventure for the day.

Isabelle appeared boisterous. I didn't slow her, just listened to her voice prattle on as I realized her exhaustion gave way to an energy surge. To keep her controlled today would be the new task I faced.

We made our way to the back door, and turned towards the coffee shop. She reached to me and took my hand as we left the hotel. I liked her grasp in my hand. It seemed right.

"Did I help you last night?" I knew her compassion returning served as a good sign of normalcy.

"We made it just fine." She went silent for a moment. "I'm so sorry, James. I won't disappoint you again."

Her conscious recall of events the previous night seemed very sweet and I turned towards her as we walked, and replied, "You didn't."

The coffee shop served as a replica of so-many others. The day would start with stale coffee, cookie cutter food, but fast service. I scanned the crowd for any who might show more than a bit too much interest towards us. My eyes settled on a few faces I watched for any untoward glances, yet few met my gaze, and fewer still paid me or Isabelle any attention.

We settled into a booth so I could watch the door. Isabelle watched me, confident I would spy danger before it found us. She ordered a bountiful omelet, and I asked for coffee and a muffin with a request of the server to keep the coffee hot, and my cup full.

"You seem to have recovered," I murmured. Isabelle pushed a fork full of omelet into her mouth.

"Excuse me," she stammered as she ate. "Yesterday should be left right where it belongs, and that my dear goes in the history books. Today we move on and see one of the greatest technical minds in the industry," she replied with excitement to her voice. I unfolded a local map taken from my motel room, as she continued her attention to her plate of food.

"Sure you don't want any?" she offered as she slid the plate towards me with a few bites left behind.

"No, thank you. I'm a bit distracted." My thoughts both frustrated and frightened me. I shook my head to clear the dismal attitude that settled in, and clucked my tongue. Here I sat with such an attractive woman, and acted like a fool. Exasperation crept through me, though I knew with the secret not shared with Isabelle, I could not stay there. The rest of the story frightened me, and that burden I wished to shed soon.

She finished up her last bites, and settled back to sip her tea. I finished my third cup of coffee.

"Isabelle, as we leave from here let's ask our driver to circle on back-streets and make our way as if we have no idea where we want to go." She looked at me and understood my concern. My comments brought her back to reality. People wanted to hurt us. They had attacked her. She'd never been attacked before in her life.

"Are you ready to go?" She began to slide from the booth and stopped.

"James?"

"Yes."

"Have you told me the whole story?" I stopped my movement. She caught it and looked straight at me.

"No. I will, though not until it's time."

As I slid from the booth, I dropped the appropriate Euros on the table to cover breakfast and tip, and took a firm grip on my cane. Isabelle stood and took my left hand.

"I'll call for a cab and pick you up outside." She helped

me out the door, dropped my hand and headed to the motel lobby.

"Isabelle, wait," I called. "Take me with you." She looked at me with a cute expression of inquisitiveness, took my left hand and we began our way to the motel lobby.

Isabelle may have thought that I had become a bit over protective, though she accepted the overture. As we reached the lobby she wondered what surprises awaited us that day.

At the front office, I used the motel courtesy phone to call for a cab, asking the dispatcher if the car could meet us in back.

We headed out the interior hallway to the rear, stopped at the exit door and watched for our ride to arrive.

The cab pulled up ten meters past the door five minutes later. We waited a few moments and came out. The driver reversed the car and came to a stop near us. Isabelle carried her bag. My essentials were wrapped in the plastic grocery bag from the convenience store. We slid into the passenger seats, and I provided the address that Isabelle carried for Dr. Hopkins' clinic.

As we left, I slid a little lower in the seat. It seemed like somewhat of a paranoid reaction, although I could not underestimate our pursuers. The driver watched in the rear view mirror.

"Look" she said. "If you two have been in there on a secret rendezvous, that's fine with me. Just don't get me involved with some jealous boyfriend or girlfriend."

We looked at each other and smiled.

"Oh no," Isabelle said. "We're on our honeymoon."

"Ok," the driver mumbled.

I looked across the seat at Isabelle.

"Isabelle," I began. She watched my face, the serious tone

of my voice not lost on her. "I need to tell you more. I haven't told you all, and I have never been a very good secret keeper."

The driver left the motel parking area. We stayed low. On the main boulevard I told the cabbie my directions.

"Take the first side street you come to. It doesn't matter if you go right, or left. Just take it. Go fast until the next street, take it, and accelerate to the next. Make three turns, and take them as fast as possible." The driver listened to her passenger. As long as the money to cover it rested in their pockets, fine with her.

Isabelle glanced at me. I had shown up at her clinic after we exchanged random e-mails, and now her life had turned upside down. She had lost the license to practice at her clinic. She abandoned her practice. She'd been assaulted. My story sounded sincere, though how could she know for sure?

A side street came up fast on the right hand side. The driver took it with no touch to her brakes, and accelerated on the quiet street. Another appeared on the left. Tires squealed as she cornered.

"One more," I commanded.

She punched the accelerator, and made it to the next right hand turn with more speed. The cab squealed around it and accelerated. I leaned into Isabelle as the car took the corner. I liked the feeling against her.

Though they overheard Isabelle at her clinic, and knew our ultimate destination, I wanted to make sure we had not been followed.

"Now what?" the driver asked.

"Stay straight. Look for a main boulevard, and turn right again."

We continued straight for about another three quarters of a mile and came to a busy boulevard. She turned right, punched the accelerator, switched to the fast lane and roared away from the neighborhood. I reached out and patted the driver on the shoulder.

"Take it easy now. I think we would have left anyone behind. I'm sure they have a scanner turned to the police channels."

Isabelle saw a place to park at a petrol station we approached and asked the driver to pull in. She pulled into a spot next to the property boundary and Isabelle directed her to stop by an old wooden fence. Large shade trees guarded the fence, their branches close to the ground. We became secluded. Isabelle handed the driver a twenty pound note and asked if she would go inside to get some coffee, keep the meter on and give us a few moments. The driver stepped out of the car. The twenty would take care of her down time.

I looked at Isabelle perplexed. Her stare held mine.

"James, I won't go any further until you tell me the whole truth." I looked out the back window to check that no one followed, and turned back to Isabelle.

"We don't have time for this."

"Now," Isabelle snapped. I raised both hands in surrender.

"The people after us want to stop us at any cost," I said.

She burst out, "Don't you think I know that? Now tell me why!"

With a sigh, I began. "My diagnosis came with very little personal knowledge of the disease. My own initiative led me to find answers. I found the usual debris of documents on trials, experimentation, and mundane notices of whom, what and where, yet no answers to my most basic questions of how to cure the illness or to make life easier for me.

Then, the stem cell arena heated up and became the news of the day. Based on information I uncovered, I decided the best odds for a successful treatment of MS would come through stem cell research and cellular regeneration. My research proceeded as quietly as possible, most of the time late at night on my home computer.

The work could also be done at work in pursuit of firms involved with new pharmaceutical developments. I even enlisted the assistance of a co-worker, likewise trained, so we could increase our output by twofold. Our real work continued unabated, though we did find time for our new line of research.

We found costs related to R&D expenses and lobby efforts, which led to the discovery of government indiscretions, philosophical arguments, and those moral dilemmas that developed around the direction of the work. Short trips to the Library of Congress occurred on a regular basis. That's where the lost paper came from. Seminar attendance became a regular past time. Then I found the most important of all."

Isabelle sat forward, and waited. "It turned my research on its ear. Isabelle, a paper came to light that reported successful transplantation of embryonic pancreatic cells that led to cellular regeneration and the cure of diabetes in 2001."

She appeared dumbfounded. Her mind must have reeled with the news.

"The first success came from the use of cells and transplant in primates, although the procedure after further refinement developed into use on a young human patient that happened to be the daughter of a very influential Congressional representative from the State of California. The girl's body did not reject the cells and new insulin secretion cells generated, with the girl's insulin injections reduced to once per week. She rose from bed. Her muscle strength and circulation increased by a factor of ninety three percent."

Isabelle struggled to find her voice.

"Why didn't it get reported?" she at last stammered out.

"A religious university located in the Bible belt conducted the research. The funds to support the work came from a federal grant. The project shut down due to financial support cancelation."

We stayed so entranced in our discussion, the knock on the passenger side window made us both jump. The cab driver waved at us. I held up five fingers. She wandered back towards the store.

"Did it get stifled due to religious objection, government concern, or other?" Isabelle choked out.

"No way to tell. It could have been the university, or it could have come from protests from various religious groups. It all became very convoluted. The university received grant funds from the federal government, so it most likely came from lack of funds. No one will comment on it." Isabelle tried to wrap her mind around the news.

"Let me summarize," Isabelle stated. "Stem cells first became nurtured close to 1995, research began to become serious in '98, and a few years later the first successful use of stem cells for cellular regeneration reduced diabetes symptoms for a human patient by ninety plus percent, yet that work was buried for untold reasons, while the world debated the morality of stem cell use. Correct?" she asked. I simply nodded.

"How did you find out?" she demanded.

"When I first stumbled into researching diabetes, I found an article that touted the opinion of a doctorate candidate at the university. The candidate had completed a Master's degree, and entered the doctorate program. In his Master's thesis he postulated that based on previous research, and the epidemic increase of diabetes, it might be one of the first diseases that could be controlled through regenerative medicine.

He wrote of the regeneration of pancreatic islet cells. His early work became credited with the first break through using primates. I contacted him about the research. At first he seemed very hesitant to talk to me, so I convinced him of why I wanted the information and then he told me more." Isabelle stayed quiet as she listened.

"Continue," she encouraged.

"When contacted, I found he had given up on his research. The university offered to forgive his student loan and give him a full time, salaried position that would lead to a teaching job in exchange for the cessation of further lab work. He agreed."

"Wait a minute. He gave up the professional pursuit of a cure for diabetes for the promise of a full time job?" she asked.

"There seemed more to it. Quite a bit more that he would not speak about. He did say it seemed odd that I had been the second person to contact him about the article, and then he became more reticent to discuss the details further. When I gained his trust, and he began to talk, he indicated he violated a confidentiality agreement he had been cajoled into signing." Isabelle sat back astonished.

"After my fifth phone call, he came clean with me. He told me a congressman, an alumnus, had discovered the research. The congressman pushed the school's chancellor to revive the program after his daughter was diagnosed with diabetes."

"So that the procedure could be performed on his daughter," Isabelle interrupted. My nod affirmed her suspicion.

"The treatment succeeded, Isabelle. I tried to get the congressman to speak to me. He wouldn't, though I did discover enough information to know that all political party support for him had been pulled. He lost his re-election bid.

His girl has since been pronounced free of diabetes. I found that from the young man who performed the procedure." Isabelle didn't speak. The cab became a tomb of silence.

"Who else contacted the young man?" she asked.

"He didn't know. They never identified themselves, just threatened his job security, and student loan to make it collectible."

"We must go," Isabelle blurted out. "This may be more dangerous than we think." The deceit and incredulous behavior, the cover up of the marvelous discovery, and the truth kept from the world became very clear to her.

The cab driver returned. As we hit the street, I studied the map laid across my knees. Based on the address Isabelle provided, I read off the most convoluted, back door way to Dr. Hopkins' clinic.

The cabbie checked her rear view mirror to make sure no one followed. Isabelle didn't say a word. Any attempt to wrap her mind around what she just heard did not make sense.

Successful stem cell treatment of disease had occurred. Though not yet accepted, she now knew for certain her technique could succeed. She had experienced some good luck with it, though she also failed. All research worked that way. Now she knew that success could be attained.

As we approached Dr. Hopkins' clinic, we began to hear the sirens. Ambulances passed first, and then fire engines, followed by more fire department emergency response vehicles. We exchanged nervous looks then saw the smoke.

"Take a right here," I ordered. The driver turned. We took a few more turns, and saw the clinic, or at least what remained of it. It now existed as no more than a mass of burned timbers.

The driver stopped a good block away. A crowd gathered and watched the smoke rise from what remained of the structure.

"There's Dr. Hopkins," Isabelle blurted out. She reached for the door. I grabbed her forearm.

"Please don't. They may be here." She gave me a cold look, yet realized the correctness of the statement. Isabelle looked at the pile of debris and tears welled in her eyes.

"This is our fault," she sobbed.

"No Isabelle, it's not our fault, it's theirs." She leaned her head on my shoulder, and sobbed.

I asked the cab driver to take us away. She restarted the car, made a U-turn, and headed back the way we came. I looked at the crowd for those who didn't seem right, sure they would be smart enough to stand back from the scene, yet not so far away they couldn't observe.

"What now?" Isabelle asked.

"Sweden." She did not respond.

"To a train station," I addressed to the driver, and turned to Isabelle.

"Let's take the Chunnel back to the Brussels Airport. We can take a hop to Sweden from there." She listened with no objections. Sadness wiped away any logical thoughts. She did not know our exact destination, just had a notion we must continue.

Chapter 18

I unfolded the map to locate a train station. I found one on the outskirts of the city. The location and coordinates I passed on to the driver. We traveled in silence. Now would not be a good time to discuss an additional location to perform the procedure. Isabelle struggled to recover from the blow dealt her.

Our travel to Sweden to make contact with another stem cell researcher excited me. As I found earlier, Sweden's advanced technology together with their liberal laws would allow the procedure. I hoped that Isabelle's contacts ran deep and stretched to the Scandinavian countries. My confidence had fallen, though hope still filled me.

The driver pulled into a full lot at the train station identified from the map coordinates and headed to the front entrance. Isabelle and I watched with care. I realized the last few days had taught Isabelle a new level of existence. I didn't like that, but was pleased to see she learned.

The driver received the fare with a handsome tip. Isabelle rested her hand on my wrist as we prepared to exit the car.

"James," she said. "Let's be careful."

"Let's get inside." I opened the door, grabbed my cane, and swung out. I surveyed the scene nearby. Satisfied, we began our tedious way up the steps. I used the hand rail to pull myself laboriously up each step. We reached the entrance doors and turned one last time to scan the scene.

Isabelle moved with shaken stride, a determined look on her face.

"I'll go and purchase seats," she said. "No arguments. I'll

be right back."

"Isabelle. Use cash."

"No problem," she answered. "I need first class, and a glass of wine. You can pay later." I sat back with a small amount of satisfaction. She would come around. She displayed shock, fear, concern, anger, and at times been distant. Her strength returned and with that would come determination. She couldn't be blamed, yet we must maintain balance and continue to move ahead.

She headed back with tickets clutched in hand.

"Platform 13," she announced. I started to stand and she leaned forward and took my hand to help me up.

"There's an escalator. Do you think we left our friends behind?"

"Yes." I wanted to put the nasty thoughts of earlier behind. This cat and mouse game had now reached a new level. It didn't matter whether politics, or economics, or philosophy drove the issue. It became more evident with each moment the game now meant life or death.

Isabelle guided me through the crowd. Our progress slowed, as I took each step with care. With Isabelle's help we made as good of time as possible, and soon stood on the platform for the train that would take us back to the Brussels airport. As we prepared to load, we slowed further. I reached forward, grabbed the handle bar attached to the car and pulled myself up the ladder. We reached the interior of the cabin and I proceeded with my walk routine using the back of each seat on my way to two open ones near the front of the car.

"Welcome aboard. Will it be a glass of wine, or a shot of bourbon?" I asked with a little humor in my voice.

"Both," she answered. I looked at her and could tell she

didn't joke.

As the train jerked into motion, an attendant began his rounds to check for tickets and drink orders. I handed him both our tickets for review and ordered two bourbons and two glasses of white wine.

As we settled into our seats, I looked sideways at the pretty woman next to me and decided we could take time to relax. The bourbon and wine would help.

About ten minutes from the Brussels station, I shook the haze away and sat upright.

"Did I fall asleep on you?"

"Inside the Chunnel," she replied. My wine glass stood half full. Isabelle's empty. I drained my glass and sat back to gather my wits.

The shot glasses had been removed long ago. I remembered the shot, the toast to Dr. Hopkins and not much more. With the stress and the shot of bourbon, sleep had come fast. I grimaced with that knowledge. On top of the stress and bourbon sat the multiple sclerosis itself. It would creep up on a person and generate unwanted fatigue. Not caused from over activity, just another symptom of the monster. This nature of the beast plagued me.

As we pulled into the station, I patted her forearm.

"All ready?" She gave me a half-hearted smile.

"I'll be fine. Just a little shell shocked," she replied.

The train glided to a stop at the Brussels airport station.

"Off we go." My hand slipped into hers.

We made our way from the train and headed to the escalator. As we maneuvered our way, neither of us spoke. Our pursuers hung as a great burden on us both. Though the stakes had been raised, we both realized the time to stop, to rest, or quiver on the sidelines did not exist. We must let others know the truth and then we could slide back into the shadows of obscurity.

At the top of the escalator, Isabelle led me towards the concourse to acquire tickets for our flight to Sweden. She spied the ticket counter of a reputable carrier and knew it would be easier for her to gather the tickets by herself. She explained her logic to me as she brought me to a seat. I reached into my back pocket to grab my wallet, and handed her my identification and some euros exchanged at the motel counter earlier that day.

"Just take it. Don't use your card. We'll pick up a car when we arrive."

Her world had changed. The masquerade played on the world stage made me sick to my stomach and now she had been dragged along. My mantra had always been to work hard, and hope opportunities would open for me. Now at a time I needed to believe and trust, I found my most important battle in life to be a lie perpetuated on the social strata of peoples from all walks of life. It seemed a facade of unequivocal proportion.

As I thought of the details, Isabelle re-appeared, her happy gait gone. Her face held no smile. She appeared drained. I knew I could be blamed for this.

"Back downstairs at the end of the terminal."

My strength had improved and we made good time. We slowed at security, but made it to our departure gate with more than enough time to spare. We presented our passes, were stamped as arrivals, and took seats near the gate.

Isabelle leaned forward with her head hung low. I reached to her, my hand on her back.

"I'm so sorry," I said with quietness.

"I'm appalled by it all." I patted her back at a loss for

words. My attempt to find some rational justice for the situation before had failed. Now Isabelle experienced the same dilemma.

We sat for several minutes, each absorbed in our own thoughts. She swiveled. She saw the cane by my side, and the shriveled legs that formerly carried me without hesitation in my world.

Isabelle had experienced it before. She understood that here sat the unvanquishable spirit of mankind. It could not be defined. A quality to it existed, as if transplanted from some foreign place.

It existed, yet no one would ever be able to understand it. Not the capitalists of the world, the power mongers, or those who wished to control their own destiny at the expense of the greater whole. Isabelle defined it as the will to survive. No greater power existed on the face of the planet. She leaned in and planted a kiss on my cheek.

The kiss startled me. I sat back with an eye cocked at her.

"I understand."

"I take it I can count you as a friend again?"

"James," she answered, "we have always been friends. Just don't break, or lose that cane. I'm all out," she replied with a tired voice I had not heard before. "I'm all right," she followed up. "Now tell me more of why Sweden?"

"Sweden," I started. "Are you familiar with a Dr. Borklund? I know of his work with Parkinson's."

"I'm aware of that connection," she responded.

"Based on the neurological similarities of Parkinson's and multiple sclerosis, I believe that Dr. Borklund moves closer to a demonstration of a link between the two. Even though Parkinson's consists of a hormonal component of the brain cells not able to produce enough dopamine, both illnesses end up with a damaged component of the central nervous system. Due to the similarities, and Borklund's pursuit of stem cell transplantation, perhaps the necessary equipment to perform the procedure can be dug up. Either that, or maybe we can be referred to another clinic." Silence enveloped her for a moment.

"I know Borklund," Isabelle stated. "I do not agree with all of his research parameters, although know he has made breakthroughs." I looked at her. A deeper story rested there.

"What's the problem between you and Borklund?" She went quiet.

"He doesn't believe in my work. At the time I first reported it, he ridiculed me and my procedure." I listened to her response without comment, and looked for a way to back track from the topic with a polished exit strategy. The loudspeaker saved me.

The intercom announced our plane would be ready to board soon. Passengers began to stir. The bustle of activity brought on by the pre-board announcement always amused me. No one would be left behind, though the activity level became like bees at the opportune moment they left their hive on their own reconnaissance.

On the jump to Sweden, I would need to tell Isabelle the rest of the story. My honesty had not shined through, and I owed it to her. Her involvement warranted it. She needed to know.

The crowd began to move to the gate, passengers polite and organized in their movement. My heart rate ticked up due to the realization that the moment of my final revelation to Isabelle approached. I must take time to find my nerve and cover the salient points.

Perhaps she would toss the proverbial towel at me, and run for home. I understood the risk. I hoped she would understand my logic.

Chapter 19

Departure from Brussels went well as we settled deeper into our seats. We spent the first portion of the flight in senseless small talk. I wanted to delve deeper into my secret. However, I enjoyed more comfort with avoidance. Then, as the trip neared an end, the time arrived to tell her.

No time like the present. I leaned closer, and whispered.

"Isabelle, we need to talk." She rolled her head, and noticed the seriousness of my look.

"I have more to tell you." She pushed herself higher in her seat, prepared to steel herself for the news to come.

"Let me revisit some of the earlier discovered papers I didn't tell you about. As controversy became more attracted to the topic, one of the greater debated approaches came out of Australia. You need to know all the facts."

Isabelle sat forward so she wouldn't miss a word. "Though the presumption held nobility, the efforts of disclosure proved disastrous."

She paid full attention.

"The research team that conducted the work believed that the study of infected adult stem cells could be a crucial link to the successful use of them as a pharmacological agent. Their study harvested adult stem cells and subjected them to disease. They kept these cells alive in petri dishes and worked to develop actual cures to diseases.

In harvesting from diseased bodies, they obtained a continuous source of diseased cells that would replicate time and again that could be treated with various chemical agents. Once they hit on a successful treatment for the disease, they allowed the cells to mature. These adult cells became resistant to the disease they had been exposed to and treated for. The process assisted cells to divide that no longer were subjected to infection by the originally introduced disease. These cells could then be transplanted into a body infected with disease originally treated for and replicate into new disease free cells. The immune cells grew, replaced diseased cells and made the body resistant to that particular disease. These new cells became true miracle cells, Isabelle. The cells treated outside the body remained cured and when transplanted into the body as disease resistant, they divided into cells that could not be infected by that disease. Cancer, cystic fibrosis, macular degeneration, even multiple sclerosis, had been beaten by resistant cell introduction that led to healthy cell re-generation. The cells became pre-conditioned to disease, and then beat it. They found a way to make disease-resistant cells. People with in-curable diseases could find cures. Diseases could be terminated not just managed." I finished quite excited. She couldn't keep silent any longer.

"Wait a second. I heard of those assumptions, though never saw any papers, or presentations on the procedures."

"Wait until I'm done."

Isabelle sat back.

"The research team applied for, and received permission from the Australian Department of Health similar to the United States National Institute of Health for the practice."

"The theory existed for some time," Isabelle murmured. "Pre-treat diseased cells with a successful reagent, transplant disease free cells to replicate and have the next best treatment available." She went silent awed by the magnitude of what she heard.

"The theory worked, Isabelle. Therapeutic agents were

used to correct cell deficiencies. Those corrected cells then replicated to healthy cells." Isabelle looked stunned.

"Then why hasn't the information been released to the world?"

"Good question and the heart of our discussion."

Her mind wrapped around the possibilities. "Wait," she said. I knew it startled her. "So treated cells were transplanted into the diseased body to migrate to damaged areas to mitigate the illness," she continued to think through the process.

Her features grew intense. "Just think, Isabelle. If cells could be treated one time within a Petri dish and be transplanted into a diseased body that resulted in mitigation, then how would that affect the long-term market for the agent that treated the cells?"

"Oh my God," she stammered out. "Does this mean what I believe it to mean?" By the look on her face, I knew she understood.

The magnitude of the knowledge overwhelmed her. Her mind reeled with the implications. *The breakthrough could be defined as one of monumental proportions, one that would change the pharmaceutical industry forever. If the reagent proved effective with the use of adult stem cell transplantation, immune cells could be introduced to replace infected or damaged cells that could regenerate in diseased areas of the body and eliminate further need for treatment of that disease. The disease would be eradicated. The treating reagent used to eradicate the disease from the cell would replace all pharmaceutical therapies. Drugs would be deemed useless in face of the treating reagent.*

"Management drugs like the one I administer to myself would not be needed. If the process could be proved and tested the process would become the industry's golden egg. The treating reagents would become the new billion dollar baby. If drug companies did not come up with the reagent, they would be ruined.

Current drugs on the market that treat, but do not cure would be eliminated. Actual remedies would replace them. A break-through would make the discoverer millions, even billions." Isabelle's quest could be achieved. She shivered with the thought.

As she contemplated the monumental news, I reached up and pushed the attendant button. A flight attendant appeared.

"Two white wines and four aspirin please." I sat back, and patted Isabelle's hand. She stared at me in shock.

"You need to stop with these surprises," she said.

"There's more you need to hear."

She held up her hand. "Wait until the wine and aspirin get here."

The flight attendant reappeared with the order. Isabelle opened the single serve bottle and poured her wine. She tossed all four aspirin into her mouth, took a big sip of wine and settled back.

"Continue," she said.

"Dr. Zachary Thimes led the research team. With the breakthrough he and his research team achieved, he wanted to publish an article in International Science."

Isabelle snorted her disgust. "Not a well, respected journal," she said. "I never heard of the article."

"No one ever did. The print house set to publish, burnt to the ground." I thought she would throw up. She retched and hung her head low. She gasped for air. I rubbed her back in an attempt to relieve her stress.

"After a lengthy investigation, the accident pointed to a faulty gas line. Three people died." She threw herself back into her seat, color drained from her face, frozen in disbelief.

"What happened with Dr. Thimes? Why didn't he republish elsewhere?" she asked. I took a large swallow of wine.

"A short time later, within a few weeks as time would have it, on their way to Perth to present at a Department of Health conference, his plane went down. Dr. Thimes and his research team didn't survive."

Isabelle gasped. She moved her wine glass to my tray, and pushed up from her seat. I grabbed both our wine glasses as she squeezed past. As she escaped towards the restrooms, the flight attendant approached.

"Will she be all right?" she asked.

"It's been a long day." There existed one last piece of information to share. I hoped she could deal with it.

The letter about the research of Dr. Thimes and his colleagues, came to me special delivery. It arrived out of the blue, unexpected and unannounced. I protected it with as much care as the article of improprieties at the FDA.

The incident at Isabelle's office turned the chase scary. The arson at Dr. Hopkins' clinic near catastrophic. Now their pursuers must be acknowledged by the sheer terror they wreaked. The plane crash was an act of terrorism.

The people aligned against them were ruthless. They would take whatever steps they deemed necessary to protect themselves. The reality of Dr. Thimes' and his research team's demise came as a terrible shock. Now Isabelle knew.

As I considered our next move, Isabelle reappeared. She offered me a small smile as she slid by. She had left to cry. Her eyes appeared red rimmed and puffy. Isabelle's beauty needed little to grace it, however now her mascara ran dark onto her cheeks, flushed there by fresh tears. She sat without a word. She reached to retrieve her wine.

"There's more, isn't there?" I reached into my left trouser pants pocket and pulled a folded envelope from its location. She slumped back, her head tossed to the headrest. Without a look at me she said, "Tell me. I can't read it."

"The letter arrived at my apartment, special delivery from New Zealand two months ago." She stared at the roof of the cabin. "It came from the wife of one of the research technicians at Dr. Thime's laboratory."

"Did he die?" Isabelle asked.

"Yes. They lived near Melbourne. She moved to New Zealand after he passed. I don't know how she found me. She never explained. She wrote of the excitement at their discovery, of how he thought of the good it could do and of the stress he endured as Dr. Thimes prepared to publish.

She told stories of multiple parties who showed up at the lab as related by her husband prior to the plane crash. He indicated a huge offer had been made to buy the lab and research. Her husband told her how the doctor promised the staff that if he sold, they all would share in the profits. She wrote of drug and insurance companies, and the ones that scared her husband the most, several evangelical groups. The letter went on to explain how Dr. Thimes refused all offers. He called the staff together to review each, though together as a group they rejected them.

She told me of how her husband revealed to her some of the negotiations, and how they turned angry, even violent. She wrote of how her husband and another technician used physical force to throw one suitor from the lab. Dr. Thimes hired a private security company to guard the clinic on a 24/7 basis. Employees received new identification badges to enter and exit. Dr. Thimes' calls to the Department of

Health went ignored.

Her husband and other employees at the clinic became sure the agency sold out. The letter explained how heartbroken Dr. Thimes and staff became at the time they found the article would not be published, and then how pleased they grew soon after the Department of Health seemed to change their mind, and invited them to the National Conference on stem cell regeneration. The document told me little of the research itself, just the circumstance of the discovery and their struggles to have it recognized."

Isabelle sat forward. "What did you say?" she asked. I stopped for a moment and thought of my last sentence.

"That the letter did not cover the specific discovery."

"No, no. What you said before that."

"That Dr. Thimes and his crew became pleased by what they thought demonstrated a change in heart by the Department of Health, due to the invitation received to the National Conference." She kept still and very quiet.

"That's not right," Isabelle said.

"What?" I responded.

"That's not right, James. Unless you have been invited as the headline speaker at a conference, a personal invitation is not extended. In order to become a speaker at a conference you must submit a technical paper for review by the conference technical committee. You said the article burned prior to publication. I'm sure additional prints and an electronic copy had been made, however the article must be published, and then the committee contacts the primary researcher to ask for further data. If that data satisfies the committee, then the author is invited to participate at the conference." She grabbed my wrist.

"They set him up. Thimes should have known. Maybe he

overlooked the normal procedures due to excitement of the recognition. He must have been overjoyed given the other nonsense he went through. The letter you received with no discussion of details of the procedure involved can now be understood. She didn't know them, yet she did provide just enough information to indicate to you the invitation to the conference they received was not sincere."

My surprised face must have displayed my shock. "They tricked them to get them to Perth?" I asked. Isabelle laid her head back.

"Yes, but Thimes should have known. The lack of publication and the chance to present must have been enough to make him go. We need to go to Australia. Borklund will do us no good. We need to find the first flight to Perth, and leave as soon as possible."

Chapter 20

Isabelle's face displayed disbelief. It appeared as the same face of beauty and intelligence I knew when we first met. Perhaps a few more brow lines from lack of sleep, stress, and concern, yet she displayed trust.

Her secret lay hidden. *Did she know what her contacts wanted? Could she turn on James?*

I reached for the phone handset on the back of the seat in front of me.

"Who are you calling?" Isabelle asked.

"We need to call ahead to see if we can get tickets to Perth."

He showed determination. No wonder he uncovered data that no one else found. He would succeed and possessed the strong-mindedness to do just that she thought. She had seen patients like him at her clinic before, though never as determined. People like James possessed an infectious attitude. She knew their quest defied odds of success, yet her confidence in him remained high.

The negotiation for the next flight to Perth went well. Isabelle bent towards me, and kissed me on the cheek. My eyebrows rose while I continued to talk, the handset pressed to my ear.

"It is a-go. All set to head to the land down under?"

"I'm not expected at work tomorrow," she answered.

"We arrive soon, have a fifty minute break and leave for Perth on a red eye. I have reserved tickets. We need to get to the counter and pay cash. Thanks, Isabelle. It's great to have you along and for you to understand." We settled back to await the next leg of our adventure.

An hour later we headed for Perth. My stomach churned. Isabelle settled into a quiet sleep with her head on my shoulder. Most assuredly, our followers had been eluded, but we knew more than ever of our adversary's tenacity.

I had become the responsible and guilty party that pulled Isabelle into this horrid adventure with little or no explanation of the danger. One moment she worked with happiness and success at the practice she loved and now that could be lost. *Did she understand the lengths our pursuers would go?*

The entire story as I knew it had been revealed to her though I questioned my integrity and the separation I caused her from her life and the plunge into this chasm where there might be no escape. For me that risk did not exist.

My bank account balance had dropped and my job disappeared. Isabelle lived a life. She pursued a career. My arrival put it all at risk. I struggled with my subconscious as we continued on our journey of truth, discovery and danger.

My head snapped forward as I woke with a start. The captain came on the loudspeaker to announce a message of no importance as we neared Perth. My watch told me it neared dawn of the next day. Isabelle stirred on my shoulder.

We each needed the rest. I enjoyed her company. Better yet, I liked the comfort and warmth that signaled the start of my emotional attachment to her.

As the plane landed at the Perth International Airport, my mind worked on our next steps. The revelation of the story to Isabelle went better than expected. She displayed her shock, her disbelief and even her anger, though none of that had been directed at me. Her intellect took over. Shock that the research crossed the threshold of disease modification and not been presented to the world showed in her eyes. The power and determination of the forces that fought us became clearer. This new path filled us both with intimidation and fear, yet her determination not to falter gave me hope.

Isabelle interrupted my thoughts. "So what's our first step?"

"Let's go to the Department of Health, and find who invited Dr. Thimes and staff to the conference."

She agreed that had become critical. "What if the person who invited them refuses to talk to us?"

"I no longer have the time for niceties. If they do not feel up to a conversation, first they will meet my new best friend, my cane, and second they can be introduced to the local law enforcement agency to answer questions."

She thought of how helpful she would be if someone threatened her with the possibility they may soon face long term felony charges if they did not cooperate. Isabelle didn't like the option, though it represented a start and their plan must have a place to begin, so she decided to go along without objections.

The plane taxied to the arrival gate. Passengers began to stand, assemble their packages, and make their way to the exit. We stood at the tail end of the line as passengers proceeded to depart onto foreign soil.

My journey seemed to have started long ago at a distant place. Quite a few new stamps now adorned my passport. I had traveled almost around the globe, and would travel the rest of the planet to reach a successful conclusion.

What might that final resolution be? We discovered how ruthless our adversaries could be. The consideration of going to the authorities crossed my mind to describe this intricate mouse trap, built to keep the material secret and let none of it escape to the world. *Could the truth be told?*

If so, could we continue our pursuit unimpeded? I knew the time did not present itself yet. I needed to assemble more data. It would have the greatest impact to continue the search and expose the truth at the appropriate time.

We exited the plane and followed the signage to the rental car area. Our followers most likely had been left behind, however I knew the next stage of the trip would be dangerous. Our presence at the Department of Health would be reported.

We rented a car with more of my traveler's checks and gathered a map and directions. Thirty minutes later we found the Department of Health. Isabelle dropped me near the steps to the entrance, and pulled away to find a spot to park. She returned a few minutes later.

At the front desk I asked for the administration department and we received directions to the fourth floor. We discussed our strategy as we rode the elevator up. As we exited a cheerful receptionist greeted us.

"Good day," I said. "We would like to obtain a copy of the minutes of the agency's recent forum on stem cell regeneration."

"That would be Dr. Rasmussen," the young receptionist reported. "On the third floor, number 3275."

We turned and headed back to the elevator.

As we proceeded, Isabelle asked, "What's the plan?"

We could play the scare tactic, though the good doctor without doubt would be an intelligent man who would see past the masquerade and follow it up with a few well directed phone checks. We had arrived at a time for caution. I stayed silent on the short elevator trip.

The doors slid open and we approached the office directory on the wall, where we found Dr. Rasmussen's office on the small map located at the end of the hallway. I gripped my cane, slid my left hand into Isabelle's, and we began our slow stroll to number 3275. As we rounded the corner to the office in question, a receptionist greeted us, and asked with some immediacy, "Can I help you?"

My response came slowly and muffled. Isabelle stepped in.

"Could you see if the doctor can see me? My name is Dr. Isabelle Giovantti from Italy."

It pleased me Isabelle took the lead, and saved me from my tongue tied moment.

"Do you have an appointment?" the receptionist responded.

"No, though I wanted to take time to introduce myself. I work with stem cell implantation procedures."

The receptionist picked up the phone and called into Dr. Rasmussen's inner office. "Doctor, I have Dr. Isabelle Giovantti from Italy here to see you." We heard a muffled response, and did not have long to wait, as the office door burst open, and an overweight gentleman in a white smock on bustled into the office. He stepped towards Isabelle with an outstretched hand.

"Dr. Giovantti pleased to meet you. Doctor Curtis Rasmussen."

Isabelle stood and accepted the hand offered her.

"Thank you for your time to see me, doctor. I'm here with my husband and wanted to take the opportunity to introduce myself." The doctor nodded as if he knew Isabelle.

My grin spread, not so much from her quick wit to get us invited into the office of Dr. Curtis Rasmussen, but due to her referral of me as her husband.

We entered his office, me with the help of my cane,

and Isabelle's strong hand. We sat close to the desk. Isabelle started.

"Thank you again, Dr. Rasmussen, to see me. My husband and I should be enjoying our honeymoon, but I couldn't pass up the chance to meet you."

"Well, I must admit, Dr. Giovantti, you have me at a disadvantage. I'm pleased to hear you practice with stem cells. Would I recognize your papers?"

My impatience took the best of me as I jumped in. "Excuse me for my interruption honey, but Doctor, do you receive a newsletter from the National Multiple Sclerosis Association in the States?"

The doctor paused for a moment of reflection and answered, "Well yes" he replied. "The mail arrives late from the States, due to the distance."

"Then you haven't seen the latest edition?" As Dr. Rasmussen began to respond, I pressed on. "Well, my wife just received recognition in the latest MS publication for her breakthrough technique in the transplant of stem cells to assist in MS recoveries." Dr. Rasmussen absorbed my rapid dissemination of information.

"Congratulations Doctor," he directed at Isabelle.

"Thank you," Isabelle replied with the right degree of graciousness.

"Doctor, do you have a compilation of the stem cell papers presented at the recent forum?" Isabelle asked.

"Of course," Dr. Rasmussen replied with eagerness. He had walked into a trap with no idea of where it lead. He picked up the phone and called the office assistant for a bound copy of papers presented at the forum. The receptionist knocked at the door. She held a binder full of bound presentation papers. Isabelle accepted the binder.

As the receptionist left, Isabelle flipped to the table of contents and ran her finger across the page as she looked for the article of interest. There did not appear any reference to the document. She flipped the pages to check the glossary. She glanced at this section, slapped the book closed, stared at the doctor and asked, "Why isn't the paper by Dr. Thimes included here?"

The color drained from the doctor's face. His jaw line tightened, lips pursed and demeanor changed. He snapped his response filled with bitterness.

"As you must be aware, Dr. Thimes and his team of researchers died due to an unfortunate plane accident on their way to the forum. The governors of the Board believed their paper should not be published to honor their memory." Isabelle clucked her tongue in admonishment.

"Doctor, didn't the Board consider that the greatest honor that could have been granted Dr. Thimes and crew would have been to publish their work?" Isabelle asked.

"Dr. Giovantti, I do not sit on the Board. They made the decision," Dr. Rasmussen replied in a shaky voice.

"Perhaps, Doctor," Isabelle stated, "it did not represent the best interest of the Board to have Dr. Thimes' paper published." All color drained from Dr. Rasmussen's face. He stood with suddenness. His thigh struck the desk.

"Damn," he exclaimed in agitation. "Doctor, you and your husband can leave. Please leave now," he stammered.

"You're right, Doctor. It's obvious you represent no more than an imbecile and a yes man for your cronies. I'm done with you, and on top of that I'm sick of you." Isabelle stood with abruptness. She extended her hand to me.

"Honey, it's time for us to go." I accepted her extended hand with a smile. "Don't worry, Doctor, we'll find our way out. Arrivederci."

As we stepped into the front room, Isabelle yanked the door shut. The receptionist's phone jumped into action. I could hear the raspy, angry voice of Dr. Rasmussen echo on the receiver.

The poor receptionist at the front desk grabbed her note pad, a pen, and spun her Rolodex to find the name and address she searched for. She scrawled a number on her notepad, jumped up from her chair so fast that it hit the wall behind her desk and scampered for the office door. She reached the door, threw it open and poured herself inside. Isabelle pulled me forward. She pointed at the Rolodex.

"We have the contact right there." I looked at the Rolodex left open to the last entry, and began to smile. What incredible luck! Isabelle moved to the desk.

"Melbourne. Randall Winston. Let's go. I'm sure he will contact him fast." She grabbed a piece of paper from the printer on the receptionist's desk and scribbled the name, address and phone number of Randall Winston on it. As fast as possible, we hustled towards the elevator. Neither of us spoke. We struggled to control our elation.

The two of us had not succeeded by incredible intelligence, just by tenacious action. We relished in the moment.

As we reached the end of the hallway, time crept to a standstill. Isabelle could feel her heart pound. I gripped the head of my cane so hard my knuckles hurt. No one raced after us. We waited with anxiousness for the elevator to arrive.

The buzzer dinged, and the doors slid open. We fell into the elevator like a couple of school-aged children filled with laughter and giggles as we staggered against the interior rails to keep ourselves upright. I wrapped one arm around Isabelle and pulled her to me with a broad smile, and kissed her lips. Words tumbled from me first. My arm stayed wrapped around her waist.

"I'll be your husband any time, but an 'imbecile' and 'I'm sick of you!'

Wow! You laid it on him." We held on to the rail. I dropped my arm from her waist, still hysterical as the doors opened on the bottom floor.

People turned and stared, yet the near delirium of our travels and the comic relief provided by Isabelle's words became too much for us to deal with.

We reached the front doors and pushed our way through. We still laughed together. Isabelle let go of my hand and went for the car, my hand grasping the handrail of the stairs and my gaze following her as she headed into the maze of the lot. *Quite a woman,* I thought as she disappeared.

We could be assured that by now, the good Doctor would be on the phone with some sort of message to his contacts.

Though we desired a direct flight to Melbourne, it did not seem reasonable. It would be too easy to pick us up at the airport on our arrival. With Isabelle fetching the car, I considered a circuitous route to pursue, one which our followers would not expect.

Tonight we would head to Kuala Lumpur. We could travel from Perth to Kuala Lumpur, spend the night and head from Malaysia to Melbourne tomorrow. Besides, that would better suit our cover as honeymooners, and if the doctor warned Mr. Winston of our potential arrival, the odds seemed good he would not be at the address Isabelle scrawled from the Rolodex card upstairs.

With that thought, I closed the last page of that chapter. Kuala Lumpur tonight it would be. We would head to

Melbourne tomorrow.

The phone rang in Randall Winston's office. He answered on the second ring. The voice neared a scream. Leave and leave now the voice demanded. *The fool* Randall thought to himself. *How much information did he give away?* He needed to leave the country now. He would leave for Sydney and from there to the States. The situation evolved into a mess and the heat would be turned higher.

What started as an easy job had turned very dangerous. The job began as a simple contract, agreed to over the phone with a representative he never met. Payment and terms had been negotiated, and money transferred. Movement of the C4 and timer on board the small plane occurred without effort. He saw the news report of the plane accident. Success of the project had been achieved.

Chapter 21

We arrived in Kuala Lumpur without incident, our path through customs tedious. The honeymooner's story continued to help. The climate weighed on us in its hot and humid state. It seemed the temperature neared one hundred degrees Fahrenheit with an additional one hundred percent humidity. It became impossible to rest and find coolness. We hurried to the taxi area.

Our arrival came at the end of the day. Once again, it seemed assured we alluded our followers. We should have thought again.

After Rasmussen's call to Randall Winston, Winston used his satellite phone to connect to the States, the call routed to another number. Simon picked up in New York. The line would be clean. He listened to the report, and hung up. *How they made it to Australia?* He made a note. He told Winston to leave possible. Randall Winston obeyed the order and would not be heard from again.

Our departure from the Health Department did not go unnoticed. The security guard at the front desk watched. A phone rang at a high rise office outside of Atlanta.

"Yes?" the gruff voice responded. The man who answered tightened his tie. Quick phone transfers were made. Discussions started. The gentleman in Atlanta spun, and looked at the wall clock. His parish waited.

Malcolm Prentiss grumbled. The situation spiraled out of control.

He expressed reticence to move ahead with recovery plans in Italy. Now, more than ever, they needed to find out how much he knew. Malcolm knew the pieces were assembled against them.

Though they had always been vocal and visual, their political maneuvers did them well, and assisted to keep them undercover. Now their guarded plans could be revealed due to this unfortunate incident. To wait was no longer tolerated.

Malcolm considered opinions of others added to the conference call. As the leader of the nationwide order he oversaw, the ultimate decision rested with him. Each week, millions of loyal followers awaited his sermons.

Their organization directed philosophies preached from coast to coast, and even on several different continents. He taught the sanctity of the unborn must be protected, and now a mass of cells that could evolve to human form must be assured safety. The foundation of the church needed to be preserved.

Malcolm's organization had adopted a program of social outrage for the media to digest, though they also exerted an interest in the political decisions made behind the scene. The plan had been perfected over the years and through millions of dollars expended through the right channels.

Their philosophy could not be threatened by a single man and his partner bent on exposure of the truth. He would not allow it. The threat and challenge had become difficult, yet Malcolm's determination to protect his flock stood greater than all else. He made a promise that day to see the project completed.

Consensus soon evolved. A number of routed calls fired across the wire. A phone rang in San Diego. Information moved to another ear. The connection ended. The message continued to Taipei, on to Bangkok, and to Singapore. The final destination ended outside of Kuala Lumpur.

The airline pathway tracked through international ticket purchases once the guard relayed they headed toward the airport, became fast and easy. Two native Malays stirred from their sleep and left for the airline arrival terminal. They would be in position well ahead of the arrival of the flight from Perth, and have plenty of time to position themselves to follow passengers as they departed. To spot a man with a cane seemed easy. Follow, do not intercept had come down from the top. Then, their orders would change.

We found a cab with a driver we could communicate with to let him know a motel for the night had become the order. Our driver spun us through downtown streets towards a western style accommodation. The streets moved in a hurry past our windows. The sidewalks still stayed crowded.

Pedestrians and bicyclists moved past our cab like a swarm of angry insects. I looked at cramped streets bordered by electronic and music stores, local markets, and a myriad of tourist attractions crammed with tee shirts, cheap brass ornaments and any ridiculous item that would attract the attention of visitors and their foreign currency.

The cab pulled into a motel. We entered the lobby ready for sleep, and booked rooms. The walk to our rooms seemed to take forever. I labored with each step, beaten down by the oppressive heat.

When we arrived at our rooms, I leaned to Isabelle, gave her a hug and left her with words that I would see her later. She looked at her watch which she had set to local time at the airport and groaned, with the knowledge it would be best to keep the end goal in sight.

There would be time for sleep when the travel came to an end. We parted and headed into our rooms, which connected by an inner door we both examined, though neither made an attempt to slip from the locked position. We both fell into a deep sleep that night, yet not for long enough.

Our flight to Melbourne departed at eight the next day. I arose by five and began to ready myself for the travel ahead. I finished my routine, extracted a map of the city collected at the airport and settled into the easy chair to whittle away the minutes until I needed to wake Isabelle.

I studied the route back to the airport, as well as the layout of the city. Before long, I fell into a light slumber. A knock came at the door.

The knock seemed rather odd at this hour. *Could it be room service?* I thought of Isabelle. She could have risen earlier and now returned with coffee or some other sort of breakfast surprise. I struggled from the chair with cane in hand and stepped toward the door. The knock came again.

"Be there in a minute." I shuffled into the entryway, "Can I help you?"

No one answered. I stepped closer to the door to peer out the peep hole. As I moved my eye closer to the peep hole the door burst open like a cannon shot. It flew backward and knocked me on the forehead above my left eye. My arms flung into the air as I fell back onto the carpeted floor.

A short statured native Malay stepped into the room. He turned and pushed the door back towards the shattered frame. Splinters lay on the floor close to me. I hit the floor hard and pressed both hands to my forehead.

Warm blood trickled between my squeezed fingers. *Head wounds bled like proverbial stuck pigs.* My head throbbed, my reality the hard floor. I lay quiet and still. My head ached and blood flowed between my fingers.

What happened and how I found myself here, I didn't remember. Someone moved about the room. The intruder rifled through the goods dumped on the bed and dropped them to the floor. Recognition of my plight dawned.

We had been found again. This attack occurred with a difference. It happened in a more brazen fashion. It scared me. As I lay on the floor, fear began to turn to anger. *How dare these people* my mind screamed out! The world peoples had been denied a revolutionary breakthrough. A moment of change so profound, a new era could evolve. My anger began to turn to rage. *Did these people know what they did?*

With slowness, I began to flicker back to full consciousness. My left eye was barely opened, covered in a haze of blood. My right eye tried to focus.

When I began to roll onto my side, the pressure of a foot stopped me. Any movement would not be tolerated. I settled back on the floor, flat on my back, and struggled to focus and clear the haze. Little by little my brain began to operate at a higher level. My head hurt. *Damn it! The bastards found us already!*

Maybe, the ridicule of Dr. Rasmussen hadn't been such a good idea, though it sure served as good fun! *I thought of Isabelle asleep next door.*

We had planned to wake by six-thirty. I wondered how close it came to that hour. *What could I do to strike back at the intruder?*

As my right hand dropped to my side, my palm fell onto my weapon. A good sized piece of wood splinter from the door jamb lay beneath it. I tested the strength of the tip with my finger. I encountered the sharp tip of a large wood splinter.

The attacker kept his attention centered elsewhere in the room. Silence surrounded me. I pulled the splinter of wood closer to my thigh, and tucked it beneath the fold of my slacks. I kept it close as I waited for my chance.

The knock on the door between my and Isabelle's room

made me start. The attacker moved fast from the other side of the room, a finger pressed to his lips. The knock came again.

"Hello," Isabelle called. The attacker grabbed me by my shoulders and pulled me so I sat with my back pressed against the bed. He whispered with vehemence.

"Answer her."

"Hold on a minute. I'll be right there."

The attacker whispered again. "Not a word or I'll kill her," he said. The English sounded broken, mixed with the local native tongue, though there could be no doubt in the point of the message He left me against the bed and stepped to the door that separated our rooms. I gripped the wood splinter under my leg.

The attacker turned the deadbolt that separated our rooms.

"About time," I heard Isabelle respond. The short intruder unlocked the door knob. He stepped away from the door. He crouched ready to attack, reached forward, and turned the knob. With a sharp pull he swung the door inward.

Water splashed into the room. It bounced off the attacker onto the floor and me. The attacker screamed in agony as the door swung wide, both hands flung to his face. He stepped back. I cocked my right leg, took aim, and kicked with all my might at the back of the man's right knee.

He fell, forward and struck the door jamb, hands still flung to his face. I reached under my thigh, grabbed the wood splinter tucked there and struck backhanded as he bounced off the wall toward me. I hit the man on the Adams apple, and could feel the hot flash of blood as it spurted from the man's ruptured throat onto my hand. The attacker fell backward against the bed, hands now to his throat and slid to the floor.

Isabelle crouched at my side. She knelt with her arms around my neck.

"Are you all right?" she asked again and again.

"Yes, I'll live," gracious for whatever miraculous concoction she threw into the man's face. I realized my head wound still trickled blood from my forehead, and must be a scene and why she reacted in such panic.

"What did you do to him?" She smiled a nervous and scared smile at me.

"I heard the door splinter earlier and what must have been your body hit. I heated up a pot of water with the coffee maker. As the door opened I fired away."

"Good job," I said. "Is he alive?" I asked with a stare at the unconscious man on the floor, the wood splinter stuck in place.

"Who cares?" Isabelle responded. The coldness of her answer surprised me, though I agreed. This man invaded my room with the intention of harm, or death. Now he lay on the floor, perhaps his own life near an end.

Our investigation for truth had taken a dangerous turn. Some one of significance now became more scared. The odds had been raised. The magnitude of our endeavors must be multiplied. We must be close to discovery of a great secret and some people, somewhere, stayed very nervous. The danger of our find scared them. We could not back pedal. No excuses could be made.

I reached and took Isabelle's hand.

"I'm sorry." She bent forward and kissed me on the mouth.

"I wouldn't have missed this for the world," she replied.

She pulled me to my feet and led me towards the doorway, with a stop at the sink outside the lavatory door.

"Let's clean you up." *Good idea.* I waited for Isabelle to scrub her hands and bent forward to the sink, rinsed my head, looked at the gash and cleaned the blood from my eye, and face.

"Let me look at that," Isabelle said. She looked at the gash.

"You'll live. Let's go. I understand the Malay police do not accept these kinds of spectacles well." I stood straight with slight dizziness.

"We can't leave by plane. You know they will watch the airport." Isabelle retrieved my toiletries. She went to her room and returned with her bag. I smiled at her as she tucked her bag beneath her arm with my goods stuffed inside. She avoided any look at the man on the floor. Air hissed from the hole in his neck.

"You know this raises our journey to a whole new level."

She turned her head, and smiled at me. "I've heard that before. Never promise unless you mean it."

We left the room with the assailant on the floor.

"Don't you have a moral duty to treat him?"

"Yes, however given the circumstances, I believe the authorities will seek his care or a body bag when found." The statement sounded cold, but after all he did not have the best of intentions for us.

"How will we leave the country?" Isabelle asked as we began our trek from the room.

"We'll need to go by ship."

She stood silent for a moment and answered. "I've always wanted to take a cruise. Our honeymoon story should be a good cover for the trip" she continued, which brought me up short. She bumped me from the rear.

"You know that means we need to share the same berth."

"Well, of course, sweetheart though I get to use the lavatory first."

No witty response came to me.

"That's fine as long as you don't leave it a mess." The vision of us together lingered for a moment. However, I needed to stay focused on the dilemma we faced, not the thought of us together. As we approached the side exit door, my common sense returned.

"Stop. We have to assume that someone watches outside. Let's head back to the front desk, ask for a cab and get lost in any crowd at the entrance." It would be a risk to leave by the front doors, yet I remained hopeful we might be able to transition with any crowd there.

We made our way to the lobby, and entered a wide area with a glossy buffed tile floor blanketed with rich area rugs and a front counter staffed by two men and one well outfitted woman. We arrived half asleep the night before and did not pay much attention.

"We would like a cab to the nearest docks where cruise liners depart." One of the counter attendants hailed a doorman and announced the guests needed a taxi with a driver who spoke English.

The doorman scurried to the front doors and whistled three times. A taxi moved forward. We exited the front doors without hesitation. Isabelle carried her overnight bag with my toiletries stuffed inside. We slid into the rear seat, and I leaned forward to give directions.

"We need a cruise ship bound for Australia please." The driver slammed the accelerator to the floor and squealed away from the hotel.

We moved on to our next leg. Neither of us knew what to expect. Maybe if we disappeared for a few days, the trail would grow cold, and we would be able to continue unhindered. We went quiet with thoughts of the tumultuous waters that lie ahead. *Would we uncover the secret that others died for? Could we find the truth?* The next portion of the journey would be filled with more twists and turns. I hoped we survived it.

Chapter 21

The air horn sounded for the call to board. We leaned against the rail awaiting our turn, and admired the massive ship that would soon be our home.

The taxi had dropped us without ceremony. The office to acquire our passes sat across the small street from the impressive vessel.

Isabelle waited outside. The female attendant booked our travel, collected the required fare and issued passes while Isabelle watched the crowd go by.

My head still ached. With tickets in hand, I exited the office and walked to Isabelle.

"Let's go." She grabbed her bag and we left to stand in line. The ship represented the beauty of luxury liners. Her cleanliness served her well. She stood stark white with an ornate brass rail that lined the gang plank and then circled each deck. On the top deck, banners flapped in the light breeze.

The ship carried the name 'Angel', with a Norwegian flag painted above the emblazoned letters. I nodded at the name, so Isabelle could take it in.

"Let's hope there's some symbolic message there." She chuckled.

"I'll take it as a good sign," I replied.

We made our way up the gangplank with my use of the hand rail to pull myself forward one step at a time. A cabin on the third deck had been booked. The cabin came furnished with a single queen bed. The thought of me on the small studio couch entered my head, but it seemed early to volunteer just yet.

We returned to the top deck, to stand on the far side of the ship, and view the horizon. The water stretched with majesty. Sun shimmered on the undulations of the sea. We grew lost in the gentle motion.

The cruise to Melbourne would take three days with intermittent stops.

Short island trips would not be a part of my agenda, but I looked forward to some quiet time. A restful period beckoned and with it a chance to gather my thoughts. *What would we find? Who chased us? Did we come any closer to the truth?*

The time had come for me to rehash our experiences, discoveries, and where it might lead. Our adversary became more determined than ever to keep us from the truth. *Where would that truth lead?*

The success of the pancreatic research and procedure had been huge. The recent success of the team from Australia could rewrite medical texts. The need for documentation that would prove sabotage occurred throughout the development process grew paramount. If it happened to lead to a path that might help me walk again, and cure my daughter, then my goal would be met. That justification became my only motivation needed to continue onward.

My mind ached with the effort to put the pieces together. Never had the desire as a path setter entered my thoughts, although the current quest threw me into the biggest adventure of my life, and the need to learn to act like an adventurer had become critical.

These thoughts made me dizzy. The huge air horn bleated its departure message. The vibration from the crescendo rattled my head. Isabelle leaned close and shouted, "Want to buy a girl a bon-voyage drink?"

My arm slid around her waist, and I kissed her lips. She kissed back into me as her arms wrapped behind my neck, with a gentle urge to push harder on to her mouth. My mouth opened and she pushed her tongue inside. I pulled her tighter with the feel of her body against mine. My hand tingled with excitement as it pressed her tighter into me. She did not resist.

The air horn blew again. She stepped back, took my hand, and led me into the massive chamber of the ship. She stopped at the open entrance to a quaint bar.

"James," she started.

My index finger pressed to her lips. "Quiet down. I'm not your patient. That kiss happened between two friends, not a doctor and patient."

She led me past busy vacationers to a table. A server appeared and we ordered drinks. We enjoyed the solitude and quiet around us. Isabelle laid her hand on my arm.

"I appreciate your trust," she said. She toasted me with her wine glass.

"You know, you might not want to thank me until this ends."

"I might not, though many people will."

"I need to think on this journey. We know that some very serious people do not want us to unmask their secret, yet who can they be? We need to get to the bottom, Isabelle. We don't know who these people are, why they want to keep their secret, even what that secret holds and where it might lead. We must be diligent and motivated. The time for complacency does not exist. They will not stop. We must persevere no matter the obstacles. We have risked so much. It must be a secret worth the keeping."

As my little speech ended, I toasted her, took a big swig

and settled back. Isabelle listened to my words. She knew I spoke with passion. She thought back to the moment she'd first been contacted. *The story sounded so good. Continue her research. It would be funded. She would assign all rights to them. She would continue her involvement as the lead researcher. It all made sense and seemed so easy. At least, then it did.*

Chapter 22

The phone flew across the room into the wall. Pieces of shattered plastic scattered across the floor.

"Damn it," Simon bellowed. "How could this happen?" Two other men stood in the room with sheepish looks on their faces as the tirade continued. Simon's voice lowered to a rumble, no longer an outraged torrent of echoes against the walls.

One of the men braved a question. He stood tall and massive. He'd experienced this type of coarse behavior before. When he played football, or when he served in the military, or when he stood protective detail over dignitaries. Austin Chambers had heard it before. He would hear it again.

"Shall we mobilize a team from Singapore?" Austin asked.

"No" came the harsh response. "We don't know where they will end up. Get me Rasmussen. That idiot must have supplied some sort of hint for them to follow." One of the men responded.

"Mr. Clemens, the time is early in the morning there. He'll be asleep." He knew right away he intervened at a time he should have kept quiet.

"Get me the doctor on the line now. Get your fat ass away from my office and never come back," the voice hissed at him cold and quiet. He knew the evilness of that voice could carry death. He turned to the door, twisted the knob and began to leave. "If you ever utter a word to anyone, I will have you killed. Leave now."

Simon Clemens looked at Austin as he stood quietly.

"Your cell phone," Simon said. Austin handed his phone

over. He watched as Simon dialed a number from memory. The phone rang several times.

"Rasmussen, listen to me. Do I have your attention? Think with care of your conversation with your two office visitors yesterday. Did you mention any names, places, dates, or other information that could have helped them?" Austin heard a mumble from the receiver. "Are you sure?" Silence followed. "If you think of any information that might be useful, call back. Good night."

Simon looked at Austin.

"Step outside. Use the phone in front. Call your wife, or significant other, and tell them you need to leave. You won't be home for at least a week. Do you have your passport?" Austin spun, and left the office. He would call no one. No wife, no girlfriend, just his mother who wouldn't remember the call anyway. On good days, she could recall his name.

Austin never enjoyed a confortable moment in Simon's presence. He breathed a sigh of relief as he left the room, stepped to a chair in the outer office, and sat.

The whole affair had not gone well. The one man they had been assigned to watch made life difficult. Austin understood he slipped the tail in Italy, been reacquired in France, lost again in Britain, turned up in Australia, been found in Malaysia and now been lost again. Simon seemed furious from chances missed. He seemed to have become even more determined to bring it to an end.

Austin's assignment to watch the man two weeks ago had seemed a bit of overkill. However, he never asked why. The job served to pay bills and he chalked it up as another mundane assignment. Austin smiled to himself, quite pleased the trip to Italy did not get assigned to him. Asking the meaning of his assignment was above his pay grade.

The door burst open. Austin jumped from the chair and hurried inside.

"Here's your phone," Simon snapped as it spun toward his face. "Get to the airport. You're on a Northwestern flight to Singapore that leaves in two hours. Other agents will meet you. Eliminate the threat. Call your contacts at job completion. They will communicate with me. As always, your pay will go to your Post Office Box. You can leave now."

The orders ended. No specific plan, no formal instructions, just go to Singapore, find these two somewhere in Australia and eliminate them. It would be more work than he had completed before. The pay would be better. Real field work pleased him. He would travel to Singapore, meet people never met before, find people lost somewhere in the outback, and eliminate the threat. It would be a nice paycheck.

There would be a lot of time to think on the flight. His military service stretched back to that nasty little war in the Far East. He knew how long the travel would take. Maybe he could upgrade from the coach seat his boss no doubt booked for him. His thoughts turned to what these people could have done. That concern vanished quickly. Success concerned him. The rest didn't.

Simon Clemens sat back. The job had never presented itself as a complicated affair. What started as the prevention of one man from the discovery of sensitive information had now turned into a horror show. Arson occurred. People died. Lies had been told. So far they had been protected, though sooner or later the top could blow, and blow it would if the truth ever hit the street.

He sat in on strategy sessions as the plans had matured to action. Assurances of the simplicity of the task had been made. It would be initiated and completed in an expeditious manner.

Now, if the secrets should ever come out, political upheaval would ensue. Corporate America would be shaken to its core. Philosophical values would be rewritten. The very heart of the Constitution would be ripped out.

He rested his head on the desk. *How could it have become so complicated?* What began as a sound business plan now imploded. They underestimated the grit of the man. The thought of failure terrified Simon. He didn't know if it could be stopped. Those at the top must have the same fear. He could hear their displeasure in each phone conversation.

The last call had turned curt and unpleasant. At that time, he became concerned for his own welfare. The rage of the voice became clear. The heat from the anger could not be missed. The intolerance was evident. Simon's boss stood on the verge of desperation. The precipice grew deeper by the moment. It must be stopped. Any long-term career would be ended if he failed. Worse still, failure placed his very life in jeopardy.

Simon walked into the front office, grabbed the land line and dialed Austin.

"Have you arrived yet?" he demanded.

"I'm at the long term garage at JFK."

Simon chose his next words with care. "Good. I wanted to leave you with a final thought for the long trip. If you cannot complete the task within ninety-six hours you will disappear. If you succeed, expect your normal rate to be doubled on return. Have a good trip." Simon disconnected. He could tell by the silence the message got through. Simon went back to his inner office, and sat. He stretched back in the chair. The job started with poor success. He waited for the next communication to tell him the nightmarish episode had ended.

Chapter 23

We finished our drinks as the crowd bustled past. Parents chased their children as seniors ambled by. The day's earlier events brought the seriousness home, though Isabelle displayed little sign of untoward emotion. She sat calm and controlled. I admired her easy disposition. Her medical training no doubt influenced her. We had experienced horrific events. What she displayed came near to heroic.

The cocktail runner came by to check if either of us wanted another libation. I thanked her, said no, and asked, "Could you tell me where I can find the nearest work room or library on the ship?"

"Fifth deck to your left as you exit the elevator," she replied.

"Shall we go check my new research room?" I asked Isabelle. She laughed with a smile.

"Lead on, my studious friend."

A smile grew on my face. "I thought I filled the shoes of your new husband."

She laughed again. "Sorry, I never do marriage on a first date," she responded with a laugh and wink. "It takes at least an expensive dinner and a good bottle of wine before I get married."

"Ah, so still hope, huh?" She tossed her head back with a fun look.

"We'll see. Just don't get me killed first," she said. Her comment, though meant as flirtation, brought me up short.

"Shall we head out?" She reached her hand to me and placed it on mine.

"James, please take that as a joke. I'm sorry," she said.

"It's all right," I replied. "You just got a little too close to reality for a second. Let's go to the library."

As I stood, the tension broke. She took my hand and we moved away from the bar. We reached the walkway around the deck.

We entered an elevator. Isabelle pushed number five, and we began our descent into the bowels of the ship. The elevator glided to the fifth floor and the doors opened with silent precision. Isabelle took my hand as we stepped out.

The hallway lay covered with a thick blue carpet interspersed with white stars. One got the impression of an endless pathway to the night sky. Two oversized glass doors greeted us to our left side with the word, 'Library' etched into the glass. The doors gave the entry a magical look as if we entered a world of untold mysteries. *The very way I feel,* I thought.

Inside, the spectacle took my breath away. The room occupied a huge space decorated with ornate furniture filled with polished shelves loaded with books. Heavy walnut furniture stood silent guard. Chairs sat close to tables, each table at least six feet long and just as wide, each chair cushioned with red leather stretched across the seat.

On the periphery of the room several computer work stations sat, with large flat screen monitors. I assumed each contained the newest and fastest processor, the largest hard disk and the best wireless internet connection available.

Stuffed chairs had been arranged across the room, each with a brass lamp hanging over the seat where the occupant could rest and read. A fireplace with an ornate gas insert sat against the far wall. The gas jet did not burn at that hour, yet I could envision the pleasant ambiance it cast.

A card catalogue stood in the middle of the room. Each drawer was adorned with silver knobs, which I guessed consisted of the pure precious metal. The library stood as an immaculate and visionary testament to the ship herself. I turned to Isabelle.

"Well I think these digs will work for me while you enjoy upstairs."

"Why do you think I will spend all my time upstairs in the sun while you get to be surrounded by this opulence?" she asked.

"I assume you will be relaxing while I get some work done."

"That works for me. You should be able to get some research completed here. Before you start, shall we retire to our digs, change, and go eat?" she asked. I took her by the hand as we headed from my new quarters back to the elevator. *Yes*, I thought, *I could work in this joint.*

As we entered our room, I took Isabelle by her shoulders and stared into her expressive eyes, asking, "Tell me. How many patients did you treat?" I looked deep into her face to watch her as she replied.

"I treated twenty-seven patients for various illnesses. Of that number sixteen reported progress, although the woman with multiple sclerosis you read of experienced the best results." I considered her response with care, though I had little doubt of her. Her expression did not change. Her stare never deviated.

"Isabelle," I continued. "What if a break in stem cell regeneration occurred? What if a disease could be treated twenty-seven of twenty-seven times successfully? What if the mystery of stem cell transplantation could be unlocked? Who would gain, and who would lose?" She didn't answer right away as she mulled the question.

"The winner would be the lab that developed the treatment. The losers would be the evangelical front that offered such a pessimistic outlook on the destruction of life for the betterment of life, and the political party that opposed stem cell usage. Another loser would have to be the pharmaceutical companies that manufacture the drugs that stem cell therapy would replace."

"What of the insurance companies?"

"No. I don't see them as a loser. They would scramble to underwrite stem cell therapy, and calculate significant rates for the treatments, though I don't think they would be a loser."

"So there would be three major losers, and three potential winners. The patients with incurable diseases would be winners," I said, and held one finger up. "The insurance companies that would profit from the treatments would be winners", I speculated and held up finger number two. "And the developer of the treatment would be a winner." I flipped up finger number three.

"Likewise, there would be three losers." I closed my fingers into a fist, and started over. "First would be the evangelicals. Second would be the political party that took a stance of not on my watch, and the third loser would be the pharmaceutical companies until their revenues from stem cell therapies replaced, or exceeded their revenues from current drugs." Isabelle returned my look without a blink. She wondered, *where did he set his rudder with this train of thought?*

"Si," she responded.

"We have our stalkers narrowed, my dear." My face grew warm and flushed with excitement. "Think of it," I said. "The economy drives the world. Sure, politics enters into the fray, and the evangelicals are more than an interested bystander. But, follow the money. Who will the true moneymakers be? If you follow the path Isabelle, you end at the doorstep of the pharmaceuticals. They must be the ones. They need to create their cash cows to survive. Who else could it be? Not the government. I don't believe they would resort to murder. Not the churches. It must be the drug makers!" She sat in contemplation.

"How did you come up with this?" she uttered.

"In the presence of greatness, great ideas happen." She blushed and turned away.

My premonitions had struck before, never this strong.

"I must get to the library. I know what data I need to gather."

She moved towards the bathroom. I stopped her and said, "I border on an epiphany. It must be the drug companies."

She stared at me in silence. "Why?" she asked.

"Isabelle, when you look at the evidence then there is only this one conclusion. Who has the money to conduct the type of surveillance used to track us over the globe? They all do, sure, but who would?" I stated. "Who would have the power to commit murder, and attempted murder, get away with it, and make it look like an accident? Any one of the three," I answered with pride. "And, who stashes the most money away to combat stem cell regeneration introduction to the world?" I held up one finger. "The largest loser would be the pharmaceuticals." I fell back onto the couch.

"The pharmaceuticals," I exclaimed. "They must be the one! Their revenue would plummet. Once-prescribed drugs that make them billions would be destroyed as stem cell therapies came online. The other two might be embarrassed, maybe even mad, though who would stand to lose the most money? It's all about capital.

Remember how I have been trained. 'He, who owns the gold, makes the rules', or something close to that. It's called the 'Golden Rule'. It's common sense that the pharmaceuticals want to try to maintain the greatest amount of gold, and write the rules on their terms."

Isabelle said, "Do you think these tactics would be approved by the Boards of these mega companies?"

"I think the bean counters ran the numbers. They make billions now. Stem cell therapy represents a gamble. Maybe they decided not to take that risk. If the mega companies lead this charge, I'm sure the Board of Directors wouldn't even know it.

The Securities and Exchange Commission runs a pretty tight ship to deal with large corporations. It might be acknowledged with a wink as the conspirators pass in the hall, though I would wager my last dollar that there hasn't been, and won't be formal action taken by any Board to approve this deception. It would be disastrous." Silence filled the room.

Isabelle wondered if James could be correct. After all, she'd been approached and asked to join their team and realize a dream. They possessed the money, *yet why would they want to control her research?*

Oh my God! She realized. If they controlled her research, they controlled when, or if that research would ever be released. *It did make sense! Did James hit the nail on the head?* She wondered.

My thoughts were cluttered. "I've got to get online. Of course, there won't be a direct link to expenditures for illegal activity, although somewhere there may be a notation of some sort of expenditure to R&D, or some sundry expense not explained away by the minutes, or footnotes."

Isabelle interrupted. "Can you do that without their knowledge?" I looked at her in mock sternness.

"You have a good head on your shoulders, but give me some credit, too. I have my ways to access data. I should be able to pull up the latest financials on, say the big five pharmaceuticals. They will take hours of examination per report that may end up nowhere. No doubt, there will be no excitement built in, but it must be done. Looks like you'll have plenty of time to work on that tan. I just relegated myself to the library for this trip."

"I'm hungry and you still need to eat prior to your research. I bet a lunch buffet with our name on it awaits us. If I don't get you for dinner, then I will take advantage of you for lunch. Let's go." She extended her hand to me to help me from my seat.

"Wait a second. Did you just say you would take advantage of me?" I asked in humor.

"I did," she answered as she tugged me upright. "I meant as a buffet partner. The honeymoon is just a cover, you realize?" she asked.

"I understand. Can't a person be hopeful?" She turned away, and pulled me towards the door. I never saw her mouth, 'I'd like to think so' as she reached for the door handle and pulled it open.

Chapter 24

We made our way to the elevator hand in hand, and wandered into the great room to find several tables pushed together covered with trays of food. The layout included an assortment of pastries, fresh fruit, and seafood all served as an impressive testament to any buffet table. I leaned towards Isabelle and whispered, "I'm glad I'll be locked away at the library. I wouldn't be able to fit into our stateroom if lunch here became a regular."

She laughed at me. "So it's acceptable for me to become as big as a beached whale, though not you?"

"I didn't say 'all right'. I just said I won't be part of it."

The food looked delicious, and our plates filled faster than either of us wished. We made our way to a table near a corner of the room.

A new energy coursed through me. Excitement filled me to begin my task. Hours of tedious research lay ahead. I had done the work before. The process did not present any new obstacles. My pulse quickened as I thought of discoveries I could encounter. The quest had become more than a fascination. It had become an addiction. To find that one new jewel of information excited me. Other tidbits would follow. It all added up to a hunt for hidden treasure.

In my excitement to leave, I rushed us away from the table. Isabelle assisted me from the huge room. We passed by a table near the entryway to the great room where my gaze turned with a casualness to its occupants. I chuckled to myself. All the cloak and dagger stuff made me paranoid. Danger appeared everywhere to me. If I would have paid more attention, I wouldn't have chuckled if I noticed the interest the occupants of that table cast at me.

My mind raced as Isabelle assisted me from the buffet, an action plan gelling in my mind. Hours could be lost with poor plans and no clear definition. I knew enough not to follow blank paths, although I needed a solid plan of attack to get started.

We reached the library doors and entered the silent chamber. No one else worked at that hour. In fact, I didn't expect to have many guests. Isabelle assisted me to a computer table, asked if I needed her to run any errands, and left me to my research with a hug.

As she left she said with a playful tint to her voice, "Don't stay up too late sweetheart. Tomorrow's another day."

The 'sweetheart' part had been nice to hear, though said in jest. I enjoyed whimsical hopes that the words might lead somewhere, yet knew my attention and energy must be spent on the task at hand.

My excitement pushed me into the research with zest, and my plan began to yield success as my professional background assisted my progress. I knew what doors to open and saved a great deal of time through the awareness of navigation pathways open to me.

My search started with the top five pharmaceutical companies as indicated by their financial reports submitted to the Securities and Exchange Commission the previous year. They represented the biggest of the big. They fell into fortune 100 Companies all traded on major stock indices with revenues the previous year that exceeded one billion US dollars.

Their Research and Development budgets could be described as massive. Even a man such as me with the applicable experience in the field could be stunned. The less populated countries of the world reported smaller Gross National Product numbers than the amount spent to develop new drugs. It made my breath catch.

My examination began with the five year histories of each firm. Profits rose as did shareholder dividends. A combination that shared those two traits would always prove a good mixture for the happiness of both corporate boards, and stock holders of these huge conglomerates that would then be rewarded with gratitude.

Some of the CEO compensation packages tied to company performance brought annual salary packages to incredible levels. Even more impressive were the golden parachutes some of these Board Members now received. It made the who's who list of the country's richest entrepreneur's look sad. The numbers shocked me. The levels of revenues did not blow me away, yet the number of very wealthy people I identified did. I wondered of their power within political sectors and realized it could be as great, or as little as they wished.

Given the size of numbers I reviewed, it became easy to understand that each company could have their own lobby firm at their bequest on the payroll and still be on the outlook for others. They had become an unimaginable force, a power of the greatest degree, and I realized if I wished to sway the forces that lived at the level I found, little could be done to even scratch the surface.

The amount of power this level of money could buy would be enormous. I couldn't even imagine how high up the ladder these numbers reached. I wondered and just shook my head in amazement.

As I sat entranced with my work, I heard the library main

doors open. It must be later than I imagined, with Isabelle back to collect me. I heard the doors close with a gentle noise. It surprised me she returned early, although I looked forward to an enjoyable night on board and a return to work the next day.

"Excuse me. Could you help me get connected, please?" The voice startled me, with its quiet, expressive, sultry, and innocent tone. I looked for the voice that drifted into my world. It came from a girl I did not recognize. No, the voice came from a woman – *a very attractive woman* I thought.

Anywhere from twenty-four to twenty-eight I figured. Auburn hair hung on one shoulder. She wore a colorful sun dress. She had a beautiful face and figure, along with legs that wouldn't quit. She reached my station and leaned towards me with one hand placed on the table top. I moved my gaze from her cleavage to her face. Green, orbs laughed at me. She knew that she grabbed my attention and seemed to take pleasure with the impact.

"What can I do for you?" She looked like an American, with no foreign dialect, wore expensive clothes and accessories. She had U.S. citizen written on her face.

"I need to get online and check my e-mail and do some work for a friend. You look so adept at your work. I thought you could offer me some tips on how to get to my carrier." I cleared my screen.

"Do you have a local service provider?"

"I use a local provider from back home. Plains dot com" she answered.

I looked at her again. Her nails had been done to perfection, her makeup applied with attention to detail. She didn't look like a girl from the flatlands of America.

"So from where do you hail?"

"Des Moines, Iowa," she responded, though I detected no Midwestern drawl. She had just the hint of an eastern seaboard tinge. I glanced at her left hand. No ring. My gaze wandered to her right hand. No rings I could see.

There appeared to be some sort of graduation ring, but her hand turned away. She seemed to feel my gaze and adjusted her hand so that it rotated further. She carried herself with beauty and had the body to back up the sexuality she wished to convey.

As I pushed back from my station, I realized I should not trust her. Her attractiveness should keep her away from the library and in the cabarets.

"So why do you sail the seas of the south Pacific?" I asked with what I hoped sounded like a casual attempt to start conversation.

"A recommendation by a college friend." she replied. "She told me how quiet I would find it and how beautiful some of the beaches would be. I explored some beaches off the beaten track," she exclaimed. "I skinny-dipped at many of them. I so enjoyed the freedom," she volunteered.

My imagination pictured the woman, naked on the hidden beaches and then I wiped that vision from my head. I regained my composure and asked myself, *why would she volunteer such information?* My radar went up. At the time, I didn't realize why, though I trusted my instincts.

"I'm so sorry for my rudeness," she exclaimed. "I'm Elaine Stafford," she said, her hand extended towards me.

"Nice to meet you, Elaine," I responded without an introduction of myself.

"And your name?" she queried. Well, now I worked my way into a corner.

"Wayne," I shot out, my grandfather's name.

"Nice to meet you, Wayne," she answered. "Hope it's not a disturbance to your work."

"No, just need to do some research for a project I didn't finish up. The trip came as a surprise." I didn't play the honeymoon card, because I wanted to protect my travel companion. My gaze settled on my cane against the edge of the table next to me. It gave me away.

"So what's your work?" she asked.

"Financial analysis work and if I don't keep up, I'm at a bit of a loss for a week on return," which didn't present much of a mistruth.

"All right," she uttered, even though she displayed no real interest. "Again, I'm sorry to intrude, except can you see if you can get me hooked up?"

"Sure, let's take a look at that monster." I turned my chair, pushed up and walked with one hand on the table to her work station.

"Do you mind if I ask what happened?" she asked.

"Parachute accident." In my mind the question arose as to why I became so secretive, yet my internal bells sounded and I learned long ago to pay attention to any of the bells that rang.

"Oh, I'm so sorry," she exclaimed. "I hope I'm not too nosy." She put her hand to her mouth.

"Don't worry. You learn to live with it." I sat next to her work station and pulled the keyboard towards me, went to a search engine I knew, entered 'plains dot com' and sent it to perform its magical find.

The screen cleared and then refreshed with an endless list of hits. I scrolled past several and saw it. Plains dot com, internet service provider from Des Moines. I clicked it and a new home page appeared. The main page asked for a screen name and password. I pushed the keyboard back at her and said, "There you go. Surf to your heart's content."

She squealed in delight, placed one hand on my thigh, wrapped an arm around my neck and hugged me tight. I did not expect that type of response and sat a bit taken aback by her display, though withstood her onslaught for a moment until I pulled free.

"Thank you, Wayne," she offered as I moved back to my own table.

"You're welcome, Elaine." I heard her on the keyboard, and smelled her perfume on me. It was a sensual and erotic smell. I punched my keyboard and went back to work.

My attention shifted to my research, though I lifted my arm to smell her presence there much too often. I became re-engaged with numbers, and found one that couldn't be deciphered at first. I studied the footnotes, looked at the size of the number, and exclaimed out loud, "Shit!" as I slapped my hand to my mouth and looked at Elaine. "I'm sorry," I mouthed at her. She giggled at me.

My attention returned to the screen. The number stared back. It approached two billion. It had been defined on the balance sheet under an expense category of product promotion. The footnote identified 'to market for research and medical technology'. I searched the term research and medical technology and came up with a laundry list of over one thousand hits.

After I began at the top, following four pages I realized what I wanted. A list of major research and medical clinics associated with well-known colleges and universities became my target. Not just American institutions, but within most industrialized countries. As I sat back the numbers hit me. I figured it out.

The number represented the cost of free drugs provided to doctors. The drugs distributed to a worldwide market at no charge. *How brilliant!* The pharmaceutical industry hired young, vivacious, and aggressive salespeople from college. *Just like Elaine, who sat just feet away from me*! These pretty young people helped establish the pharmaceutical giants of the industry as the biggest drug dealers anywhere.

With the thought of Elaine as a pharmaceutical sales rep, I snapped forward and cleared my screen. At that very moment a hand fell on my shoulder. I jumped in surprise.

"Oh, I'm sorry," she exclaimed. "I didn't mean to sneak up on you! You looked so relaxed. I'm done with my e-mail. Would you like to go have a drink?" she asked with coyness. My thoughts danced with the most recent find.

"What?" I stammered. She laughed at me.

"Would you like to get a cocktail? Would you like to go and have a drink? It will be my treat." I stared at her without expression, and didn't say a word. "Oh, come on. You're on a cruise, by yourself. Take a break. Come join me and enjoy some exotic mixture of juices and rum. It will do you good." I shook my head as the real world began to return.

"Did you just suggest a drink?" I asked.

"Yes, a cocktail," she responded as she bent lower towards me, with an ample view of her cleavage. I snapped back to consciousness.

"Right now, I need to pass. Maybe we can do it later." She looked disappointed.

"Fine," she replied. "You never know what you might miss," she shot back. She turned and started towards the door.

As she reached for the handle, I said with abruptness, "Hold on. I'd love a drink. I'll take you up on it." She swung back to me with a smile on her face.

"Which one?" she responded.

"Drinks," I answered.

She pouted and added, "First. Never know what might come up later."

The time had come to push away from the work table and begin my walk toward her. She stepped aside with grace and held the door for me.

"To the elevator and onto the second floor," she said. "There are great views, a comfortable bar and very good drinks." I made it to the elevator with little effort, hit the up button, and we waited together. We exchanged small talk of our cabins, flights, where we visited and the food. The elevator arrived.

"Elaine." She turned, and looked at me.

"If my legs get a bit weak, could I ask for your hand to give me a little balance?" She smiled a radiant flash of beautiful teeth.

"Of course," she replied. "I hope you'll reach for more than just my hand," she responded with a playful glint in her eye. I thought fast. *It's for information. Get as much of it as possible. Be pleasant. Be funny. Do not open up. Don't mention Isabelle.*

The odds that I stumbled into someone not as sweet and innocent as she portrayed herself circulated in my head. Maybe I did too much research. Maybe my paranoia had escalated. I didn't know, yet my thoughts screamed at me, *Be cautious! And be careful!* A serious cat and mouse game began.

Did she know of me? It seemed obvious, she did. *How did she stumble onto me?* These thoughts and more flew across my mind. I must be careful and smart. *Let the game begin*, I thought as the elevator doors slid open.

A cushy chair across from Elaine at the bar she became my short-term new place of rest. The cocktail waitress appeared. Elaine ordered a Mai-Tai, and I, a beer.

"So, you must agree, you can have more fun here then cooped up with a computer."

"As a matter of fact, time with a beautiful woman and a beer, I have to say yes." She giggled with a hint of embarrassment, a light flush to her cheeks and her head lowered.

"Oh, come on Elaine, a woman such as you, I'm sure, can make claim to many such compliments. I bet you're the rave of Des Moines. In fact, I bet you're prettier than the Iowa cheerleaders and even beat the Nebraska wheat huskers when they come to town."

Our drinks arrived. True to her word Elaine reached into a pocket of her sun dress, pulled out a twenty and paid with a smile.

"Well thank you for the compliment, although the Iowa cheerleaders look very pretty and if Nebraska comes to town, they come with their fellow corn huskers and leave the wheat husks at home." *Very good,* I thought.

So she knew that the Nebraska collegians carried the name corn huskers, not wheat huskers, though that didn't prove much. The Corn Huskers were a popular college team that many people in the country would know.

Elaine's Mai-Tai arrived garnished with pineapple and slices of oranges. She slipped each fruit piece from the rim and ate them. I sipped my beer from the chilled mug and watched my partner. As she tipped her glass up for a sip I caught sight of the ring on her right hand. It identified North Carolina State as the college and had been set with a pretty blue rhinestone.

"A school color?" I asked. She flipped the ring to look at

it and replied.

"Yes. The Tar Heels and they have very pretty cheerleaders." I thought of the location of North Carolina State. To my recollection they occupied the center of Research Triangle. One of the more prominent medical research centers in the country, an excellent location to recruit medical technicians, and pharmaceutical sales representatives.

"I received my Bachelors in English Lit there. When I graduated I returned home to Des Moines. My mom got herself injured and I have been at home ever since." And *what does an English Literature graduate do in Des Moines, Iowa?* I thought, yet left that question on the table for later.

Elaine's next question took me by surprise.

"Can you recover from your injury someday, Wayne? I mean here we sit with that band ready to play and that quaint little dance floor with our name on it. I'd love to think you might be able to dance someday. Think you'll be able to?" I thought with care of my response, although I wanted to keep the moment light.

"Haven't you ever danced around a pole Elaine?" She looked at me rather shocked and gasped. "It's quite simple. I use my cane as a prop and rotate around the stick as an extra appendage. I make every effort to stay upright and not go ass over tea kettle as my partner dances close to me."

She still looked at me like I joked, except then stated with determination, "You're on. I want a dance the next song. You can demonstrate your pole dance routine to me." I would be happy with that. The sooner we moved away from a hypothetical recovery, the better I liked it. She knew how to handle herself. The conversation needed to stay light and happy, and move to a good time versus my supposed injury.

It had come time to go on the offensive.

"I'm sorry for your mom, Elaine. What's up with her?" Not the most fun and fanciful direction the conversation could go, yet it threw it back to her and she needed to respond, whether truthful, or not.

"She suffered a car accident. Her back and hip never recovered. Dad tries to help as much as possible, though she needs more care then he can give. He doesn't know what to do. That's what brought me home. My sister helps out when she has time, but she is a mother, and has a couple of young kids. My brothers live near Chicago and St. Louis. Because I'm the youngest, I returned first. I haven't regretted it at all." If she made the story up, she prepared well.

How long did she recite that little speech? It became easy to see her older sister and children on the front lawn of their home. "When my mom got injured I went home, except she insisted I finish school and graduate. So I did go back and get my credential to teach, and returned to Des Moines so I could be with her." She sounded good. I wondered if I misjudged her. She explained it very well. She almost made it believable.

Careful, I thought. She knew her story and could drag me in. *Stay on your guard.* We both sipped our drinks. I looked at her graceful eye lids and high cheek bones. The lips wrapped over the rim of her glass.

"So Elaine, why did you go to the deep south? You're a mid-western girl. Why not head to Iowa, Nebraska, or Oklahoma?" I asked.

"Needed change," she replied. "My home town lies outside Des Moines. I went to high school there and I've known the same people all my life." She sipped her drink.

"Tell me of yourself, Wayne. Where do you work? Where did you go to school? Do you have a girlfriend back home?"

she asked with a twinkle to her eye and a small smile.

"New York, New York and no," I answered. No specifics, no long stories, simple and straight forward.

"How long ago did you hurt yourself?" she asked. I expected the question.

"Twelve years ago."

"How?" she asked. It didn't surprise me. I hoped my face didn't display any frustration with the question.

"It happened on my first jump. I landed too hard and snapped my right leg. The pressure compressed my T7 and T8 together. I've been a gimp ever since." She went silent as she played with her lower lip. I knew her next question before she asked, and pretended that it surprised me.

"Can't they fix it? What of new therapies?" she asked in innocence.

"None exist." The band began to play. I reached across the table and grabbed her hand. "Time you learned to dance with an old man with a cane. Come on." I pushed away from the table, her hand in mine.

We moved to the dance floor. Soon I twirled around my planted cane, with a graceful turn of my arm around her head. She seemed impressed. She giggled and laughed as she turned with my moves. I led her and loved it.

The band played a Latin derived song and it beat and surged with an active rhythm. I smiled and tugged her hand to my chest. She threw her head back and laughed more. I reminded myself we had not become friends. *Be careful.* The song ended and she threw her arms around my neck in laughter. We turned and headed from the dance floor. I made it back to our table her hand in mine.

"Well thank you, sir," she said. She bent forward and kissed me full on the lips. I separated from her lips with reluctance. She looked at me with a small pout on her face.

"More of that later?" she asked. I could just nod at her.

At that very moment Isabelle appeared.

"Well honey, I guess I just can't leave you alone," she said. She pulled a chair up to the table and sat. I spoke first.

"Bonnie, please meet Elaine. Elaine, Bonnie." They both acknowledged each other. Elaine didn't say a word of my mention I did not have a girlfriend. I knew Isabelle would pick up on the name mistake, and go on guard.

Isabelle and I needed to move away as fast as possible. I had decided without a doubt, Elaine attached herself to me, not by a casual chance encounter, but as more. With Isabelle's appearance, she now knew that a handicapped American man and a deeper complexioned woman traveled together on a ship that sailed from Malaysia to Australia.

"It's time for me to get back to the library. Good night, Elaine," I offered as I pushed back from the table. Isabelle stood without a word to Elaine and followed me from the room.

We exited the bar, and headed for the elevator. I didn't say a word until we entered the elevator.

"She's a plant," I said.

"I figured," Isabelle exclaimed. "I went to the library to check on you. I didn't find you so I came up here to get coffee. I should have stayed away, although I thought you might want help to escape from that kiss." I chuckled.

"No, I could have fought my way out," I replied with a smile on my face.

"Yeah, right," she responded as she slapped me on the shoulder.

"If she stumbled onto us by accident, or by other means, it doesn't matter. Whoever wanted to find us, will know by tomorrow," I added. The last comment sent us into silence.

The elevator doors opened on the fifth deck. We left the car, and made our way to the library doors. As we entered, I turned to Isabelle, and asked, "Do you run into many pharmaceutical reps that provide their wares for free?"

She raised her eyebrows in mock astonishment. "Good heavens. A new drug released on the market represents candy to the babes. Manufacturers give them away as fast as they can, so doctors become addicted to the sweets and start the prescription flow as fast as possible. You have to remember that doctors represent the best place for new patients to get hooked. We play to the market, so the drug companies play to us. Without us they would lose business. Doctors represent drug pushers for the biggest suppliers around. What have you found?"

"Some figures of interest from one of the big five. It's buried within their financial report, though they do report almost two billion spent on product promotion."

Isabelle laughed. "They call it product promotion? It's more like drug pushers promotion. We as doctors represent the biggest peddlers around. We give them away, we prescribe them and we do all except sell them. Nothing stops us from being pushers. We get patients addicted to their drugs."

The thought had occurred to me before. *Doctors had become pushers*. The market couldn't be better defined.

"And if a new cure came on the market for a disease treated by a drug manufactured by the pharmaceutical industry, what would happen to the market?" She sat close to my work table.

"The market for that drug would die. The manufacturer would lose millions, yet make additional millions more from any replacement." She understood the point.

"Yes," I said with enthusiasm. "The market for the replaced drug would be remade. The use of stem cells could increase at an exponential rate. Management drugs would be yesterday's history. Long term maintenance drugs would be wiped out. Diseases would be cured, not just managed. The drugs performing the cure would need to replace and exceed the returns from all management drugs."

"My God," she whispered. "If diseases could be cured by stem cell treatments, the block of their use by the FDA would be revealed. The Evangelicals would have a fit! The party in power that tried to stop their development would be destroyed." She looked at me wide-eyed. "You're wrong James. The pharmaceuticals don't want to kill stem cell research. They want to control it. The Evangelicals or the political party in power must be our enemy." Isabelle now understood. The ramifications could not be underestimated. We both stayed silent lost within our thoughts.

"Let's go. There is plenty of time tomorrow to ponder this. I'll sleep on the couch, though I get first shower," I joked at her. She again mimicked a slap at my shoulder as I ducked away. "Let's go," I announced again. "Elaine might come back soon" She did make contact with my shoulder with that slap. We laughed together and headed to the door.

Elsewhere a phone dialed.

"Yes" came the answer.

"We've got them," a voice reported.

"Where are they?"

"On an ocean liner in the South Pacific called the 'Angel.' She's registered in Norway on her way from Malaysia to Melbourne."

"I'll have a man on his way to Melbourne. Make sure you keep track of them. " The line went dead.

Elaine closed her eyes that night and wondered if her report would be good enough for a bonus. She grew tired of the travel that came with the territory as a sales rep. Not what she signed on for. *Too bad*, she thought. *He'd been a perfect gentleman and the dance had been fun.*

Phone lines began to work overtime. After news reached Simon that the pharmaceuticals may cut them out, he moved to tap their lines. Now a lucky break paid off. Given the different time zones, it would have seemed a little odd to the casual observer. New instructions had to be given, orders issued, updates passed on in a cool, mechanical manner.

They acted in a methodical way. The wait and now the big break had arrived. The cruise destinations of the 'Angel' quickly printed out. A team soon had been dispatched to intercept the ship on one of its island hops. The break now worked for them. The time arrived. Airline tickets had to be reserved. All attention turned to the 'Angel.' A great sigh of relief seemed to envelop so many. Now, they hoped their tedious and dangerous pursuit could be brought to an end.

Chapter 25

My legs dangled from the end of the small couch as I woke the next day. Isabelle inhaled deeply in her sleep. Based on the light I saw from the small portal, I guessed it neared 6:00 in the morning and time to rise. I pulled the blanket tight over me for a moment, stretched my legs and wondered what kind of day it would be.

My feet swung to the floor. I wiggled my toes. I stood with my arms raised above my head. My fingers stretched. I looked to the bathroom door and took one cautious step towards it.

Isabelle rolled slightly, not yet awake. I didn't regret my act as a gentleman the night before. I would have liked to have followed my more basic instinct, though knew other priorities existed and chuckled. There would be time to play later. I sensed the heat present the night before. She appeared seductive and ready to accept my overtures, though I refrained. *Later*, my mind called out. There would be another time.

My feet slid with no noise toward the door. As I reached the bathroom entrance, I realized my cane rested next to the couch. I looked at it and shrugged my shoulders with a decision to leave it where it stood.

The cold water greeted me with a shock. As warm water began to glide through the pipes I relaxed, scrubbed yesterday's exertions from my skin and emerged renewed. I dried myself, shaved, brushed my teeth and slid out the door with the towel wrapped around my waist.

"Hello," Isabelle greeted me. Her presence startled me.

"I'm sorry if I woke you. I tend to rise with the sun."

She glanced at my half naked body and replied, "No problem. I'm up at sunrise as well. Let me take my shower, get dressed and let's head to the breakfast buffet. Nice outfit," she finished as she brushed past me. I glanced at the towel wrapped around me and smiled.

Fresh clothes came from my fancy new luggage bag Isabelle picked up for me at one of the many gift shops on board. I grabbed a new pair of shorts, a polo shirt, boxers, and sandals from the bag. She'd been a busy girl. I dressed, folded my towel and sat on the small couch, waiting for her return.

The clothes made me look like I planned a golf day, though comfort was the main objective for the day. I heard the water run in the bathroom. It brought images to my mind I knew not to indulge, yet my age did not get the better of me yet, even though I cracked as such to Elaine the night before.

My thoughts turned to Elaine. It now seemed a given the wheels would have started to roll to try to stop us on, or before our arrival in Melbourne.

The water stopped. I listened to the noise of her movements, and settled back on the couch and continued to think of my encounter with Elaine. We would need to take every precaution possible as we left the ship. I did not know for sure she tried to set me up, but we could take no chances. We could not afford to let our guard down. Our antenna needed to stay raised to new heights.

The bathroom door opened and Isabelle stepped out. She had draped a light robe on. I wondered where that came from, though women could always find a way to fit another item into their bag. Men couldn't. We crammed all the items we could into a bag until no more room existed to cram. I looked at my new bag I had just rearranged, that bulged at different angles and knew I fit that category.

Purple and violet colors streaked her robe. She smelled fresh. She had pulled her hair back so the gentle curves of her cheeks and shiny inquisitive eyes showed. She caught my stare. She stepped to me and leaned forward, with a soft kiss on my lips. I pushed back against her. She pulled me up.

"Still on that kiss from Elaine last night?" she asked.

I looked at her pretty face and replied, "Just a little."

She chuckled with humor and stepped back. She slid one arm from her robe and shrugged it off the opposite shoulder. It fell to the floor around her feet. She stood naked before me. I took in her beauty and in a husky voice said, "She didn't come close to you."

She chuckled and extended a hand to me. I took her hand and wrapped an arm around her waist, pulling her into me. I kissed her in a deep, passionate manner.

She reached for my other hand and turned to the bed. She led me around to the side of the bed. She threw the blanket back as I sat. She slid under the covers as I kicked my sandals off, pulling my shirt over my head. I used the side of the bed to push myself up, undid my belt and let my shorts fall to the floor, my boxers following. I turned and dropped into bed next to her, pulled her towards me, and kissed her again.

"I guess I can never be your patient," I whispered to her.

My roll continued onto her and in eagerness we made love. She intoxicated me and all the emotions of our time together surged forward.

We lay silent together for several minutes after the passion ended. I held her close and whispered to her. As time ticked by the comfort we enjoyed in each other's arms could not be broken. At last I stirred.

"Well, if they didn't know where we had hidden before, after those cabin shuddering moans, they know now."

She pushed me to the side of the bed with a laugh.

"Yeah, I didn't pull a solo," she laughed at me. "You get out now. I'm hungry and want breakfast. I'm done with you."

The time had come to re-enter the bathroom.

"I'll be just a few minutes, then breakfast?" She stunned me. Her beauty went more than skin deep, unlike Elaine. Though Elaine carried a physical beauty, what lay underneath showed her true colors.

The predicament we faced re-entered my mind. I had accepted we would be watched and followed. Our response must be planned with care and had to be two fold. We must get separation from our followers and get away from the ship unnoticed. We had two days to figure it out. It would take time, though I remained confident.

Isabelle entered the bathroom to freshen up. She exited the bathroom after a few moments with her hair up on her head. She was quite a sight.

"Let's go," she announced. I reached for my cane, turned to open the door, looked into the hallway, and stepped out the door with a glance one way and then the other.

"All set," I said to Isabelle as she left the room and we began our journey towards breakfast.

"You seem preoccupied," she offered as we boarded the elevator.

"I can't get thoughts of earlier out of my head."

"Back to work," she said.

We entered the buffet room, and found tables set and

food arranged with grandeur. I looked to see what passengers occupied the room. Several tables sat open. We made our way down the fresh fruit aisle and headed for seats. I watched for Elaine. No unusual glances came our way.

We found an obscure table away from the food and seated ourselves. Our conversation turned to current events of the day that seemed so far removed. It quickly became a nice way to escape the continuous dialogue of the plight we faced. There would be plenty of time for that later.

We enjoyed breakfast and relaxed. The easy comfort I spent with her could have continued unabated. The conversation flowed, the smiles came, and neither of us acted pretentious, as I had experienced in the past. It was simple.

Breakfast finished, I sat back with my cup of coffee. I began to consider items I wanted to accomplish. My eyes wandered to the other side of the table.

"We need to get away from the ship unnoticed."

"My thought also."

I raised my eyebrows at her and asked, "Do you have any great ideas?"

"I figured I would follow your lead," she replied.

"Rather a mess isn't it?" I queried. "Can we use any of your doctor credentials to shield us? I'm sure those credentials must be good for some purpose." She stared at me with a blank look.

"I'm sorry" I blurted out. "I didn't mean to speak of your profession like that. Please accept my apology."

"Under one circumstance," she answered. "Do not ever use that pitiful tone of voice again," she finished with a laugh. I exhaled and smiled at her. "The look on your face should have been frozen in time," she said with laughter. I chuckled with her. At that moment I looked up at the door and saw Elaine escorted by her entourage enter.

"Time to go," I said. "Don't look up, there's a side door to your right." She stood with abruptness. Without a look, she extended her hand. My hand slid with ease into hers. I stepped around the table towards the side door.

With one last glance at the entryway, I burned to memory the faces flocked around Elaine. Three others entered with her. One woman, not as attractive as Elaine, and two men built like middle linebackers.

We found ourselves in what must have been a service alleyway that led back to the main corridor. Isabelle pulled me along. We reached the corridor and turned away from the entrance to the buffet. We walked to the elevator, pushed the button and waited. The car slid to a graceful stop, passengers disembarked and they headed for breakfast. We entered and pushed number 5 for the library.

"What do we do now?" Isabelle asked.

"Stay away from them," I answered. "I have to complete as much of my research as possible before Melbourne. You check on the ship. Use that pretty head of yours, and come up with some winners to escape once we arrive."

"What if Elaine comes along to the library again? Will I find the two of you lip locked?" she asked with innocence. I hoped I detected just a bit of jealous reaction in her last question, and quickly smacked that thought from my mind.

"Not after earlier. No more lip locks, at least with her," I replied with the slightest tilt of my head and shy grin on my face.

"Find me in the work area away from the main room of the library if you look for me."

The elevator arrived at the library floor.

"Good luck," she offered. "I'll try to find the infirmary

and check on the lay of the ship," she said. I made my way to the library, pushed the heavy doors and entered my domain for the day.

Isabelle stayed on the elevator to the top deck. She kept a wary eye peeled for unwanted company as she exited and began to look for a directory of the ship infrastructure. She found a map of the ship's layout and began her search for the infirmary. There on the seventh deck, tucked away within the bowels of the ship. It would be poor publicity to locate the infirmary at the center of ship activities. People on a cruise ship didn't want to think of illness or injury so they hid the sick room away where no one would stumble on it.

She returned to the elevator and punched deck seven. She arrived, surprised to see small guest rooms located on that deck level. Not like the more elaborate state rooms on the decks above, just smaller rooms, at smaller rates.

She looked for the floor guide as she exited and found the doctor's office at the end of the hallway. Her journey commenced. It seemed like she walked several city blocks when she came to room number 745 marked with the word 'Infirmary.' She heard no response to her knock and tried the door knob, which turned without hesitation.

A familiar smell and sight greeted her. Chairs sat against the side walls. A glass partition separated patients from the nurse's front reception desk. No one presided at the desk. She stepped to the window and slid it open.

"Hello," she called to the empty space. A small bell hung by the desk. It must have served as the announcement of new patients. No one answered her verbal request for help so she reached up and tugged the bell by the thin string that hung from it. A voice answered from the back.

"One moment, please."

Isabelle waited as the receptionist hustled forward. A middle-aged, heavyset woman appeared from the back. Isabelle guessed her age as late forties with an additional twenty extra pounds on her frame. *No wonder*, she thought. The buffet would add the weight if that served as the on board fare for staff.

"Can I help you?" she asked.

"Well, I hope so," Isabelle answered. "I'm Doctor Giovantti on the cruise as a guest. I hail from Italy. I hoped to take a look at the medical facility and exchange a few moments of time with the professional staff, if at all possible." The receptionist extended her hand and introduced herself.

"I'm Sarah Thompson, an LVN from Tampa, Florida." She looked at her watch. "I'll check with Dr. Williamson, though I'm sure he won't have a problem," she finished.

"I would appreciate that," Isabelle answered.

Nurse Sarah moved towards the back. She turned at the door and said, "Doesn't appear we're too busy. I'll check with him. Be right back."

Isabelle looked at the patient files behind the front desk. They had been color coded and sat within a vertical file. The office appeared neat and efficient. She expected the same from the doctor. Nurse Sarah returned and beckoned.

"Come on back," she said. "Doctor said no problem and he would like to meet you." Isabelle opened the patient door and stepped into the back area.

The doctor leaned against a counter top cluttered with bandages and glass containers of cotton balls, gauze, tongue depressors and assorted other supplies. He wore a white smock over a tropical shirt and casual blue jeans. He also carried extra weight, enough to support Isabelle's earlier conclusion.

He peered at the items before him, an order form at hand. As Isabelle entered the room, he smiled broadly.

"Doctor Frank Williamson," he announced. Isabelle grasped his hand and introduced herself. Doctor Williamson appeared to be a cheerful man, with a large gentle face and soft hands. He stood just shorter than Isabelle, close to five feet eight inches tall and appeared near forty.

"And to what do I owe the honor?" he asked.

"I'm here to enjoy the ship with my husband, however professional curiosity got the better of me so here I am," she answered. "While he's upstairs, I wanted to see the on board doctor's office. The pool and sun make me grumpy." Her gaze circled the room to show her interest. The room looked tired.

"What do you do in case of an emergency, doctor?" she asked with a casual demeanor. He laughed.

"You can see I'm not equipped to handle an emergency, huh?" he asked in humor. "My worst emergency to date involves a steak bone caught in a throat, or the ever incessant common cold and sore throat. With good fortune, that's the worst of it." She figured.

"And what's your procedure for the worst case scenario?" she asked. "Let's say an emergency appendectomy." He answered with a laugh. "Let's hope it never arises, though if it did we would broadcast an emergency pickup at sea. The patient would be care flighted, or the closest vessel would be re-routed by the Coast Guard to our location. I have the ability here to perform the most basic of procedures and hope I would never need to perform any surgeries."

She expected this. They continued to chat for the next few minutes. She found he graduated from a prestigious school in the northern portion of the States, became bored with a traditional practice and looked for a more luxurious environment. He'd been on board for two years and loved every moment. He laughed with a pat of his stomach and alluded to the delicious food and night life. They enjoyed some polite conversation and then Isabelle excused herself.

As she walked the long corridor back to the elevator a thought came to her. She would share the plan with James later, yet now wanted to check the food preparation area.

She reached the end of the corridor and climbed aboard the elevator and made her way back to the first deck. She exited and went to the ship's directory on the wall. Food preparation could be found on the 11th deck. She turned to head back to the elevator and bumped smack into Elaine and her entourage.

"Hello," Isabelle said with coldness to her voice.

"Bonnie, please, I just kissed him. I didn't mean to intrude. Can't we let it go?" she pleaded.

"I already have," Isabelle answered as she stepped past them and made it back to the elevator. She stepped inside the open door just as it closed. A noisy group of adults and two children waited. They punched the sixth deck. She reached past the kids and pushed 11.

They began their descent to the sixth floor. As the doors slid shut she leaned against the back wall, her breaths racked in ragged rasps. *She must be more careful!* She did not want to bump into Elaine and her friends again.

The doors slid open at the 11th floor. Activity swirled at a mad cap pace. Orders flew around the room. Tables filled with pre-prepared food had to be rolled from coolers destined for two large elevators at the end of the room that would be transported to the buffet area.

Bacon sizzled, fruits of all kinds were cut and peeled,

juices swirled and pancakes flipped. As she stepped away from the passenger elevator she stopped and watched. The room buzzed with organized chaos. It would be a good spot to get lost within. A woman with a ship uniform on stepped forward.

"Can I help you Ma'am?" she inquired.

"Just curious," Isabelle answered. "I'm a physician from Italy on vacation just having a look." Isabelle grabbed her wallet and flipped her identification.

"Of course you may. As you can see we stay rather busy." The woman took a hair net from a box attached to the wall and handed it to Isabelle.

The room hummed with activity. She wandered with no purpose across the maze. As she approached the cavernous elevators she saw where prepared food waited for transport upstairs. There she spied what she wanted. Large doors on rollers stretched from the bottom to the top of the deck. *They must be used to restock the ship,* she thought. The roll-up doors looked huge. Three stood there. *Perfect.* A cook moved to get by. "Excuse me," Isabelle called. "How fast does the kitchen get restocked at port?" she asked.

"It happens almost as soon as we dock." he answered.

They now had two ways to escape the ship. She couldn't wait to share her information with James.

Chapter 26

The entry doors to the library opened and slid quietly closed. I kept my attention on the screen and silent. Her voice called my name.

"I'm here." Isabelle appeared a moment later.

"Good place to hide," she stated. "Do you want to avoid more lip locks, or just some privacy?" she asked with laughter. I should have remembered, women didn't forget and none forget in 24 hours.

"You just missed her. I sent her away a moment ago. Think I wore her out," I joked. She walked to my location, and slapped me on top of the head.

"Sweetheart, the way that girl fit into her clothes, I doubt if the wear came from your side," she shot back at me.

"Ouch," I joked with a mock grab at my chest. "Some women have a mean streak," I carried on the prank.

"Honey, you have no idea," she said. I realized the time came to move on.

"What did you find?" I asked.

"Two ways out," she replied. "One way, you need to get very ill. I guess I should ask if you fear helicopters." I looked at her rather surprised.

"No, I'm all right with birds that go up, if they stay in the sky and do not come down in surprise." She continued, "The second, we get cold. We sneak into a cooler in food preparation, wait for supply re-stocking trucks, and get out when delivery drivers get occupied elsewhere." I put my chin in my hand.

"Those are very good, my dear. Why do we have to

wait within the cooler?"

"I saw an area where we could disappear and make an unexpected reappearance if necessary without much commotion." I thought of the options.

"What if we just made our way down the main gangway?" I asked. She looked at me in exasperation.

"Forgot that one," she responded with sarcasm.

"I don't like cold, and I'm a lousy actor. I assume I would need to get very ill for a helicopter ride out?"

"Fine, you come up with the escape plan," she exclaimed in exasperation.

"No, no, no, Isabelle. Those are great ideas. I wish we didn't have to play masquerade to get off this tugboat." We sat in silence.

"What do you think of my last plan?" she asked. "We acquire some heavy winter gear, sneak into food prep area as breakfast rush starts, hide, and sneak out as the first trucks roll on board. We sneak into the back of one of the trucks, escape from the cooler unnoticed, and get transported to the food warehouse, sneak from the back of the transport vehicle and get away. How do you like that?" she asked rather pleased with herself. I didn't say a word for a moment.

"I like it. Are there door openers on the inside of the cooler doors?"

"Of course," she answered. She had caught a quick glimpse of one of the servers with a loaded fruit cart exit one of the big coolers as she snooped below. The door opened from the inside as the service attendant exited. There must be a latch to exit the cooler.

Both plans rattled around in my grey matter. Either sounded sufficient to provide us the necessary cover to get away.

"OK, then. Let's go with the cooler route. I never liked to fly anyway." She agreed and stood to leave.

"Well, I get to shop for winter gear," she announced. "You know girls, and their desire to shop." I looked at her rather surprised. "Well, the demands of a doctor don't take up all my time as you should know," she said with a smile. "Besides, Milan calls itself one of the fashion capitals of the world." I thought back to the many beautiful stores I had seen there.

"Glad to know you're the kind of gal that can have a real life."

"I do have my bad habits," she answered. "I'm headed to shop. Can I get you a large, or medium?" she asked.

"You can't tell by now?" I responded.

"Wouldn't have it any other way," she answered as she exited.

A smile crossed my face. I liked our banter back and forth, though now the time had come to get back to work and focus on our great escape. The plan seemed like it would succeed. With luck we could slip away undetected. We must do just that. With the numbers I found, I now was more convinced the issue revolved around economics and the power that money could buy, and if it came to money and power, people could be corrupted. Even if it meant the life of their fellow man would be placed at risk.

My head hung low at the conclusion I had arrived at. It seemed a natural progression. However, the situation meant not just the murder of your fellow man, but betrayal, and not the betrayal of just one man. It had become a betrayal of the masses, a plot of the highest order. It involved as yet untold powers and the maintenance of economic status for the few. I shook my head. It threatened to overwhelm me.

Could it be, I had been set on the course for some divine reason that I didn't understand? It had become bigger than me alone. If my assumptions stayed correct, it would shake the foundations of the scientific community.

The look of disbelief on Isabelle's face had convinced me. As a relevant professional, she still couldn't believe. No one would want to believe, however now that we came so close to the revelation of the whole sordid affair it had become a matter of time. I knew it, believed it, and trusted in it. It now, would also take a huge amount of luck for the final revelation.

Isabelle took the elevator back to the first deck. She unloaded, and looked at the directory to verify the location of stores. She checked that Elaine did not lurk and found the shops she wanted on the second deck.

The luggage bag and new clothes for me had come from a gift shop on the top deck just away from the pool. On the deck Isabelle now found herself, jewelry stores, knick-knack shops, shoe outlets, any retail outlet desired could be located.

A shop that interested Isabelle sat just adjacent to the elevator. She checked the hallway and crossed it with a confident stride. The outlet carried everything from gloves to parkas to sweaters.

She found a salesperson, and announced her husband and she had plans to hike the peaks of New Zealand, and they needed cold weather gear. The sales rep jumped in. Isabelle sensed they must be paid on commission, and figured they didn't sell too may parkas as they sailed the humid climate zones of the south Pacific.

Isabelle loaded up. Gloves, sweaters, parkas, hats, thermals and even chap stick for the cold. Her picks pleased her. The gear would be delivered straight to their cabin and she made those arrangements to avoid hand transport. She paid cash to avoid a credit card track and headed back to the library.

She entered and announced herself, very pleased with her recent excursion. The large room echoed back at her. She made her way to the work room. As she entered, she sensed a terrible wrong.

Silence greeted her. No noise came from James' keyboard. She took a few steps into the room and called hm. Silence answered back. She stepped forward and looked towards the workstation James worked at. She gasped, as she threw her hands to her mouth.

She saw the flat screen monitor on the work table. She heard the hum of the tower. The screen had been shattered.

Spider web cracks spread on the screen. James did not sit at the work station. She called again. Silence returned. She moved to the workstation.

Then she saw him. His toes pointed straight up. She rushed forward. I lay flat, my head turned to the right. She bent and checked for a pulse. She put her hand out to check for respiration.

Blood pooled on the floor from a wound on the back of my head. She stretched her hand and applied a small amount of pressure. Her fingers came away sticky with blood on their tips.

A large egg shaped protrusion started to rise there. She pushed her arm under me, and heaved me to my side. She tilted my head so I didn't put pressure on the egg shaped lump. She checked for a pulse again. It beat stronger. As she leaned over me, I stirred. I started to raise a hand and she stopped me.

"Stay still," she ordered. "I'll get a bottle of water."

"And some ice," I mumbled. She smiled. She rose

and left the room. As she left the elevator earlier she saw a soda dispenser at the end of the hall, and a neon arrow that pointed to an ice machine.

She hurried to the soda machine, and bought a bottle of water. She ran to the ice machine. Extra buckets sat atop it. The top one she filled with ice. She grabbed some paper towels, plopped the water bottle into the ice bucket and rushed back. I lay on the floor where she left me. She hurried to me, and placed the ice bucket on the floor.

"What happened?" she asked.

"I picked up a headache somewhere," I replied with a struggle. I reached up to feel the lump on the back of my head. Isabelle stopped my hand.

"Leave it alone," she said. "Suffice it to say, it's big. You look like you have two heads," she joked.

"Great," I grunted. "More brains, more head room needed." I tried to sit up. Isabelle kept her hand on my shoulder and pushed me with gentleness back onto my side. "What about the screen?" I asked.

"Destroyed," she replied.

"Damn," I uttered. "They saw it. We have even more trouble."

"As if that hadn't been a thought we didn't already have," she exclaimed.

"Can you help me to that chair?" I asked.

"Sure you're ready?"

"You need to know what I found. The government can be defined as a player. Huge donations have been made to political parties from the medical industry."

"Pharmaceuticals?" she asked.

"Through indirect routes," I answered. "They've hidden it. It's happened on an international basis. Our friends at Ashton and Alpha must be a part of it. They want favors, and they also fund the Evangelicals." Isabelle threw her head back.

"What happened here? Do you know who hit you?"

"No, though it wouldn't surprise me if one of Elaine's entourage did it."

"Can you tell me more?"

"As your associate thought, the FDA became stacked with appointees that have been bought and sold by the Evangelicals. The Pharmaceuticals paid, the Evangelicals provided the people."

"Good Lord, we're chased by one of the biggest industries around and a very dedicated and ultra conservative organization. We must be crazy," she finished, her voice a quiet murmur. "It's too much James. They can bury us and get away with it." She went silent. "Why all of them?" she at last quizzed.

"Get me to the chair first." She held one of my hands. She slid her arm behind me to offer stability.

"All set?" she asked. "Hold onto me. I'll get you up, and lower you into the seat. On three, we'll go. One, two, three!" she announced. She pulled me up and then with slowness she began to lower me to the nearest chair.

When she had me a few feet away she told me, "Move your arms around my neck. Hold tight. I used to mud wrestle. I'll be fine." She began her arduous task. "Now," she said as I dropped the last few inches. She moved her arms from behind me. I released her neck, and settled back into the chair.

"Did you mud wrestle?" I asked.

She smiled, with a rub on the back of her neck. "No. I knew you wouldn't hold on," she uttered.

"Pretty smart," I mumbled.

"Let me check your head," she said. She leaned forward and placed one hand on the back of my head. The egg stood out large, though the blood had already dried.

She removed her hand, and I quipped, "Nice position doctor. You can check my head any time." She knew I grew stronger and a little closer to human. She smiled at me as she knew her cleavage showed to me as she leaned to check the back of my head.

She picked up the ice bucket, placed the water bottle next to it and began to make an ice compress for the growing bump on my head. She wrapped the temporary cold compress together and handed it to me.

"Hold that on your head," she told me. With care I reached back, and held the ice in place, and winced as the ice made contact with the point of the obtrusion. I held the cold compress without pressure on my wound. Isabelle wiped the blood from her hands on a paper towel.

"I think you'll survive. Now, do you remember anymore?" She asked. "Work proceeded. The door opened and I thought you had come back earlier than expected. I continued to work and didn't even look up. I heard the foot falls. They walked up to me and stopped.

About that time, I began to make some smart ass comment and then the lights went out. Whoever paid me a visit smashed me hard. I fell to the left from the chair and on to the floor. They must have seen the data on the monitor and smashed it.

The data can be recovered easy enough, though they didn't want it publicized. I faded out fast because next I knew you arrived. Nice top by the way," I added with a little grin back on my face. She looked at her blouse. Yes, it would have given him a nice shot of her cleavage.

"You better get your mind out of the gutter Mister, and more on what this means," she replied. I became serious again.

"What I found can be fatal to them. It backed up data I found yesterday stuffed within financial reports of several of the pharmaceutical industries biggest, like Ashton, the group I met with to put a data mine agreement together."

Isabelle struggled with the news. They had been a primary partner of her old company.

"Isabelle. I have names. U.S. Congressman Belfay. He represents a district from the middle of the Bible belt. He is their political connection."

"What about Evangelical ties?"

"The Coalition for Life located in Atlanta, led by Malcolm Prentiss. I found payments made by shady subsidiaries of Ashton, some located on shore and others off. They have assembled a super-conglomerate of industrial power players.

Offshore accounts send money as huge campaign contributions to political candidates, all the same party, legal with current campaign practices, but then it started to come together.

With their brevity at efficiency, offshore banks made the mistake. They consolidated accounts, and made notations where the money came from in their summary reports. They have to. Offshore governments would close them down if they did not maintain impeccable records.

One of the beauties of offshore banks is their preciseness. It's too bad for those that want to hide there. They never can escape. The foreign governments of the countries where the banks register count on the bank's revenues, and part of the attractiveness of the banks has to be their efficiency and honesty with which they operate." Isabelle didn't say a word as she thought of what she heard.

"How did you get to those records?" she asked. "They must be very, very valuable. They wouldn't be left for the average investor to access."

My smile widened. "Do you remember what I told you I did?"

"A financial analyst," she replied.

"And what do they do, my dear?"

"They analyze financial data," she retorted.

"Yes, and so much more. We track bank accounts for our buyers. On any order to buy a million shares, or more, our buyers must make sure of fund availability before they execute the buy. Analysts then come into play. We research. We know how to unlock doors quicker than anyone, anywhere. Whether it is company research, or financial records we chase, it doesn't matter to us. The order happens. We perform the research. That includes foreign banks. We check for accounts that may hold millions of dollars, so a buy order can be placed."

Isabelle stared at me. "So how did you get in?" she asked again.

"In my work we study banks from the Caymans, Switzerland, Singapore, Canada, Mexico, and the new states of former Russia. We learn the intricacies."

"So, you broke in."

I didn't respond with anything she would be happy with. She studied me.

"How's your head?" she asked.

"It hurts."

"So, you broke into foreign banks, downloaded

balance sheets, deciphered deposits, and the movement of money from where it came to where it ended up?" she asked in a matter of fact tone.

"Yes," I answered.

"Do I want to know?" she asked.

I looked hard at her. "You have to know."

"The money came from the Ashton/Sheldon and Alpha conglomerate and several other well-to-do medical suppliers. They seem to have formed some sort of distribution house they all contribute to in order to conduct their business under the radar."

She sighed with a look at the floor. "How much?" she asked.

"Fourteen billion dollars," I answered.

Isabelle groaned. "They will kill us and not even think about it," she said.

"That's why we need to stay ahead. Thank goodness I locked the other articles in the safe in the room."

The pressure had become too much. It threatened to suffocate her. She blew. "Damnit James! We aren't in a game! Fourteen billion dollars! The government! Who knows what else? They'll kill us. Tell me what you have, damn you! I know you haven't told it all to me! Tell me, and tell me now," she shouted.

I tried to hush her. "They'll hear you."

"Screw you, James!" she shouted. "Tell me. Tell me all of it. It's my life, too!" I looked hard at her and reached back with a gentle touch to the back of my head. She slapped my arm down.

"You'll live. Now tell me!" she demanded.

"Please don't shout anymore. It hurts my head." I sat back. She stood enraged. She needed to hear all the mysteries. The details would scare her, though she needed to know.

My head ached. It seemed like a squished pumpkin smashed on the street at Halloween.

"Remember, you asked. I think Congressman Belfay and Malcolm Prentiss formed a team with Ashton, Sheldon, Alpha and others in the conglomerate of the pharmaceutical industry to stop stem cell research."

She looked at me with no emotion on her face. "What proof do you have? You just said you found documents that prove the powers that be have plotted to stop stem cell research," she said.

"Yes, correct. With the numbers reported, but disguised on the annual reports of the drug companies, it became clear the political machine used money from the pharmaceutical industry, and the outrage of the evangelical front also paid for by the drug pushers to create an added hysteria about the ills of stem cell research." I kept silent for a moment so my last statement could soak in. She took time to digest and gather her thoughts.

"Tell me the story. All of it," she said.

"The pieces started to come together yesterday."

"Yeah, well I figured that much out," she shot back.

"When my diagnosis, and thereafter research began, what happened at work didn't make sense to me. All of a sudden without much reason, they fired me. Sure my research reached into new areas, but my job performance was maintained at a high level. As long as I satisfied my quotas, why was I fired? Then it began to dawn. I had come too close.

Consider that some of the largest traded companies on the American exchanges include pharmaceutical firms.

They can be defined as monsters. It was too easy to reach an agreement with them that allowed me to continue my research unimpeded. I assumed it would be a complementary agreement. My work must have become a threat. If my research came too close, they would know right away. They put the deal together to keep tabs on me. I don't think they ever expected me to go so deep. They underestimated me."

Isabelle wanted to vomit. *Did they play the same game on her?*

"Yesterday, big numbers from the pharmaceuticals started to come to light. Numbers not related to research. These didn't involve profit and loss, or mere financial procedures. These funds were targeted for investment within 'social' programs as defined on their statements.

Let me define 'social' programs for you. They consist of legitimate charitable organizations. These include evangelical groups, and various non-profit medical associations, care groups, emergency response teams, support organizations, and more. Non-profit, charitables in need of public or private donations to keep their doors open. They were chosen by a select committee within the company to report to the Board of Directors for final approval. It's a PR game. Conglomerate participants appear gracious and donation recipients happy and reliant. It served as a perfect recipe for assistance from welling recipients of 'donations' for collaborative pursuits when needed.

Those particular numbers grew significantly. They comprise a portion of the balance sheet as authentic expenses. Later financial reports showed the percentage donated specifically to evangelical groups. Over the last several months that number began to decline, while other non-profits stayed static or increased slightly. The funny thing was that political donations increased substantially, while other non-profits were on the decline.

Some sort of radical change happened among the groups, which meant less money donated to evangelicals. Another part that caught my attention on the financials indicated that as cash flow to evangelicals declined funds moved to offshore accounts increased. Monies that would have targeted the conservative religious groups started to be funneled offshore and consolidated for transfer back to the States. Yet these monies did not fund the before mentioned social programs. Those funds became targeted specifically for political contributions."

"My God," she uttered. "Do you mean to tell me these monies had been first shuttled to evangelical factions to use to defeat the advancement of stem cell research followed I assume by the right to life argument however, those funds later became set aside to buy political favors?"

The look on her face showed realization and a shock of the brutality of the cash game.

"A decision had to be made somewhere along the power channel within the pharmaceutical conglomerate to spend more for political manipulation than in support of the bad behavior of the evangelicals."

Isabelle blanched and choked. The bile rose. She didn't know if she wanted to get sick or cry.

"To control the development of the stem cell industry, the pharmaceuticals pulled the social program money back from the evangelical bodies and targeted it by way of innocent covers that shuttled funds to political action committee needs and left the evangelical groups high and dry. The drug companies changed their priorities.

Evangelicals became incensed. The pharmaceuticals could

point to the evangelicals as the blockade to advancement. The politicians would be the heroes as the pharmaceuticals stood ready to reap the rewards and not suffer the potential catastrophic failure of the so-called treatment drugs they manufactured. They could phase out their treatment drugs on their timeline, and replace that revenue stream with the 'cure' stem cell treatments offered. The politicians who supported them would be the clear leaders of the breakthrough. The evangelicals would be the fall guys. They were thrown under the bus. The pharmaceuticals changed their champion to the politicians to assure their success. The evangelicals had served their purpose."

She realized now the completeness of why she had been targeted. If they controlled her research, they controlled her success, or failure. She understood the reason for their get together with James and why Alpha had become involved. It served the same purpose. They could keep tabs on him and on future developments. They controlled James. They controlled her. They controlled the evangelicals. They controlled the politicians. It could be defined as a brilliant plan. One in which each member of the conglomerate had to be players, and all ended up winners.

"So it became more worth their buck to buy political influence to control the stem cell direction then to push it to the evangelicals for their outraged, emotional attacks," she stated.

"Yes. I'm sorry to break your belief, yet the short, sweet, and simple answer is, yes. The politicians, like Congressman Belfay sold to the highest bidder. The conglomerates paid better."

She now understood.

"The Ashton/Sheldon conglomerate at first let the conservative antagonists bellow at the top of their lungs. The conglomerate stayed quiet, although they provided the cash to encourage the results of debate. As it was determined that the moral outcries began to have a lessened impact, funds were re-directed to purchase a more assured result through political channels."

"Oh my God" she uttered again as she moved her hand to her mouth. The irony of the explanation left her aghast.

"The drug conglomerates have pulled off the greatest deception ever. The protection of fetuses and the philosophies of moral conservatives, which the evangelicals bellowed to anyone who listened, was never the objective. It's all about money.

Big money and the power it will buy to make even more money. Billions of dollars made by the Ashton/Sheldon conglomerate every year and they hid their agenda in groups such as the Coalition for Life to deflect the vision. The transition from the evangelicals to the politicians is now evident.

Money, Isabelle. The story lies there. Money sent to politicians to support re-election, so they can cheer the cause of the pharmaceuticals.

The moral conservatives put up a front. They represent no more than a dedicated tool that believe they follow a moral direction. They get used as no more than pawns on the chess board. The drug companies use the moral conservatives. When that message started to languish, they switched to the politicians, and the people that suffer from diseases and injuries get screwed." I fell silent. Isabelle stared at me.

"So what does this have to do with me?" she asked.

"You're a pawn on the board as well. You're needed. Your success needed advertisement to increase leverage. The closer you came to success, the closer the pharmaceuticals come to their goal of the replacement of management drugs with cures, not treatments. They would continue to control the market, have their political support in line and be able to point to the evangelicals as the bad guy. The religious right sees you as a target. The pharmaceuticals love it that you have become a target. It takes the heat away from their desire to play both sides of the street. With you as a target, Belfay and others can hide in oblivion. The games played to fix FDA decisions disappear from radar. The pharmaceuticals stay clean.

The hysteria raised by your success the pharmaceuticals used as a tool to wave in the face of the Coalition for Life. Remember that Italy represents a very religious country. Good heavens, the Vatican is in Rome. The police on your porch presented no obstacles. I would bet Alpha requested them.

The whole thing can be defined as a game of deflection. I would bet the Ashton/Sheldon conglomerate became thrilled with the energy diverted to our chase. Meantime, they buy their influence at the political level, and groups such as the Coalition for Life become none the wiser until too late."

"How did you start to put these pieces together?" she asked. She remained somewhat dubious, yet knew the basis of the argument made sense.

"The data I've found within the last twenty-four hours began to mold the previous data I collected in New York into an undeniable conclusion. The money from the Ashton/Sheldon group works its way to Belfay and others along a very convoluted path. It began to scream louder at me. All the pieces began to fall together, Isabelle. They all added up. The financials I've reviewed confirm it."

"All right, let's see if I've got this straight," she said. "You say the outrage yelled by the religious right about stem cell use raises smoke to hide the ill intent of the true story. It's very real to those who have a moral argument to oppose the research, but used as a tool of diversion by business. The rabble rousers get cheered on.

The pharmaceutical industry plies politicians with lots of money to get their support to stop the development until ready. Politicians accept money with open arms and continue to stoke the fire of moral conservatives to keep the pressure from themselves and the pharmaceutical industry. Correct?"

"Yes. All, except the politicians stoking the fire of moral conservatives. I think the evangelicals do that on their own, even with reduced donations from the pharmaceuticals. Sure, the politicians love their involvement, but the moral right can provide them and the pharmaceuticals with cover as long as they continue, whether on their own volition or in concert with others." Isabelle sat back and sighed.

"And the players you have identified include Congressman Belfay from the political side, Malcolm Prentiss from the evangelicals, and a huge conglomeration of pharmaceuticals led by Ashton and Sheldon, that also includes Alpha."

"Yes."

"James, what proof do you have?" she asked. I pointed to the back of my head where the egg shaped knob seemed to have grown into a new appendage.

"Not enough," she said.

"I know, I know. I just wanted to lighten the moment."

"Ha, ha," she responded. "Not quite enough to make me laugh. You've got to have proof, James," she said.

"Does this work?" I offered.

The time for another revelation arrived. I handed her a

printout I carried folded in my back pocket. Not a research paper, but a financial document. The page reflected a very detailed balance sheet dated four months ago.

"Look under the line item, 'miscellaneous expenditures.'"

Many sub-items had been listed beneath the primary line item, one titled 'New Product Development' highlighted in yellow marker. Isabelle let her eyes find the right side of the line item where a very large number appeared. She read six billion, seven hundred thousand dollars.

"All right," she said. "You must realize that these kinds of expenditures do not represent anything uncommon with the R&D of new drugs." I again reached into the back pocket of my trousers, and produced another sheet of paper. I handed it to her.

"Look at the highlighted line," I said. She took the paper with a sideways glance at me. She saw the page numbered as 'page seventeen.' She picked up the first page, and looked at the page number. It read 'page seven.' She looked at me in curiosity, raised the most recent page I handed her and found another highlighted line, 'Research, and Development.' Her attention traveled to the right hand side of the page. The number printed there shocked Isabelle. She counted each comma and each decimal place. She lowered the paper and looked at me.

"Fourteen point nine billion dollars," she said. She again picked up the other page and reviewed the lines. "How long have you had these pages?"

"The first I printed in New York, about a month before I left. The second I printed earlier today, before I received my knock on the head."

"Do you know what it means, James?" she asked.

"Yes," I responded. "The number on page seven should

have been defined as lobby efforts, or political contributions. On page seven you see the true costs of new product development. The R&D line on page seventeen defines political expenses, hidden as R&D. They adjusted the financial Isabelle. They moved the large number back in the report in an attempt to hide it." She stared at the paper. Several seconds later she looked up.

"The government has been sold," I said to her.

Chapter 27

"I found the critical data in a Bank of Canada account. The monies earmarked for social Program Expenditure were distributed to several different sources. After a follow-up, I tracked a few to legal firms in Detroit and a public relations firm from Kansas City. The total number of separate entities was large.

The real tickler came on the deposit. The sheer size of the deposit meant that amount of money could not be moved all at once without attention. So, the movement went to, and from an investment company that specializes in hedge fund acquisition and divesture.

The deposit continued until monies were transferred to several private accounts, and onto sources such as the legal and public relation firm. Then another strange occurrence happened.

The total funds moved from the Bank of Canada are well in excess of what could be tracked to hard expenditures. The excess appeared at the public relation firm out of Kansas City. I looked at that company's books. As far as I can tell it went to combat federal fund expenditure for further stem cell research, led by Congressman Belfay. The excess went into his PAC, or Political Action Committee."

Isabelle held up her hand. "Wait. You said private funds?"

"Yes," I replied. "Guess what? In a private fund the money can be directed to different accounts not managed by a large security company. No federal reporting was required. A total of twenty-three separate accounts were used.

After thirty days in the hedge fund, the accounts were liquidated. The money from these accounts did not make its way back to the originator of the funds, or the Bank of Canada for distribution to social Programs. The money had already been divested towards expenditures to prevent federal fund use against stem cell utilization or for political positioning through Belfay's PAC."

"You found all this from your research?" she asked.

"It is all public information, my dear. They have to report those expenditures." It pleased me the work made an impact on her.

"What kind of expenditures?" she asked.

"Television production companies, public relations firms, market research outfits, newspapers, media outlets, magazine advertisements, you name it. They represent the normal realm of advertisers for name generation in political campaigns." It took her breath away. The work she dedicated her principles to had been sold to not even the highest bidder, but the most corrupt. Any hope within her vanished.

"What now?" she asked.

"We need to get the hell away from this boat. We'll be lucky to make it."

"Let's not be seen then. I would prefer to stay alive if it's all the same to you" she said.

"You talked of the doctor."

"Yes, though again you need to get very ill, very fast" she said half to herself, half to him.

"We need to make an office call. If a script for some pain medication can be had, I could develop a severe allergic reaction, and require an airlift."

"At least you might get some aspirin," she responded. "Wait a sec. I thought you weren't too excited about a helicopter ride? What gives?"

"Not a helicopter getaway. There must be a handicap exit

to leave the ship. Let's find out." I stood, and almost fell. Isabelle placed a hand on my arm to still my sway.

"Keep a gait like that and we should get prescribed the handicap exit by the doctor. I don't believe anyone would question your request."

"Sounds like a plan. Let's go."

As I stood to my full height, a wave of nausea passed over me and then disappeared. My head hung low.

"Will you make it all right?" Isabelle asked.

"Dizzy," I responded. "Let's go slow. Hang onto me."

"Pleased to," she responded. She smiled at me and tucked my forearm tighter around her arm. We headed from the work room to the front door. As we exited, Isabelle checked the hallway. She led me towards the elevator. We waited while I rested. Isabelle helped me aboard and selected the infirmary deck.

The doors slid open on the doctor's office deck. I groaned as I looked at the long hallway.

"Would you like me to get a chair?" Isabelle asked.

"No, with your arm, and the handrail along the wall, I'll make it." I shuffled my feet with slowness. The rail came within reach as we passed under the archway of the hallway.

Isabelle stood at my side the entire way. At last we came to the doorway. My energy had drained away. I stood about ready to hit the floor. I leaned into the door, my forehead against it. Isabelle put her hand on my back.

"Let's get you inside," she offered. As the door swung open, I slid inside, and fell onto a seat. It hadn't been graceful, yet I made it. Isabelle followed me into the reception area. The same nurse greeted her with a big smile and a hello.

"Hi," Isabelle responded. "We need to see the doctor. My husband took a nasty fall and knocked his head pretty hard. I don't think he needs stitches, though some codeine would do well to help with the pain."

Nurse Sarah moved much faster than earlier.

"I'll be right back," she responded and vanished. Isabelle took a seat. The door to the exam area soon opened and Dr. Williamson emerged.

"Let's take a look," he stated. "Oh my, nice one," he said as he bent to me, and looked at the egg shape on my head. "Can you get to a back exam room?"

"Yes," I responded. The walk down the hallway had worn on me.

"Okay let's get him up," the doctor said. "Sarah, can you help us here please?" She rushed from her desk and wrapped her arm though my right one. The doctor counted to three and everyone surged forward with a pull that lifted me to a vertical position. Isabelle stood back as Sarah took me from one side and the doctor from the other. I dragged my feet on the floor as they half carried me, half dragged me to the exam room.

As we approached the exam table, Sarah and the doctor rotated me and leaned me back. Isabelle stepped forward, lifted my feet and pushed me onto the table. The doctor and Sarah pulled me backwards. As my bottom slid onto the exam table, I leaned backwards onto the exam table.

The doctor asked Isabelle what happened. Her voice sounded as if it came from a great distance away. The gloved fingers of the doctor touched the back of my head. The fingers never touched the bump, yet the simple pressure generated a sharp throb. The doctor turned to address Isabelle.

"Looks like a contusion of the scalp. What did he hit?"

"A computer monitor in the library. I found him on the floor."

"Did he lose consciousness?" the doctor asked.

"Yes, for a moment, or two."

"We don't have an MRI on board. He split the scalp. As soon as you get him to Melbourne, I would recommend an MRI at the local hospital."

The doctor left the exam room, and returned with some beta-dyne antiseptic, and large cotton swabs to clean the wound. He applied antiseptic, wiped it away and took a closer look.

"No stitches necessary," he reported. "Big bump that will cause a nasty headache. I will give you a prescription for the MRI in Melbourne."

"Would it be possible to get a script for some codeine as well?" she asked. "We don't have a pharmacy on board, though I can get you a dozen pills as you leave here. He'll be fine. He will have a nasty headache tomorrow, and tell him to please watch his step if the ship rolls. It takes a while to get used to that."

"Let me get him a wheelchair," Sarah volunteered. She disappeared and returned a few moments later with a chair.

Doctor Williamson leaned to look at me.

"You good to go?" he asked. "Let's get you into the chair. You ready? Take your time. There's no rush."

"I'm ready." With the doctor's help I moved to a position where I could sit on the table.

Isabelle smiled to herself. My voice grew in strength. She stuck her hand towards Dr. Williamson. He handed her several packets of pills, which she dropped into her skirt pocket.

"Thank you so much. Can we use a handicap exit when we leave ship?"

"Of course you can. I would recommend it. The handicap

exit can be found on the lower deck. Don't forget about that MRI, have him take it easy on the codeine, and the mid-ship bar serves a nasty Mai Tai that may help him with recovery."

Isabelle began to move me from the exam table. The doctor helped pull me towards the wheelchair Nurse Sarah had retrieved. She rounded up the chair and now had disappeared somewhere within the exam rooms. They pulled me up, and turned me so I could sit back into the chair. I settled in with a sigh. Isabelle reached beneath the chair to release the brake and we began our roll.

We exited the doctor's office and re-entered the long hallway. I thought of a hallway that never ended from a horror movie I viewed once. My trip in a chair went much better this go around. Isabelle made quick time to the elevators. I could get used to preferential treatment like this. As we arrived at the deck for the Mai-Tai bar, I looked at Isabelle, and said, "Thanks."

She looked at me, and smiled. "Don't worry. I always dreamed of involvement in a life and death struggle with the biggest pharmaceutical companies around, the biggest and most conservative churches and the United States government. You know how to show a girl a good time."

My look must have been rather crestfallen as she offered to buy the first round. "Can I buy you a Mai Tai?"

"I didn't think you'd ever ask." The sun blinded us as we emerged from the elevator. The bar we wanted with chairs arranged by small tables sat near the elevator. I began to push the wheels of the chair with Isabelle close behind. I grew stronger. I spotted an open table and wheeled to my desired position, while I waited for Isabelle to sit. The waitress appeared and I ordered doubles.

"Want to take care of the headache all at once, huh?" she

joked.

"No. Just want to get you drunk for later."

"Well, you must feel better." The Mai Tais arrived. We settled back to revel in the warm sunlight and our tropical drinks.

"So do we go with me in critical condition, freeze ourselves, hit the handicap exit, or just say the hell with it and leave by the main gangway?"

"I like the gangway." She sipped her drink.

"All right, time to get serious."

Isabelle held up her hand. "I couldn't be more serious. Do you think they will try to kill us?" she asked.

"Yes," I answered. "These are very serious people with a lot on the line. Isabelle, significant political ramifications that may go deeper then we even realize have been hidden." Isabelle took another long draw.

"These taste good," she announced. "Would you like another? I never liked the cold," she stated. "I bought lots of nice winter wear today, though we'll still get chilly. You'll like your jacket. It's bright red." I realized she might be a bit tipsy. The waitress walked by. Isabelle held up her hand.

"Two more, please," she ordered. I leaned forward and told the waitress we wanted singles for the next round.

"Why can't we throw a double whammy at them, and just leave on the gangplank like we own the place?" she asked. "They'll never expect the brazenness and it just might work." I looked at her with a shake of my head.

"Have you forgotten who we are up against?"

"No, I haven't. Look, they will expect us to find some alternative way off. What if we just surprised them and walked out?" I looked at her with care, and wondered how much the alcohol spoke.

"They'll watch the main exit, Isabelle."

"Perhaps," she responded. "What if we gave them other options to think about? What if we set them up?"

"How can we do that?" I asked.

"Just suppose," she started, "that they discovered the winter clothes I bought. They will and you know they will. Suppose they find that my tour of the ship earlier today included a visit to the food preparation area? Then, they find I visited the infirmary as well. They will discover these things."

"Yes, they can find all that out, though this afternoon we returned to see the doctor because we needed too, not because we wanted to scout the place out."

"Si and they will know that. They caused the injury that forced you to see the doctor. It would be a perfect cover. They will know you have been hurt. They provided another escape hatch they have to watch. Now we have the handicap exit as well. Let's spread them thin and bluff," she concluded. "Let's give them so many options they have to cover, they can't cover them all."

It started to make sense. I considered if it could be the Mai Tais talking, yet a plan had started to gel.

"You know, they will have someone stationed to watch the gangway," I offered. She bit her bottom lip.

"They will watch the main gangway if they have enough people, but right now we have four different options for them to cover. They would have to cover the cooler route. Next they would need to make sure you did not get shipped out via helicopter evac, there would be the handicapped access to cover, and then the most blatant exit, the main gangway" she finished with excitement. She took another sip of her drink and said, "Let's head to the room."

My drink finished, we began our exit. I wheeled rapidly. Isabelle cast a look at me as we continued towards the exit.

"James," she called. "You can move."

"It's the alcohol. It reduces the inflammation. Acts like jet fuel. Not a long term effect, though for a very short period, lets me scoot."

"How long does it last?"

"It varies. As long as I don't drink too much I can move pretty well."

"Does it help you walk as well?" she asked.

"It does sometimes. It's the same story line." That piece of information she filed away for another moment. It might be handy later.

We left the bar with me in the lead. I punched the number for the appropriate deck at the elevator and we waited.

"What if we poured a few drinks for you and then we left ship? Could you walk or would you just roll faster?" she asked.

"If we didn't overdo, the drinks would help both."

As Isabelle pushed me onto the elevator, she leaned closer to my ear, and whispered, "Now it's time to bait the trap. Bet we catch some pretty big rats," she chuckled. "Do you suppose they have bugged our room?"

"You can bet on it."

"Well, they must have got an earful earlier," she said with no shyness. "Let's play a little game." I liked the sound of that.

The packages Isabelle purchased earlier that day rested on the bed as we entered our room. I turned to look at her and she pressed a finger to her lips for silence. She went to the bed.

"These should keep you warm," she said as she pulled a

pair of still-packaged thermals from one of the bags. She reached into another bag and produced a new jacket, a heavy lamb's wool sweater, wool socks and even a scarf. She produced her own menagerie of goods that included a scarf, sweater, jacket and a pair of ski gloves. She turned to me and motioned for me to speak.

"What about my gloves?"

She reached into a bag and found a black pair of well-padded gloves, a pair of winter socks for herself and motioned me to keep up the verbiage.

"Well, that should keep me warm enough."

"Ah, the Alps of New Zealand should be beautiful. What time do you think we can get to New Zealand?" she asked.

"We'll check in Melbourne. I think a quick cab fare will get us to the airport." She smiled and whispered, "Now we have the cooler route for them to cover, plus the handicap access and the main gangway. We've got them spread."

"What time do you think we can get to the cooler?" I whispered back.

"I think we should be downstairs at 5:30." She smiled at me. I gave her the thumbs up of approval. So, now they knew our suspected plan of escape. We had baited the trap. It became time to start the process to get away from the ship.

Chapter 28

We began to rattle bags and make erroneous noise for anyone who listened. At that moment a knock at the door froze us.

I motioned with my head to the bathroom. She stepped back and closed the door as she slid inside. I moved with caution to the door.

"Who's there?"

"Room service, compliments of the ship."

"One moment, please."

As my hand reached for the door handle the door burst open. Splintered wood flew into the room. I had learned from my last experience and stood to the side of the arc of the door's swing, as it flew open. The man stepped inside.

Déjà vu struck me like an electric charge. I caught sight of a pistol. The intruder made the mistake of a quick glance back into the corridor.

My instinct told me to grab the sweater from the bed Isabelle purchased for me. With one shuffle forward I threw the sweater over the man's head, my arms outstretched at arm's length.

The sudden counter attack startled the intruder, not to mention it blinded him. He raised his hand, and pulled the trigger of the pistol. A bullet flew into the pillows at the head of the bed. Feathers erupted into the air.

I grasped the sweater sleeves tighter, wrapped the sleeves quickly around the intruders' neck and snapped my arms away from my body. The sweater clamped on the intruders' throat. The gun fell to the floor.

Without hesitation, I released my right hand and brought it hard across my body and struck with a furious blow that crushed the man's throat.

The attackers Adams apple smashed backwards and I heard the sound of a moan. My right hand quickly rose and grasped the sweater sleeve around his neck. I yanked with all my strength on the sweater wrapped around his throat.

The intruder flew head first past me onto the bed. I didn't know if he lived or not. At that moment I didn't care. Rage filled me and I wanted to inflict pain on my attacker, as I struck with my right fist square into the back of his neck.

After repeated blows, my hand began to hurt. I struck one last blow and dropped on him with my right knee, and heard the dull thud and knew with satisfaction that pain had been inflicted. I fought to catch my breath. The intruder did not move. I heard gurgled respiration.

The bathroom door swung open and banged into my foot as it hung from the side of the bed. Isabelle gasped and stepped to the still open room door to shut it against what door jamb remained. She turned back to me. I rolled from the intruder onto the bed, and then stood with a slight weave from the exertion.

"Is he alive?" she gasped out. "Are you all right?"

My breath came in ragged gasps. My head hurt anew. I pulled the sweater from around the man's neck, and recognized him right away as one of the big bodybuilder types who accompanied Elaine into the buffet two days earlier.

I beckoned Isabelle to me. She leaned with her cheek next to mine, so I could whisper close to her ear.

"We need to go now. Any ears hidden in the room heard the commotion. We need to mingle in public areas. We need to stay up all night and be surrounded by a crowd.

Let's gather our things and check it somewhere. We need to move."

She didn't ask any questions, just started to stuff our goods back into the bags they were delivered in. The man on the bed did not move. His breath sounded ragged. I knew he would be sore for days. I also knew he wouldn't roll off the bed to stand anytime soon.

My knees balanced me against the bed. The gun lay on the floor, a nasty testament of the fear others began to feel from what our search might reveal. I could see the gun had been fitted with a silencer. The gun looked like a 9 millimeter with a clip pushed into the hand grip. I stared at the weapon intended to take my own and Isabelle's life, and realized we would be lucky to leave the ship alive.

As I stared at the gun, a desire to touch the weapon filled me. I reached to the weapon and lifted the gun. Its' weight surprised me. I rotated it and engaged the safety. I let go of the weapon, and it fell onto the bed. Isabelle turned to face me.

"We can use him," Isabelle whispered.

"Explain," I murmured.

"Tie him up first. Gag him. Do not let him regain consciousness" she replied. I reached for the pillow the bullet blew through, and pulled it to me. A ragged gash in the wall stared at me.

With a shudder I realized that the hole had been intended for my head. I ripped the pillowcase apart into length wise strips, and accumulated several to wrap the unconscious man's wrists and ankles. I circled his head with a strip, and slipped the knot into his mouth. He would not make any noise any time soon.

Isabelle watched in silence. I looked up at her as I

finished.

"Do you want to hear my idea?" she asked. I smiled to myself. Her enthusiasm shone like a welcome beacon as a display that she moved past the event and onto our next quest.

"Let's finish here and move first. We can talk as we walk."

"Let's go upstairs. Remember these walls might have ears," she murmured. I wondered what the tones of the recent struggle meant to our listeners. *I considered if they could be one and the same?* At least no one beat at the door. Not just yet.

The eavesdropper listening to their conversations slammed away the headphones and switched the speakers to low so everyone in the room could hear the commotion. They listened with intentness. The sounds of struggle were obvious and then silence. The three of them looked at each other.

"Do we have another contact on board?" one of them asked. The man who adjusted the ear phones hushed him to silence. He turned the volume up as loud as he dare. He glanced around the room. He ordered an associate into action.

"Mickey, go. Get to the hallway. Monitor whoever goes in and out. Now!" he shouted. One of the men who surrounded the speakers turned, headed to the door and left the cramped cabin. The other two continued to listen.

The man on the headphones grabbed a cell phone and pushed the memory code for the pre-loaded number. The phone rang once.

"I need to make a report," Eric said. "An attempt on suspect's life just made. Shot fired. Do you know of other contacts on board? Repeat, do you know of other friendlies on board?" he asked.

"Negative," was the response. "Identify shooter. Continue surveillance."

Congressman Belfay swallowed the rest of the highball in one gulp. So, others had also picked up on the danger. The line went dead.

Belfay understood the speed in which this little episode had so quickly spun dizzyingly out of control. He turned the chair and looked out the office window to the outside world. The lights of the night settled on the city. He could see the monument in the darkness, brightened by the blinking red light atop its point to warn away wayward aircraft. The dome of one of the most recognizable structures in the world stared back at him. There stood his place of work.

At that structure he'd been anointed with the authority to represent people of all colors, genders, and ages. *How did such a good plan become so convoluted* he wondered? It must be greed.

He began to serve the country with the light of honor in his eyes. Now it had been clouded by the pressures of money, the destroyer of integrity. He had been trapped like so many others. *Could there be another way out?*

He snapped back to damage control. *What idiot could have made the call to take him out?* They had to know that Armstrong couldn't be killed without more public relation nightmares. *Didn't they realize they must find out what he knew?* They must determine if and what information he passed on. He must discover the party as soon as possible. The game of cat and mouse had reached a sensitive and complicated point. They could be ruined if Armstrong talked with media sources. Then it would become a matter of denial and cover up.

It could be done, at more cost, and bad publicity. There could be enough information for some media hot shot to track the secrets they kept and prove to the world what they covered for so long. It had become more dangerous, and worst of all it took them another step closer to discovery.

As we prepared to leave the room, Isabelle left sales slips from her purchases scattered on the bed.

Before we left the room, the attacker groaned. I grabbed the gun on top of the bed. Isabelle mouthed the word 'No' at me. I reversed the gun, held it by the barrel, stepped towards the man and struck him behind the right ear with the butt of the gun. The blow thudded in the room. I hoped I hadn't killed him. I stepped to the dresser, opened one of the drawers, dropped the gun inside and closed it. I didn't want any of the past history of that weapon attached to me.

In the next drawer of the dresser rested a folded extra blanket left by room service. I snapped it open and threw it on the prone body. If a maid happened to appear, she would see the bulky form of a body. I hoped it served as enough to satisfy anyone's immediate curiosity. As we left our room I placed the 'Do Not Disturb' placard on the door knob.

"Let's walk and talk," I said to Isabelle as we left the room. At the elevator, it opened to let a guest off. The man gave each of us a quick glance, waited for the door to close as we loaded, and stepped towards a quiet area in the alcove area. He pulled a cell phone from his breast pocket and pushed a key.

"Yes" came the response.

"They go up as we speak." Silence met the report.

"Go to their room. See if you can get in. Call me back." Eric ordered a second man from the room. "They are going up. See if you can acquire them and stay with them." His cell phone rang as he completed instructions.

"Door locked. No noise from inside. A 'Do Not Disturb' placard on the outside. There are signs of a forced break in. Too many risks from foot traffic in hall to enter."

Eric Mowers digested the information. He had been assigned this case on a high priority basis. *Someone had the power to make things happen.* Eric didn't know at first, but he identified the boss quickly. Eric never left things to chance.

"Report back to cabin. Second agent dispatched to find them." They would have to make assumptions on the attacker.

Chapter 29

We unloaded at the top deck. It neared four thirty in the afternoon.

"Do you have any desire to head back to the library?" Isabelle asked. "None," I answered. "What do you say we catch some fresh air? I need to clear my head. Can we just look at the view?"

"That sounds good to me."

With her hand in mine, we headed to a spot where we could be alone, and watch the ocean. We needed to consider our next move.

Neither of us spoke as we stared at the horizon. I thought of my daughter and getting back to my inconsequential existence. Isabelle wondered if anyone missed her, what she could accomplish at the clinic, and what she had been promised. It all seemed so long ago.

With spite in my voice I uttered, "Those bastards that want to stop us have no idea what they do."

"Or the millions who could be helped in the world," Isabelle said.

My hand dropped from hers. "My daughter represents my primary concern! It would be nice to help others, but my daughter can be my only objective," I spat out.

Isabelle pushed back, staring at me.

"I understand your desire to help your daughter James, yet the situation can overwhelm you. You can help your daughter and offer hope to others."

My next words came in an unsteady voice, "Since her mother and I divorced, Brenda represents my one and only concern. At first diagnosis I thought just of me. I became obsessed. Then, things changed. My daughter had the same illness. I always carried the dread of what I may have passed on to her, and then it came true. If others benefit so be it, yet my true allegiance will always be Brenda."

"James, you must overcome for everyone, not just Brenda. You should be so proud of your love for her, yet others exist. Others just like her and you."

"This represents so much to me, Isabelle. I have always been told I would never achieve. This chance can't be ignored. To prove to my father, I can."

Isabelle stepped to me and grabbed an arm.

"It must be about more," she said anger in her voice. "To prove you can do it? So you can satisfy your desire to your father, and just for your daughter? That's not good enough James. That's not acceptable."

"I'm sorry Isabelle" I uttered. "I want you to understand. We have been through hell. Moments ago someone tried to hurt us again. It feels like we have come so close. I want it bad, but do I want it for the wrong reasons?"

"Yes!" She slapped me hard across the face. "I'm done. I will help you get away from the ship and after that, no more. I can help so many. It could be just the start. You should know, James. I have been approached to make a deal with the pharmaceutical conglomerate. They want me to continue my research. They offered to fund me. They asked me to keep tabs on you, to know how close you came to them. I haven't told them. It's time for me to go home. I have work to do for everyone."

My shock immobilized me. I had put my trust in her, made love to her, and developed an attraction to her. I couldn't wrap my mind around the horror of it all. *My God!*

The ultimate betrayal had been committed. Had it been played out on me?

"Isabelle, have you betrayed me?" I uttered past dried lips.

"No! I didn't tell them. They must have decided that to kill us was their best solution. Do you think I would approve that? I don't trust them. I do trust you, though you must think bigger, James. I understand your passion for your daughter. However, it must be bigger than just her. The scope towers over us all. You must accept that. Take hold of your compassion. Use it now for more than just your daughter."

My mind reeled. I released her arm. Isabelle's revelation shocked me. The words she spoke struck hard. *Could I be that selfish? Could I be so petty as to turn my back on so many?*

"Isabelle," I said. "You're right. I'm sorry to have been so, greedy. Will you help me get off the ship?"

She reached around my neck and hugged me.

"Of course I will. Don't give up on your daughter, but others with similar hopes and dreams also fight the battle."

"To give up on others never had been my intention. My priorities are simply different."

She stepped to me and kissed me.

"Thank you for your effort at strength for everyone."

My thoughts turned to the new information I had found and the excitement I would share with Isabelle. Now, that was gone. I would miss her presence when she left, yet I must continue. My daughter and father also entered my thoughts. *It will not be the same. The time had come for me to achieve.*

My voice sounded tired when I addressed Isabelle, "I understand your desire to leave, but can we share some thoughts before you split?"

"Go ahead," she responded.

"The best option appears to be the use of the lower exit when we dock. I'd like to head to Christchurch as soon as I can make it to the airport."

"What about our friend in Melbourne?" Isabelle asked.

"He'll be long gone. I'm sure the good doctor called as we left." We stood silent together. I spoke first. "With your help, we can get away. Can I count on it?"

Isabelle reached towards me.

"James, I hope you understand me. Of course, I will help. We should go together. We can even use the same taxi to the airport. We can separate there. You head for Christchurch. I'll head back to Milan."

We would still work together short term. *She would be good on her word.* I considered the options and spoke first.

"So, is it a plan for the lower hatchway?"

"No," she said. "I think more creativity is needed."

"What do you mean?"

"I think you need to have a serious setback," she said.

"No," I said. "We've covered that before. I will not leave you behind." She looked at me over the sunglasses she put on.

"Who said you?" she asked.

"You just did."

"I said, I think it's time for you to have a relapse," Isabelle repeated. "I didn't say it would be your body." We didn't exchange a word. Then it hit me.

"Tell me," I said as I leaned forward. She proceeded to knit together a very deceptive escape plan.

We needed to stay on deck all night. We would make use of the intruder who lay unconscious in our room, distract our watchers with a helicopter extraction, and then they would also have to cover the food preparation area and the handicap exit. For the next several minutes, Isabelle unraveled her story. I listened to every detail.

My excitement grew. I leaned back so fast I almost went over backwards. Isabelle grabbed my arm. As I steadied myself, I planted a kiss on her lips.

"You're brilliant," I said.

"And what else?" she asked.

"And beautiful," I added.

"That's better," she said as she nestled against me. "I'll miss you."

"And me you," I replied.

We discussed our plan further as the sun settled into the horizon. As dusk fell, we moved to execute our plan.

Isabelle led us back to the promenade deck and a cabaret she spotted earlier on the trip. The music played, the audience seemed boisterous and a sign announced an open mike for comedy night. The crowd would be so into the nonsense from the ship's guests, little notice would be given to a handicapped man and woman or of that man and woman as they left the party. It couldn't have been better and what we both hoped for.

We sidled into the cabaret and found seats at a table along a wall close to the entrance to the restrooms. A server approached with the usual efficiency of cruise line staff. We ordered fruit juices without any alcohol. We knew there wouldn't be any sleep that night and didn't need alcohol clouding our judgment, or make our eyelids heavy. We settled into the cushions of the lounge chairs to wait for darkness to envelop the ship.

The night crowd grew rowdy. Several times, Isabelle reached to hold our glasses as audience members passed by and knocked our table on their way to the restroom. We kept a wary eye on our watches to make sure we didn't overstay our targeted departure time.

We downed several fruit juices. I looked at my wrist watch and tapped it several times. I wanted to get Isabelle's attention and let her know, the time for our departure arrived.

We pushed back from the table and stood, and I reached to Isabelle and took her hand. Together we exited the club as close to the wall as possible and made our way to the elevator.

On its arrival, Isabelle selected the deck located above our floor. We left the elevator and headed for the stairs so we could take them to the deck level of our cabin. As we began our descent, Isabelle took my hand. It had always been easier to go downstairs than up. I wanted to make sure we didn't create a scene any time soon. We reached our deck after our descent down the stairs. Isabelle cracked the door and peered out. No unwanted guests waited there. We crept with stealth towards our cabin.

Isabelle inserted her electronic key, turned the door handle and we entered. The attacker lay on the bed, covered as we left him. I moved to the bed, and pulled the blanket back. The man squirmed. The bonds held tight, and if he moved too much they tightened further, adding pressure to his already damaged throat, which forced him to gasp for air, a painful sound to endure.

He lay still. His hair had matted to his scalp from sweat. A small smear of blood shone where I had struck him behind the right ear. The time to begin the process of our escape arrived.

Isabelle slipped into the bathroom and grabbed one of the complimentary bottles of water, opened it and poured it into a glass on the countertop. She opened several packages of codeine pills she carried from our visit to the doctor's office and dumped them into the glass of water. She stirred the water with the end of her toothbrush left on the counter and exited the bathroom, glass in hand.

As she exited, I rose from the bed, and began to loosen the strips that tied the man's neck and undo the wrap that bound him to the headboard. As the bonds loosened, I rolled the man from his front to back. Their prisoner awakened fully and stared up at me as I held a finger to my mouth for silence. I loosened the knot on the bind around his neck. As the knot came free, I pulled it off. I held the gun to the man's forehead, confident the fear of the weapon would stop any screams.

Isabelle handed the glass of water to me, and I held the glass to the man's lips. I slanted the glass to the man so he could open and with a grateful look, he began to swallow. I tipped the glass until it was empty. The man sputtered and coughed. It wouldn't knock him out, though it would make him sleep.

As the man finished drinking, I pushed him down. He began to struggle, but as the binds grew tighter he gave up and let me roll him to his side without further resistance. Isabelle's face grew pale. She had been sworn to care for man's ills, not to cause them.

The man went silent once again. I had no empathy for him as he lay flat on the bed, as I looked to the bullet hole in the wall. I reversed the gun I held and swung at the man. The room echoed with the thud of the butt of the gun as it struck the back of the man's head. Isabelle gasped, as she raised her hands to her mouth. I turned and begged her silence.

My hand went to the back of my head with a show to her

that turn-about could be fair. I checked my wrist watch. It approached three-thirty in the morning. Next step was to call for an emergency response team. I checked the man's pulse. Not rapid, though strong. Between the knock on the head and the codeine, he would be unconscious for some time.

I pulled the binds from their places, gathered them together and dropped them into a laundry bag, left on the top shelf of the small closet for guest convenience. I stuffed the bag into a dresser drawer and turned back to the man, grabbed him by the arms and half-pulled, half-rolled him to the floor.

His feet pointed towards the bathroom door, as if he came from that direction, lost balance and fell forward. It would be up to the doctor to determine the fall, and by then we would be removed from any investigation. I placed the man's gun in the middle drawer of the dresser. No reason to take it with us. As I arranged the body on the floor, I looked up.

"All right," I whispered. "Are you ready to start the party?"
She whispered, "Si."
"Good luck. I'll meet you at the bar upstairs at 5:30. Be careful." I reached to her. She fell into my chest. I squeezed her, released and reached for the door. I pulled it open past the shattered frame. With all the commotion soon to start I doubted it would be noticed. I pulled the door closed, took one last look into the room, and left.

The hall stood empty. I wall walked to the elevators and pushed the button. It arrived within moments. I took it up to the top deck and exited into the darkness of the new day.

The temperature had turned comfortable, not hot and humid at that early hour. I wore shorts, a polo shirt, and deck sandals. I moved onto the deck and towards the rail to gain a hand hold, so I could use the rail as a guide toward the bar I wanted. It would stay open all night. A clock displayed the time at four fifteen. She should be on the ship's phone to make the call about now.

Nervousness churned her stomach. She picked up the cabin phone, and dialed the emergency number. An operator answered. Isabelle launched into her panicked tirade.

"You must help me! My husband fell. He's unconscious. I need a doctor. Please hurry!" She cut away, stepped towards the door and threw it open. She then moved to the bathroom to throw water on her face. She didn't wipe it off, to leave an appearance of runny mascara and wet cheeks, then turned and dropped on her knees next to the prone man. She waited for the rescue team.

Within minutes, she could hear the elevator doors open and foot falls rush down the hall. A team of on-board paramedics burst into the room.

"What happened?" one of them asked.

"We just arrived back at the room. He went to the bathroom, started to come out, must have stubbed his toe, and fell into the dresser." James' cane lay next to the body. One of the attendants saw it and took immediate note.

"Are there any medications prescribed to him?" he asked.

"Yes. He uses a MS management drug. No allergic reactions," she stated. The other paramedic entered the room and pointed to the lump on the back of the fallen man's head. The bump near his right temple, incurred by James' earlier strike, now receded and had all but disappeared.

"Did he hit the dresser? When did he lose consciousness?" he asked as he applied a blood pressure cuff to the man's arm.

"About three minutes ago. I tried to revive him. I'm a doctor," she explained. The first attendant grabbed a portable radio from his belt as Isabelle answered.

"We need a stretcher as soon as possible. Call the doctor. We're on our way to the infirmary. Have the doctor meet us there in five minutes." He clicked the radio off.

The attendants struggled to put a neck brace on the man. As they finished, two other medical technicians appeared at the door. They pushed a stretcher with a back board loaded on top. They handed it into the room.

They rolled the man onto the backboard with care, supporting his neck throughout the entire roll. On the count of three, two of the attendants lifted the board into the air and stepped their way out the door to the stretcher. One of them said into the room.

"You can come with us to the doctor's office," he offered. Isabelle pushed away from the wall.

She grabbed her carry-on bag as she left the room. The attendants had already gone.

Eric sat at the radio and listened. He heard the commotion. He turned his radio to the on position and spoke in a hurry.

"Target injured. He's on the way to the doctor's office. All personnel, report to cabin as soon as possible." He stopped and placed the transmitter down.

Isabelle arrived at the infirmary with the medical technicians. Dr. Williamson bustled in a few moments later, hair disheveled, shirt un-tucked, yet ready for service.

"What's up?" he asked the team.

"A male, mid-thirties, suffered a contusion on head. We found him unconscious. Respiration and blood pressure in normal range. He lost consciousness about seven minutes ago" the attendant reported as he glanced at the clock. Dr. Williamson looked at Isabelle.

"What happened?" he asked.

"He missed a step as he left the bathroom, tripped and hit the dresser hard" she replied.

"Has he regained consciousness?" the doctor asked.

"No," she said. Guilt nearly overcame her and then she considered this man tried to kill her and James. She experienced guilt no longer.

"Get the Captain on the line," Dr. Williamson barked as an order, not a request. "Move him into exam room one." Dr. Williamson turned and headed to the exam room. The moment Isabelle hoped for arrived. She turned and headed for the office door, left open with all the commotion, and slipped into the hallway.

The call to the captain had been picked up. "This is First Lieutenant Randal here. What can we do for you doctor?" he asked.

"Lieutenant, we need an evacuation helicopter here as soon as possible." Silence returned on the radio. At last the voice responded.

"Doctor, we arrive in two hours. Can't it wait?"

Dr. Williamson exploded.

"Lieutenant, I have an unconscious man here with a possible severe concussion. He needs medical help I can't provide on-board. Would you like to explain to the Captain why you denied that care?"

"I'll order the helicopter right away, doctor. I will let you know its ETA as soon as possible." The doctor clicked the radio off.

"Let's make him comfortable," the doctor ordered.

Eric clicked his radio off. He heard the exchange, his radio set to the same channel. Mickey entered the cabin. Eric barked, "Get to the helipad. Confirm patient transported from ship." Mickey turned and vanished.

Doctor Williamson marched to the head of the patient table and ordered the neck brace removed. He scrubbed and whirled to begin his exam. He came to a sudden stop.

"Who brought this man in here? Who is this man?" he asked the attendants. In his earlier haste, Dr. Williamson had reviewed the EMT report and not examined the patient in detail. He'd seen dilated pupils, unconsciousness and head trauma. Now he observed the patient's physical features.

One of the emergency technicians flipped a chart.

"James Armstrong," he announced.

"No," Dr. Williamson said. "I saw Mr. Armstrong earlier today."

Just then the exam room door burst open. The Captain entered with authority. He asked for an immediate update.

"We have a misidentified patient."

"What's the injury?" the Captain demanded.

The doctor responded. "He has a contusion of the skull with small amount of blood loss." He opened the patient's eyelids and performed a quick check. "Pupils are dilated. He suffered a probable concussion. I called and ordered a helicopter."

The Captain grabbed a radio he carried in his breast pocket. "This is the Captain to main deck. When can we expect the evac?"

"Twenty minutes. They should be on the deck in twenty-five." The Captain clicked his radio off.

In a small cabin below, Eric reached Mickey on the walkie-talkie. "The patient is to be evacted in twenty-five minutes. Confirm transport by helicopter." He disconnected.

Back at the exam room, Dr. Williamson stepped to the Captain. "Captain, we have a misidentified patient. I examined a James Armstrong earlier today. James Armstrong is not on my exam table."

"Who identified him?" the Captain demanded.

"I don't know. I would assume it was his wife."

"I need to speak with her," the Captain said. Dr. Williamson looked at the faces in the exam room.

"Has anyone seen Mrs. Armstrong? Did she make the report?" Dr. Williamson asked. Heads looked around the room. One of the attendants left the exam room to look in the front office.

He re-entered and reported, "No sign of her."

The Captain strode from the room. He switched the power back on his radio. Security picked up.

"This is the Captain. Issue an all points alert to find passenger, Mrs. James Armstrong. Get me her and her husband's cabin number. Meet me there. We have a misidentified patient and a woman that has disappeared."

Eric couldn't reach for his walkie-talkie fast enough.

"Mickey, come in, Mickey come in," he screamed.

Mickey responded back.

"Check the stretcher. Confirm patient as James Armstrong" Eric rasped out. A second man needed to be sent to the handicapped exit area of the ship.

The Captain and on-board security officers arrived at the same time at the Armstrong cabin. The Captain knocked, and received no answer. He turned to one of the security personnel, who reached into a pocket of his shirt and extracted an electronic pass key. He inserted it into the lock, opened the door and four bodies piled in. The Captain ordered a sweep of the room.

"Sir," one of the security guards snapped. "The door frame is shattered."

The Captain examined the splintered wood that made up

the door trim.

"Sir," barked another security guard. "Gunshot sir," he said as he pointed to the headboard.

The Captain strode to the security guard.

"Do you have any visible blood?"

"No, Sir. I'll have the bullet hole swabbed."

"Gun," one of the other agents announced. He stood at the open drawer of the dresser where James left the weapon. The Captain looked at the gun. He knew this had become a much more complicated affair. He reached for the radio and flipped it on. At that moment Eric stepped into the room.

"Captain a word if you please before you place that call."

The Captain stared at Eric. The Captain had been former military and served in the Navy. He noticed the look of professionalism, the cut of a man who got his way, a man like himself who expected others to follow orders.

They left the room for the hallway. Eric moved a few steps from the cabin door. The Captain followed.

Eric flashed credentials at the Captain. The Captain caught site of a picture and the words 'National Security Agency.'

"What's going on here?" the Captain asked.

"This is a matter of National Security. We have been ordered to track Mr. Armstrong. We picked him up by your online ship's manifest. We scrambled to your first port stop and came on board there. We have bugged the room. I apologize that we had no time to inform you. We heard the shot, determined he survived and continued our surveillance. We believe the man readied for medical evac is not James Armstrong."

The Captain took it all in.

"So, you have tracked him a great distance. I don't

need to know why, though I do need to know where we can find Mr. Armstrong now!"

My journey along the hand rail had taken me outside the target bar. I hung on to the rail with rapt determination, and calculated the distance to the nearest table and chairs within the confines of the bar. I counted eight to nine small steps. I had left my cane behind as a prop. It had made sense, though now I began to regret that decision.

With as much dignity as possible I stepped forward and dropped my hand from the rail. I bent at the waist to maintain my balance, my sight fixed straight ahead. I lifted my left foot and moved forward, my arms out from my sides. I slid my right foot forward and stopped with both feet together. The ship rolled a bit, though it didn't bother me. I repeated the process to make it halfway. I took a deep breath and moved. A few more steps and I would be there.

Thoughts of Isabelle filtered into my mind. She had been such a trooper. Her life came unglued and I could be blamed for that. My feet shuffled forward. Two more steps and I could lean forward and grasp the back of the chair nearest me. The process had been slow, yet I made it. I lifted, stepped, and repeated the process. As I leaned forward the hardness of the rattan chair came in contact. The chair had no wheels and stayed in place. I moved my hands to the table top and used the nearby chairs and tables to make my way deeper into the recesses of the establishment.

As I reached the end of the bar, I looked at my watch. Another ten minutes until Isabelle arrived. I ordered my first drink, a double bloody Mary, no celery. The drink appeared. I sipped it. A few more like that and either I would walk from the bar, or they would need to drag me away.

I sipped with casual nonchalance. Isabelle appeared. She

leaned to me and pecked me on the cheek.

"Five minutes to spare," she announced. I winked at her in approval.

"Good girl. All set?" I asked.

"Si," she replied. "You will leave via helicopter soon." I thought of the guise and how our adversaries would react. I would like to see that.

As they stood in the hallway, Eric asked the Captain, "How many different ways to leave ship?"

The captain considered all possibilities. "The main plank way of course, the EVAC helicopter, handicap access below and the food re-stock area." Eric considered each.

"Captain," one of the security guards called. He held several of the receipts Isabelle left on the bed. The Captain stepped forward.

He checked each and said to Eric, "Food prep area. They mean to get out via one of the coolers. They plan to leave by use of the trucks." Eric headed down the hallway towards the elevators. The Captain motioned to two of the security guards to follow.

As they walked, Eric handed facsimile pictures of Isabelle and James to the Captain, and security guards. "Watch for them," he said.

Chapter 30

We watched the sunrise from the bar after being up all night. Beautiful oranges and golds melted into the horizon.

"How do the legs feel?" Isabelle asked.

"Won't know until I get up and walk," I replied. "And to speak of which, the time has come to find out. I'm off to the restroom. Could I get another one of these?" I asked the bartender.

"And what for you, my dear?" the bartender asked Isabelle.

"Could I get a tea?" she ordered.

"Be right back," I said as I moved off with the assistance of the chairs and tables within the bar as hand supports. My legs had grown stronger, though not good enough. Another drink just might get the job done.

Back at the bar, I found Isabelle with a mug of tea in her hands. I struggled into my seat and started the new drink.

"Not quite there, yet," I reported. "Let's head out after I finish this one."

"Are you sure we need to go through the handicap area?" she asked.

"Tell me why we shouldn't," I replied. "By now, they are headed to the helicopter. If I had enough people I would watch the big doors in food prep. If they searched our stateroom, they found the receipts. That leaves room for us at the handicap exit."

"But they know," Isabelle objected. "If they bugged the doctor's office, they know of our interest in the handicap exit."

Each option ran through my mind.

"Excuse me, bartender," I called.

"Yes sir," he asked as he moved closer.

"Do you know the weather forecast for Melbourne today?"

"Warm. Last forecast I heard said about 82 degrees Fahrenheit. It should be almost 58 when we dock."

"We should be able to leave with hats and sunglasses on. Scarves and gloves are out." Isabelle agreed. "Let's try and be as inconspicuous as possible," she said. "Wait here. I'll ditch the clothes and be back with hats and glasses." She returned a moment later with ball caps and sunglasses.

The last of my drink quickly disappeared.

"Ready?" I asked. She took a deep breath.

"Let's go," she replied. I pushed away from the bar and stood. My legs had improved. She slipped her hand into mine and we began our walk from the bar. I had my cap and sunglasses on. She stopped for a moment and slipped her glasses on. We headed towards the elevator to take it to the lower deck. As she slowed at the elevator doors I continued, and pulled her along.

"What's up?" she asked.

"Let's go to the main exit. You're right. The best defense must always be a good offense and right now, I feel pretty damn offensive," I declared. "Let's give it our best shot and get away now." She looked at me over her sunglasses. *He knows how to survive.* She trusted me. We walked together to the main foyer.

Even at that early hour, a group of passengers prepared to disembark. I figured they had gotten up for one last hurrah before they left. Like I should talk, I laughed. Two doubles to start the day. Yeah, though I justified mine as medicinal.

My walk proceeded with confidence. Isabelle held my hand as a form of restraint. As we reached the exit door, I stopped. The ship docked. Activity bustled near us. The time approached six in the morning. The ship arrived right on time. We could hear the gangway fastened to the side of the ship.

"Are you sure you're ready for this?" I asked her. She smiled.

"No time like the present," she said. We exited towards the stairway.

Isabelle adjusted her cap on to hide her hair. With her help, I took several strong strides to the stairwell where I grabbed the rail. I began to take the steps with confidence with her behind me. A line of cabs waited for passengers at the bottom of the stairwell. As we reached the pavement I turned, and smiled at her. As I did so I stumbled on the last step. I fell forward. My hand reached to grasp the hand rail. As I did so I heard the echo of the loud pop. *It happened!*

As I spun back to Isabelle a look of disbelief crossed her face. Her hand pulled from mine. She fell hard. Asphalt from the area where the taxis had parked kicked up as other strikes splattered black, hot flecks of asphalt on my face. I fell forward, went to my knees, and forward to my hands, my nose to the pavement.

My God, someone had shot at us! Isabelle was shot! Terror filled my mind. Another shot poured itself into the step above our heads. I thrust an arm beneath Isabelle and pulled her away from the steps to the pavement near a cab.

She moaned in obvious pain, yet still lived. I rolled to my side and ran my arm beneath her neck to cradle her head. Blood stained the left shoulder of her blouse. Another bullet whizzed past my head. Passengers behind us began to scream and fall to the stairway.

Chaos erupted. A ship crewman stationed at the bottom

of the stairs reached to grab Isabelle and stopped in mid-motion. A bullet struck him in the neck. His hands flew to the wound as he tried without luck to exert pressure and stop the blood as it flowed.

The cabs that lined up at the foot of the stairs blocked the view. The shooter could not get another straight shot at us. Bullets flew over the cabs. Other passengers on the stairs continued to scream. I raised my head, and yelled. "Call for help!" Passengers fell flat on the exit stairway. I looked back at Isabelle. She had paled, though maintained consciousness. The hat sat skewed on her head, her sunglasses left on the ground near the bottom step where she fell.

"You have to go," she whispered. "I'll be all right. The bullet went through my shoulder. I'll be all right. You must continue. It's up to you. Succeed James, succeed! Go now, you must go!" Crew members raced to the scene. They yelled for others still on board to call for an ambulance. I looked at Isabelle and lowered myself to her left ear and whispered "I will succeed and I will find you." I kissed her on the cheek, and pushed away.

Crew members began to arrive on the scene, shocked. They pulled at me and began to treat Isabelle's wound. They applied pressure to their deck hand to no avail. A major artery had been ruptured and continued to pour blood. My worst nightmare materialized. Someone tried on board. Now, they waited for another chance and took it. On my hands, and knees I looked into Isabelle's eyes. I could see the pain, yet also the conviction.

"Go," she said. Crew from the ship streamed to assist, emboldened to come out of shelter by sirens as they approached. Bent at the waist to keep my head lower than the cab roofs, my crawl took me to the cab parked ahead of me.

I pulled the door open and prepared to enter. The driver lay on the front seat, terrified. With a burst of strength I pushed from the cab and crawled forward. I wanted to stay low and continue to the first cab in line. My exertions pushed me past the next cab to reach the first. The painful crawl took me to the first cab, where I pulled open the passenger door and fell on the seat length wise. The driver turned and began to shout at me. I reached deep in my shorts pocket and pulled two hundred dollar US bills out, and threw them at the driver and shouted, "Get me to the airport!" The driver grabbed the bills, threw the car into drive and squealed from the scene, anxious to leave it behind.

All emotion had drained from me. My partner lay hurt and I left her on the street. Dread crept over me. It fouled my mouth, and left me hollow inside. The act embarrassed me.

How could I have done that, my mind pounded? I lay prone on the back seat of the cab, and struggled with my thoughts. Emptiness filled me. I had considered the moment, but discounted it with the hope it would never occur. Now, it had happened to someone I cared for. I had left! *Would she, could she, ever forgive me?* The emptiness inside threatened to suffocate me.

The cab moved onto the nearest expressway. I lay numb. The thought struck my consciousness again and again. It made me sick to my stomach. I had been a fool to think we could move through our day invincible. I was no spy, or hero, or secret agent, just an ordinary guy, who had tried to play a very serious game, and worse, play it with other peoples' lives and now they suffered. I escaped free and uninjured. Scared, but not on a dirty piece of asphalt, my blood spilled onto the tacky surface. *How could I have been so cavalier?* As the cab rolled on I continued to beat myself up.

From my prone position, I asked, "Can you stop at a pharmacy?" The driver agreed. As I watched the overhead street signs flash by, my realization returned to the task at hand. Isabelle told me to proceed. I wouldn't fail her.

The cab driver exited the expressway. He spun the car through a few quick turns and came to a stop. I looked up to see we arrived at a local pharmacy. I asked the driver if he would wait. He let me know he wouldn't. I struggled out and threw a twenty on the front seat in disgust. The twenty covered the fare from the dock, but after all I had already thrown two hundreds at him. The driver reversed from the spot and burned rubber as he left the store. I stood alone.

The sun beat hot on my back as I shuffled toward the doors of the store, careful to maintain balance. As I approached the curb I saw a spot where push carts stood. *That would help*.

My stretch reached the push bar of the nearest cart. My hand gripped the cart so it didn't run away from me, and I breathed a sigh of relief as I stepped up onto the curb. With the cart gripped, I pushed it to the automatic doors and entered the store with my temporary walker. The prescription counter was at the rear of the store. That's where I would find canes.

With determination not to make a fool of myself, I proceeded to the rear. As I approached the pharmacy counter I spotted canes and made my way towards them. There were several to choose from. I looked for one of proper height and strong enough to damage someone's shins again if the need should arise. After a check of each stick, I chose a sturdy one that appeared as if it had been cut from the tree limb of a mesquite tree. I pushed the cart with one hand while I used my chosen extra appendage with the other and headed to the checkout area.

As I exited the store, a cab pulled up and dropped its most recent fare. I made my way to the cab, held the door for the woman who exited and slid in.

"Where to, fella?" the cabbie asked.

"To the airport, please. I want the easiest way to Christchurch. What do you recommend?"

Without a pause the cabbie answered, "A private air tour would be the ticket. One of my friends runs a tour of the New Zealand Alps. Off the beaten track, but if you want a great price he'll give it to you. Even better, he'll be able to leave near the time we show up. He runs from a private airport, not the International. Would that be all right?" he asked.

"Perfect" I answered. "Take me to your friend." The cab pulled away with me as I headed for my next adventure.

My trail needed to go cold as fast as possible. I needed to display caution when contacting the woman who had sent me the documents after her husband's death. I would worry about that when I arrived in Christchurch.

Chapter 31

The cab driver took me to a small airstrip near the airport. Along the way he asked if I had my passport and appropriate identification. The driver rambled about the beauties of the Alps. I listened to the diatribe as no more than background noise.

My thoughts turned to Isabelle. I thought of her last look at me and her poignant plea to go, her quirky smile and laughter, and of how funny she had been after the Mai Tais. I thought of her beauty and the moment I relished within it and wondered if I would ever see her again.

"We're here," the cabbie announced. He jumped from the driver's seat and began a brisk walk into a ramshackle old office. The airstrip appeared to be no more than a dry, pot-hole-ridden path hidden away on an abandoned pasture.

Dust blew across the field. It couldn't have been better. I assured myself that if I looked hard enough I would spot prairie dogs in the sage that surrounded the field. The place represented a great opportunity to get lost. I smiled to myself with the realization that I found the proverbial needle in a haystack.

My extraction from the cab seemed clumsy, as I exited to stand. It was a proud accomplishment as I turned to admire the scene. The shop was down trodden. Before it, sat a new Cessna twin seat. The appearance looked good and it pleased me that at least the piece of equipment I would travel within appeared sound. My cabbie exited the door of the dilapidated office, followed by a short man with a bandana wrapped around his neck.

"Hey," the driver called. "Here's the pilot I told you about. He'll take you to look at the Alps and land you at Christchurch. Cost you five hundred bucks American," he added. I looked at the pilot.

"How does four hundred American and a nice tip when we arrive sound?" The pilot agreed and extended a meaty hand. I turned to the driver and handed him two American twenties.

"I assume that covers my tab?" I asked. The man grinned and shook my hand with a strong shake.

"Yes sir," he replied. He turned to leave. I grabbed his shirt sleeve. He turned back.

"I'd appreciate it if you didn't remember me," I said as I handed the driver another twenty.

"Never seen anyone like you all day," he said.

My amble to the plane began. The pilot followed.

"Want to see the Alps, huh?" he asked. I shuffled forward through the dust without a turn to face the pilot. I spoke after a pause, "I'd like a bird's eye view. I'm more interested in my arrival at Christchurch." The pilot asked of luggage. I let him know I had none. He seemed pleased.

I clambered in, aided with the assistance of the handles attached to the struts. As I strapped in, the pilot turned the engine over. The propeller sputtered to life and the pilot coaxed the plane forward. We began our bumpy taxi. The pilot communicated to the small tower of our intention and we soon turned, bumped along the runway and lifted off. I settled back and waited for the touch of wheels to the solid ground of Christchurch.

My head nodded to my chest, until I awoke fully and sat forward.

"Over there." The pilot directed me to look to my right

as we flew. I saw majestic peaks of some of the most beautiful mountains ever. They stood covered with snow, most assuredly encapsulated year round.

Here at the bottom of the world, I could only wonder how my world turned so upside down, as I peered out the window with my dreams still alive, but on shaky ground. I started with little more than a hope of treatment that now, spiraled into a nightmare.

My dream seemed destined to failure. I knew there had been no certainties to begin with. It had been just a dream. No claims of success could ever be made. I wanted to find a way to pursue ordinary, simple, mundane tasks that millions in the world did every day without a second thought. I thought it would be simpler than it had been. All I wanted had seemed so uncomplicated.

A sigh escaped me as I gazed out the window at the wonder of nature. Sometimes, I wondered of my place. *Had I been shortchanged? Had nature thrown me a curve ball I could not hit?* I discounted those thoughts. *I will not be proven wrong.* A way would be found. My body told me what worked and didn't work. My mind knew the limitations better than any neurologist, or specialist that tried to tell me why my legs didn't obey.

"Seen enough?" the pilot asked as I peered at the beauty below.

"Yes." I wished Isabelle could be a part of this. She would understand the thoughts that rolled through my mind. The plane banked as my vision pulled away from the side window.

"Can you tell me, how long to Christchurch?" I shouted to the pilot.

"We should be there in fifty minutes." I settled back in my seat and thought of the steps ahead. I wanted to act fast. The people behind me would not be distracted by their missed deed and would watch Isabelle's treatment at the local hospital and try to gain hints from her. It seemed assured it wouldn't take them long to pick up my trail.

With satisfaction I smiled to myself, *I must be closer now.* Their actions had become more brazen. I must find the secret they tried to keep hidden and I must find it fast.

Eric stood with the phone pressed to his ear. The Congressman on the other end shouted at the mouthpiece. Eric held the phone away and could still hear the crispness of the torrent that bellowed at him. He demanded to know where he had gone. Could he be found?

To all of these questions Eric uttered he didn't know. It seemed possible he headed to New Zealand. That much came from their eavesdropping. He didn't know why. He would follow up with the local cab drivers, the hospital and the airport. Rage built in the Congressman. All the political power structure he had built would crumble. There could be no excuse. He couldn't risk a murder charge tagged to him. *Who could it be that had fired the shot? Could it be those damned emotional evangelicals? Could it be the drug industry? The insurance conglomerates? Who?* Instructions never involved murder. Obstruct. Deter. Dissuade. Physical violence had never been part of the formula.

The voice regained control. "Go to the hospital. Check the condition of the woman. Check if she'll be coherent enough to speak. Where did she get shot?" the voice demanded.

"Shoulder shot."

"Get to the woman. Find out what she knows. Find the man." The line went dead. The Congressman stood and lifted a high ball glass from his desk to the domed structure out the window. *Oh, what a great country. Everyone must keep their cool.*

The plane touched with a lightness that spoke to the expertise of the pilot who guided the craft to an area away from the main terminals and shut it down. He pointed to the small terminal I needed to check through, shook my hand and wished me good luck.

The agreed upon fare was settled along with a healthy tip and I began to make my way to the terminal. I passed through the lone security check point at the facility. I displayed my ticket and passport, answered that I traveled on pleasure and scooted past.

As my passport scanned through the electronic reader, it sent hit records across the Internet.

"Got him," the technician said as he reviewed screen output. He hit the print screen command as a department manager scurried to the printer for a hard copy. The manager dialed a cell phone as he walked away.

"He just arrived at Christchurch. He checked through security at 9:47 New Zealand time." The brief message erupted into a flurry of action. The efficiency of the response would have startled the layman that watched.

The commotion I created, I had no idea of. My mind was set on one goal. I needed to see Candice, the woman that sent the parcel. That package arrived without notice to my apartment. I knew there must be more to the story than just the pages I received.

The pages did not present a technical document, but was more of a daily journal, so I could understand the team had broken through. They had found a way. I shared that with Isabelle. Now I wanted answers from the woman who sent me the information.

As I left the small terminal I spotted the larger terminal

for arrivals and departures of regular commercial airlines. An airport shuttle waited in front of the terminal I exited. I clambered on board and asked the driver if I could hitch a ride to the rental car area.

A few minutes later the shuttle departed. The driver dropped me, and gave me directions to the rental car counters. I struggled to enter the terminal. Right near the doors, I found the rental car companies.

I made my request for an older model car, without a GPS system. I explained I had never been trained as a technocrat and just wanted a simplified car to see a friend. The clerk understood and she booked me into a later model vehicle equipped with no GPS system.

That pleased me. I didn't know if GPS could be used to find my location, yet if followed, they now wouldn't have that luxury. I asked for a map of the city and made my way to the exit doors.

My legs grew tired. I progressed with caution, yet with deliberate attention and with steady patience I made it out the doors to the courtesy bus. The bus delivered me to my car. I had used a credit card, though no longer cared. My steps taken had not worked. I had no reason to believe the rental car experience would be any different. Why keep it up? I convinced myself I had not become a defeatist, just a realist.

The courtesy bus driver dropped me at my rental car. I walked with care to the driver's side door. I may have been motivated to move faster if I knew what turmoil my credit card use generated. The bee hive had been disturbed and the bees would not be stilled.

Eric stood in line at the Melbourne Airport. His cell phone rang.

"Can you get on the flight?" No pleasantries were offered.

"I'm at security now, with ticket in hand." The line moved ahead, and he moved with it.

"Good. We had a hit on a credit card number at a rental car company in Christchurch. Go. Check-in there on arrival. See if you can get a car description and destination. Call me with further information." The line went dead.

As I pulled away from the rental car lot, I displayed the rental documents and identification to the gate attendant. I spread the map before me balanced on my knees. It appeared I had 20 kilometers to travel. I would enter the community, stop to call and arrange to meet. A get together at her home would not make sense. We needed a public place among a crowd we could get lost within. A local café would be perfect.

The landscape along the expressway was beautiful. I watched the road signs around me. I thought of Isabelle, and wished she could be with me. *How could I check on her condition?* I wondered, as I sped along.

As I drove into the pleasant suburb, I saw what I hoped for. *Perfect.* A shopping mall sat nestled off the expressway. There must be an eatery inside.

Given the hour, I was surprised to find the mall lot crowded. I found the main entrance, pulled into a spot and began to make my way inside to public phones. I looked at the instructions on the phone, found local information, deposited coins, picked up at the rental car counter and dialed. I asked for the name as listed on the package.

"Hello?" answered the pleasant voice.

"Good day," I responded. "You sent me a package a few months back about your husband's research work. I would like to treat you to lunch and find out how you tracked me down. Can we meet now?" I didn't have time for diplomacy. I had questions that needed to be answered. I hoped that by her first contact with me she would entertain those questions.

I heard her respiration. At last she answered.

"Yes. Where are you?" she asked.

"Meet me at Sun Ridge Mall. There's a small café called 'The Water Crest' across from me." I waited.

"I know the location. I will have a white scarf on. Give me 60 minutes." The line went dead. I hung up and wandered to the café.

My steps slowed. I gave maximum concentration to my stride. I lifted each foot from the marble floor with care and moved my new cane forward for balance. No one waited at the front counter. The attendant had vanished on one of their mundane chores. By habit I slid beneath the entryway and headed towards a table tucked away with a view of the front. A waitress appeared and I ordered tea and settled into my new environment. My instincts told me to stay calm and be patient. The wait would be worth it.

Candice entered fifty minutes later. I took that as a good sign. She must be anxious, a white scarf wrapped over her head to cover her hair.

She appeared shorter then I imagined, wore blue jeans and a red turtleneck sweater. White tennis shoes completed her ensemble. I looked into the mall without any sign to her. One shopper passed by. No others approached. I raised a hand to wave. She turned and looked at me and headed over. As she reached the table she extended her hand.

"Candice" she stated. "You called me a few minutes ago?"

We shook hands firmly.

"James," I responded. She took a seat at the table and folded her hands.

"How did you find me?" I asked. She smiled at me with intelligent, deep blue eyes. Her face showed signs of age, lined with the look of sorrow. She appeared much too young to be a widow, perhaps no more than her late twenties.

The waitress appeared and Candice followed my lead and ordered tea. As the waitress departed, she began.

"Come, come James. You don't think all computer specialists reside in America?" she responded. So, I had an answer. A computer hack or professional analyst found me.

"How did you do it?" I asked.

"Not much trouble," she responded. "I trained in Singapore. I went to Malaysia for gainful employment, and found a multi-national that told me they had an interest in file protection. They hired me to set up fire walls, and add an encryption system that would capture the user name of any potential threat that tried to gain access. My husband and I met in Thailand and came back to Australia with the children for what we thought would be a safer environment." I listened to every word.

"How many children do you have?"

"Three. A set of twins, and an older girl," she answered. *Good,* I thought. She had children. That would be much more believable and hold up to questions more than a single girl who wanted to test the waters for personal gain.

She sipped her tea.

"So you found me based on some of your old corporate lessons?" I offered. She agreed with me.

"After Wayne's accident, I wanted to know more of the industry he worked within. I conducted a lot of searches tied to stem cell research. I always ran a check on those who accessed the same information. It's what I trained to do." She smiled at me.

"One of the user names that always appeared I came to know as yours. I tracked your user name back to your true identity. Given the abundant information maintained by several organizations within your own government it came easily to me."

"Wait a minute" I said, a hand held up. "You mean to tell me that based on the data I accessed on a regular basis and the degree of personal data maintained by government organizations located thousands of miles away, you found my IP address and gathered personal data on me?" I slumped back. *No wonder they knew of me and my objectives.* It now made crystal clear sense.

My recovery required a few moments. She sipped her tea and waited for me to regain my composure.

"So tell me. When did you relocate to New Zealand?" I asked.

"The house the kids and I have now, my husband and I bought together prior to the plane crash," she answered. "My husband told me stories of threats everyone at the lab received. We knew it would be best if we isolated the kids."

"What kind of threats?" I asked.

She replied in a quiet voice. "Before the trip to the conference we received phone calls at the house. They said Wayne needed to rethink the position he had taken. They put the question to him as, "Are the lives of your children or your work more important to you?"

Shock must have been apparent on my face. "My friend has been shot," I told her. "I understand and congratulate you on the courage it took to move your children from danger."

"It didn't do Wayne any good." We both sat lost in our thoughts. "How's your friend?" she at last asked.

"I don't know. They shot her as we disembarked a cruise

ship in Melbourne. I'm scared to check. I'm sure they will try to trace any call made to check on her condition."

"Let's finish our discussion and you can call and check on her without their knowledge of your location." She smiled. I mouthed thank you to her.

"Tell me of the suitors to the lab," I pressed. Candice's face became stern.

"Wayne became very uncomfortable with the approach of the evangelicals. He claimed they showed aggression, rudeness and arrogance. He enjoyed the pharmaceutical people. The government people acted as regulators, there to make sure the work would be conducted by the rules. There were a few foreign governments and other labs."

I required restraint from jumping in and asking more. She fidgeted with the silverware on the table. She squirmed. "Did you review the information I sent you?" she at last asked. I wanted to exhale the mood had become so stressed.

"Yes."

"It's just the precursor" she said. "The notes I sent you are Wayne's informal notes, he jotted down as more of a journal than anything else. He made me promise that if it ever became necessary, I would share it with someone I trusted. James, I have followed your research. I have read your e-mails. I can view what you have done on the Internet. I know what you want to achieve. I want you to have Wayne's formal work notes." The offer humbled me.

"James, they did it. They differentiated stem cells. These cells did not differentiate into tumorous cell masses. They succeeded, James. They generated new cells without any anomalies. They achieved success within the true definition of regenerative medicine."

I had heard it before. With many trials, the researchers

thought they found the miraculous cure, though their successes used lab mice and could not be replicated in human subjects. The look on my face must have betrayed my thoughts. Candice reached forward and placed both her hands on my arm, as I leaned on the table.

"James" she whispered. "They used human test subjects."

My wildest dreams had been exceeded. It meant a cure could be obtained.

"But, the work of the lab had been reported as the use of different stimuli and reagents to make stem cells immune before replication."

"At first, and then their objective grew more aggressive. They moved from the production of immune cells to the differentiation of virgin, non-diseased cells. They did it, James. That objective was their baby to present, and then they never had the chance."

Chapter 32

My amazement must have been clear to Candice. What I just heard would shock the world. It would change research everywhere. My mind reeled.

The entire industry would be moved past expectations. She stood with her hands still on my left arm. I had begun to slide from the chair. I wanted to call Isabelle and tell her the news. Our hopes and dreams had been met. Sure, Isabelle's own work came close to a tremendous break through, but these folks achieved it. Candice had just told me her husband's lab found a way to successfully accomplish regenerative medicine through stem cell implantation. If they could treat cells and successfully transplant them, any disease could be cured.

She released my arm.

"Do you have Wayne's notes?" I stammered out.

"Yes," she answered. "Do you want them?" I stared at her.

"Of course," I answered. "I will get them to a law firm. Your husband and colleagues will get the credit." She shook her head.

"That doesn't matter to me. If the information ever delivers a successful retail product a college fund needs to be setup with fifty thousand US dollars for each of my children. That's all. Wayne would be pleased." I looked at a simple woman who made such a simple request. I agreed with a nod of my hand.

"You can be assured of it."

"Good" Candice said. "Let's get those documents sent

to the States and set you up to make a call to your friend." Maybe a way out had been found.

As we began to leave the café, I took her by the right arm.

"What happened to the test subjects?"

"They've gone underground. I think they got scared for their lives. I tried to contact several of them, but phones had been shut down and calls were not returned."

"How many test subjects?" I asked.

"Nineteen," she answered.

"And you never made contact with any of them?" I asked in surprise.

"None" she responded. I wondered what happened to them.

We exited the café. Candice assisted me to a bench, left me there and headed to her car. She returned with a luggage bag on wheels towed behind her. She stopped to help me up and we headed deeper into the mall.

"Where are we going?" I asked.

"There's a UPS store up there." I stopped.

"No go. If we send these to my apartment, they can be intercepted."

"That's why you will open a UPS box at another location."

"How much cash do you have?" I asked.

She looked at me in surprise, and answered, "About one hundred dollars."

"If I need to, can I borrow some? I do not want to use a credit card and I promise I'll send it back as soon as I hit New York. I used a card earlier today which, in retrospect I shouldn't have done." She agreed.

With Candice's offer of her right arm for balance, we entered the UPS store. I went to the counter and told the desk attendant I wanted to open a box at the Manhattan store, and send the bundle of documents to that location. The clerk listened and repeated back the instructions and disappeared to the back work area to make arrangements.

He returned a few moments later to announce my new box number at the New York store and that the documents would be shipped that day for delivery in the next three business days. The arrangements pleased me.

We left the store minus the baggage we brought with us content with the knowledge the documents had been secured. Candice helped me into the mall and back to the entry hallway we entered through. We progressed with care, my legs tired, though I had taken on a new life and grew encouraged with each step.

I would have proof that stem cells could be used for medical break troughs. We stopped at the pay phone I used earlier. Candice reached into her purse and extracted a small cylindrical black tube type of device. She attached it with what looked like strips of Velcro to the handset.

"Do you know the number of the hospital?" she asked me. I shook my head I did not. She dialed a number for information and handed the phone to me.

"Speak in a normal voice," she whispered to me. The hospital receptionist answered. I asked if Isabelle Giovantti could speak on the phone. They connected me to a nurse on the surgical floor, who told me that Dr. Giovantti had not regained consciousness from the surgery, that her condition had stabilized, and they expected an upgrade to a guarded condition. I hung up, and handed the receiver back to Candice. She broke away the tube device from the hand piece and dropped it back in her bag.

"A decoder and voice masker," she said as she saw the look on my face. "They will never be able to trace the call. It came in as a woman, not a man."

She smiled at me. I looked at her with a blank stare. "A toy I developed for my former employer. It never went to market, yet it just translated your voice into an electronic signal with feminine overtones. The code translation broke the signal the call originated from into a random binary code. They will not be able to break that unless they send it to Washington D.C. and run it by one of their mega-computers. By then you'll be long gone. They will find nothing but a pay phone at an obscure mall location. All clean," she finished. I smiled at her.

"Candice, will they be able to find you?" I asked. She threw her head back and chuckled.

"No." she replied. "James, a pleasure," she said as she extended her hand. We stood at the exit doors. The time for us to part arrived.

"Candice, I don't know how I can ever tell you the meaning of what you have done." She looked at me with a serious look on her face.

"Send an e-mail to this address at the time monies get transferred to my children's college funds," she answered. She handed me a business card with her electronic address on the back. I took the card and placed it in my shirt pocket, and threw my arms around her neck and gave her a long hug goodbye.

We turned and left in separate directions. I began my slow gait towards my car. I began to think of my getaway from Christchurch, as I reached the car and slid around the vehicle.

My trip to the airport went without complication.

I spotted a hotel next to the airport and pulled in. I knew I would be charged extra, but had a concern that the rental car counter could be watched. I would call the local office in New York and let the company know where the car had been parked. My life and the materials Candice left me meant so much more.

As I approached the front of the hotel, a cab pulled to the curb to discharge its fare. I whistled at the driver, who looked up and proceeded to me.

"I would like to get to International carriers please," I announced as I slid in. The driver took off to International departures, dropped me off, and sped away. I made my way to the doors, towards a Northwestern counter. I wanted to avoid Quantas. Not because I didn't trust the airline. Quantas never crashed. I figured that the most popular airline might be the one with the most eyes trained on it and, the one to avoid.

The line moved along with other passengers, as I looked for departures on the big board behind the counter. I spotted an early departure I would like to get on if available. At the desk I asked about flight 42, which stopped in Taipei, Honolulu and ended at Los Angeles. The best part was that seats were available and the plane departed in fifty minutes. I could book straight through. I paid the fare, received passes for Taipei, Honolulu, and Los Angeles. My trip home had begun.

The counter attendant asked if a wheelchair would be easier to get to the gate. I acquiesced and accepted the offer. I hoped to get past security and to the gate as the flight closed. Perhaps my luck had changed. If I knew the activity that my reservation stirred, I would think again.

The printer clicked without pause. Another hit had been recorded against the passport. Orders changed. Personnel were redirected. Cars turned around. Eric received the message.

The office in Melbourne burst into energy. "Get me to the States, and specifics on the plane destinations, times of arrival and time on the ground," he barked in the phone. "Hello. We've got him. He's at the Christchurch airport." He moved the phone away to bark a few more orders. A printed paper with the flight information was handed to him. The plane stopped in Taipei, then continued on to Honolulu, with a final stop in L.A.

"Had they found why he went to New Zealand?" He received no response. His attention reverted back to the phone.

"Can we get someone on that plane?" he asked. "Where's the nearest team to the airport?" he shouted. People scurried across the room. Chairs flew back from work stations. Phones rang. It looked similar to the floor of the New York Stock Exchange as they neared the close of the day. "Nearest team to the airport?" he shouted again. The call to the States went through quickly. He spoke to the Congressman.

"I'm sorry, sir. We do not have an idea at this point. He booked a flight back to the States." The Congressman kept the call on speakerphone. He turned his stereo up with a remote control to muffle the sound. He asked if Eric heard from any teams on the ground.

"The closest team cannot make it to the airport for another seventy-five minutes. The plane leaves in forty-five." He issued new orders.

"Get a team to Taipei. If they can't respond, pick him up at Honolulu. Do not allow him to reach the mainland." The line went dead. He made the last statement with cold brutality, which did not escape those who heard it.

My slumber from Christchurch to Taipei had been

desperately needed. The intercom with an announcement from the pilot fully woke me.

"We arrive in fifteen minutes. Those leaving us, please complete your Customs form." The announcement came on a second time in Chinese.

What would be my next move? I wouldn't disembark for any reason in Taipei. I wouldn't need to disembark in Honolulu either, though I would have to watch passengers that loaded. *Perhaps I could switch seats.* Los Angeles represented the greatest challenge. I would need to switch planes. My followers would have a chance to find me. I rested my head back to think of how I could disembark in Los Angeles.

My impatience grew as I waited in Taipei. I watched passengers re-board. No speculative glances came my way. It seemed likely my trail grew cold. My departure from Christchurch occurred in a hurry, and I knew that if the airline traffic had been monitored and records reviewed, I ran the risk of them on my tail in Taipei or Honolulu. I must assume they would find me. Where they would pick up my trail I did not know, yet I knew they would.

Given the balmy conditions and sudden gusts of wind, our departure from Taipei went well. I settled back, wishing I had taken some of Wayne's documents on the flight. A migraine grew in my left eye, the original eye affected by optic neuritis.

As a flight attendant passed, I asked if I could get some aspirin and water. I surveyed the crowd. Many vacationers headed to the sun to escape the dampness of their island. A few business types sat in the crowd. No one appeared suspicious. *Honolulu would be the point they would pick me up*, I thought. The documents sent to New York worked well. My own safe arrival presented greater difficulties.

Relaxation began to overtake me as I settled deeper into my seat, purchased some earphones as the attendant came by and decided to get lost with an onboard movie. I thought of Isabelle. I missed her laughter and most of all her presence.

Thoughts of our conversation that led us to a separation of ways filtered into my mind. I understood her moral decision, yet felt she missed mine. Yes, we both had held back out of fear of betrayal, although we came to respect and admire the other. Our stubbornness led to the final confrontation and separation of our ways. Now, I wanted to speak with her, yet knew without the encoder device Candice used at the mall, it would be dangerous.

My timeline had been met. It appeared I would be on schedule to help one girl I loved, but I had lost another along the way. I sat up straighter. Did I love Isabelle? She had stayed with me on the crazy journey. She had supported me until our last discussion, even when she discovered the deceptions. She accepted me for the man I became, not the man I had been. Yes, I had fallen in love with her.

My first call in the States would be to check on Isabelle. They would know soon enough I arrived back home. My thoughts turned to my departure in Los Angeles.

I thought of how to break the news. What would it mean to the power brokers who expended so much energy to stop me?

The cabin intercom woke me with the announcement of our arrival in Honolulu. I sat forward and pulled the earphones from my head. I looked for the nearest restroom sign and rose from my seat. My legs had grown stiff and sore. Pain radiated into my knees as I moved with care. As I traversed the aisle, passengers became more excited. The crowd rustled about, baggage appeared from beneath seats the more industrious stood and opened luggage compartment doors to access items stowed there. The plane came to life and with it, my instincts.

As the plane touched down, I exhaled a deep breath and thought of my next move. A flight attendant passed by. I touched her arm.

"Yes, sir?" she inquired.

"Ma'am, I've been sitting in the same place for a while now. Could I upgrade to first class and find a seat upstairs?" I asked.

"Let me check with the gate at arrival. I'm sure our ground crew would be pleased to upgrade you" she finished as she hurried away for final preparations.

If I could move upstairs, perhaps I could stay away from any curious looks. I would take a shot that might keep me secluded. I crossed my fingers and waited for good luck and a seat upstairs.

The plane pulled up to the ramp. Anxious discussions went on around me. The level of excitement grew. The last of the passengers passed. At that moment the flight attendant reappeared.

"Good news," she announced. "Two seats remain. The upgrade will cost twelve hundred dollars to first class. Would you like one of the seats?"

"Yes," I answered as I began to wrestle my wallet from a back pocket. I pulled twelve hundred dollar travelers checks from my wallet I had stashed there. With good luck I would arrive home soon. I thought back to the funds I stashed away in Christchurch and smiled as I became very pleased with myself I did not deplete my reserve fund.

"I'll be right back with your new seat assignment." She turned, and headed from the plane. It pleased me the first part of my plan had fallen into place. Now I needed to move on to part two.

The attendant returned a few minutes later with my new seat assignment.

"Can I help you to your new seat?" she asked.

"As long as I can find a handrail up the stairs, I'll be fine." I pulled myself up with the help of the seat back in front of me. I followed the flight attendant to the stairway to upstairs.

A rope that crossed the stairwell lay dropped for those who left first class. With a lean towards the hand rail that ran along the wall parallel to the stairs, I began my ascent. My climb up the stairwell was slow. Each step had to be navigated with care. I reached the floor of the top deck where the flight attendant waited. She extended a hand, which I accepted as she helped pull me up the final step. My breath came with some exertion. She continued to hold my hand as she walked me to the third row and pointed to the aisle seat. I reached the seat and fell onto it with a sigh of relief. The attendant asked if I would be all right.

"I'll be fine as soon as I can get a bottle of water, please." She darted away and returned with a bottle.

My appraisal of first class began. Now the real work started.

No other first class passengers yet boarded. Soon I would be surrounded by others, though now enjoyed the isolation and surveyed the area for any clue that could provide me an exit. I looked and waited. The game had moved to the next level.

Travelers began to board fifteen minutes later. I settled in, and watched with amusement as the crowd entered the first class cabin with the crew bustling about. I had not been showered with this type of attention as a coach passenger. I would need to try first class more often, at least to the point my bank account could afford it.

The usual assortment of honeymooners returned from their passionate hours as they still clung to each other as they boarded. Other assorted business types, families and recreational travelers also boarded first class. None appeared suspicious. Perhaps my hide and seek game might protect me.

Down below, two people listened on their cell phones, handsets pushed tight to their ears. Both reported no sign of the suspect. They walked the aisles a second time. Stragglers boarded. The watchdogs found their seats. The suspect had not been identified.

Their reports did not sit well at the offices they reported to. Orders had to be snapped to verify passenger lists. James' description flew across electrical connections. Questions flew about.

How could it be possible to lose him? Did he use a different identification? New search teams had to be called up in Los Angeles. The search intensified. He must be found and detained. His entry onto the mainland represented the worst case scenario.

As the intensity of the search swirled, I relaxed with a glass of French wine in hand, and relished in the surge of power applied to the aircraft's engines that would lead me home. I began my return to what I hadn't considered until now. I had four hours to think about my options, and must be right. I must anticipate and prepare. My very life and the outcome of failure or success depended on my next moves. I could make no mistakes.

As foot traffic to the first class restroom declined, I rose and started my trek. I reached the door, entered and turned to latch the entry. I turned back to face into the room with a gasp at the sight. The opulence took my breath away.

The room appeared massive. At least half-dozen restrooms from coach would fit within this room. Towel bars glistened in the light cast by a small chandelier. A low couch rested by one wall. Cabinets lined the sink area, no doubt crammed with fresh cloth towels and bottles of hand lotion to replace those that awaited passenger use. Linoleum that lined the floor gleamed with a polished shine.

"Excuse me?" I asked the first flight attendant that walked past me after I returned to my seat.

"Yes, sir," she replied.

"You have to excuse me," I started. "I'm just a poor Country Boy on my way back home, but that's one of the most beautiful bathrooms I have ever been in. Do all first class airline restrooms look that nice?"

"We pride ourselves on the nicest facilities in the fleet," she said. I hadn't finished as she began to address another passenger.

"Do you have to clean that place?" I asked her as she faced me again.

"They get swapped out for cleaning when we land." She continued her dialogue as the perplexed look on my face seemed to have turned into a permanent grin. "The units are simply plug-ins. They can be lifted into and out of place for cleaning at our final location. The design came from our internal engineers to assure we offer the greatest level of customer support to our clients. Our airline received numerous awards for the advancement, and comments such as your own prove the system works. A fresh unit will replace that one when we land." My answer to get off the plane had been defined.

"More than I ever needed to know of restrooms," I said with a smile. She laughed with a flip of her hair.

"You're welcome," she responded. I had a way off. Now to consider how to make my escape locked away within the restroom.

The remainder of the flight passed in relaxation. I enjoyed the service, food and comfort that first class afforded me. On the first deck, it did not go as well for my two followers. To start the flight, their ears heard a tirade they seldom heard. Their commander wanted to know how they could be so inept. A crippled man slipped through their grasp. He couldn't understand how it happened.

The records had to be checked and double checked. The rage in Eric's voice could be overheard through the cell phones by passengers nearby. The listeners tried to muffle the sound, though the anger on the other end of the line could not be masked. The message came across loud and clear.

I hoped to hide away in the restroom, be extracted when the plane arrived in Los Angeles and escape. I doubted it could be that easy. My pursuers had already proved what lengths they would go to in order to halt my discoveries from release to the world. I had no reason to believe they would stop their pursuit now.

My anxieties pushed me to the edge of my seat for the remainder of the flight. *No opportunities for mistakes, or oversight of even the simplest detail existed.* These thoughts and more ran through my mind as we made our final approach to Los Angeles.

The men on the lower deck searched their heads. *Where could he be?* They verified he purchased a ticket for this flight, and that his seat had been occupied. They grew more anxious to find their prey. They became even more anxious to appease the rage of their superior. His anger preceded him. People knew him for his tenacity. He did not fail. They did not want to bear more anger and become part of his failure. They dreaded the outcome. As the plane neared touchdown nervous energy on board swelled.

The plane landed with the usual soft jostle of her passengers. The interior over head lights came on to indicate approval to stand. Some passengers jumped the gun, and reached for their carry-on bags as the plane neared the disembarkment gate. I stayed seated.

Unbeknownst to me, one of my followers began to move forward. Though flight attendants asked passengers to remain seated, it did little good to stem the tide. One of the men from the rear of the plane indicated to his partner he would disembark and watch the passengers as they entered the terminal. The seated watcher waited for the crowd to thin.

Though passengers swirled about me, I did not have a desire to make a rapid exit. I had no reason to hurry from my seat, and the crowd needed to thin or disappear for me to make my way to the restroom to hide out. The flight attendant I spoke with earlier approached as she gathered litter and other debris left behind.

"Do you need some help?" she asked as she began to patrol my aisle.

"No thanks, I'm fine," I replied. "It just takes my legs a few minutes to warm up. I'll be ready to go in a few moments."

"Take your time. We won't be ready for our next trip anytime soon" she replied. *That's what I plan on.*

Below deck the passengers emptied. The follower still on board stood at last. No handicapped man had disembarked. He stretched, and looked around. No one else appeared to be left on board. He stepped to the aisle, opened the luggage compartment and grabbed a small carry-on. He slipped the bag strap over his head and one shoulder. As he approached the front of the plane, he stopped.

The rope that blocked the stairway lay across the stairs. *The first class section* he thought with irritation. *What an idiot! He had been in first class! No wonder they hadn't spotted him.* He assumed another team watched the passengers that disembarked, so if he had departed with first class, they already had him.

He better check the area. He started up the stairway.

At the top of the stairwell he stopped and peeked around the corner of the wall to observe the passenger compartment. No one could be seen. The flight attendants had left the top floor emptied. He stepped onto the foyer of the top deck. He saw the restroom door and stepped to cross the hallway and grabbed the pull handle to look inside. He pulled the door open and stepped inside. As he did, his nose exploded in a ball of fire. He began to fall backward out the door, and then flew forward back into the bathroom, pulled by a powerful grasp.

When the flight attendant finished her cleanup duty and departed, I stood and headed to the restroom. I entered the restroom, turned and slid the door to the closed position. I looked at the door latch sign and decided to leave it unlocked. The 'Occupied' sign in the on position would not bode well for curious onlookers. I cracked the door to watch the exterior.

The bathroom appeared ornate as I remembered. I moved to the small sofa and wondered how long it would be until the room would be unloaded. I sat on the sofa in the dark and saw a small port window. A little light in the room wouldn't hurt, so I moved to open the cover on the window. Light streamed in, as I opened it, and then I froze in place. They had found me.

The slightest footfall in the foyer could be heard. I turned, and moved to the door, and looked out the small crack. My breath froze. I did not recognize the man, although his demeanor could not be mistaken. He had a professional look about him. It was the look of a killer. I realized I watched the intended instrument of my death.

As quiet as possible, I slid behind where the door would open. It would provide me the smallest of cover, and my only hope of surprise. I waited to attack.

The wait didn't last long. Within a few seconds the door began to open inward. I poised myself. *I must attack without hesitation.* As this final thought entered my mind, a foot entered. With an unusual calm, I stepped past the door and swung a hammer head strike at the man's face. The blow struck and the tissue beneath my fist dissolved into mush.

Without a thought I stepped forward and grabbed the man by the front of his shirt and heaved. The blow to the face followed by the immediate forceful change in direction threw the man into disarray. I stepped to the side as the man's body flew past, let go of the shirt and watched as he fell to the floor. I grabbed a hold of the door to steady myself and pushed it closed.

The man lay on the floor while his hands grasped his nose. I dropped on him, and swung a leg, so that I straddled either side of him. The man on the floor knew weight had dropped on him and moved to rid the weight. The pressure exerted upward could not be missed, as I placed both my hands on the back of the man's head and pushed his face back into the floor. Pressure against the man's nose into the floor must have been enough, as he stopped immediately. I let up just a bit.

"Lay still. Do not resist. Do not talk. Do not cry out. Understood?" I said in a low voice. I rewarded his positive head nod by a slight release of pressure against his head, and leaned forward to say, "We'll be taken off soon. Stay still. Do not try to escape. Do more of you wait on the plane?" The man heard the question and nodded slightly in a negative response.

He had been compromised. The mission neared failure. The thought of escape burned through his head. The guy wouldn't kill him. That would be a mistake. If the situation had been reversed the outcome would be different. Now, he must find a way to escape.

The sun blazed through the portal window. By its position I guessed it neared late afternoon. *If this maintenance crew acted like others, they would pull the restroom unit before five so they could make their way home.* Just as my thought finished, the entire bathroom unit shifted. Maintenance crews could be very predictable. The unit slid from place.

We transitioned to space. A tall fork lift slid the unit outward, the hydraulic arms extended to their maximum reach. The bathroom unit unhooked and slipped from its berth on the side of the plane. The forks tilted back so the small structure would slide to a flush position with the extended arms and be lowered to eye level of the operator. I tightened my knees on the man's ribs as the unit continued to slide from position.

With a quickness that betrayed his size, the attacker rolled with a violent throw. It caught me unprepared for the sudden counter attack. I sprawled off the man's back. I tried to push his head into the floor, but he had braced in preparation for such a reaction. I fell with a gasp of surprise.

In desperation I threw my arms out. In panic and with pure blind luck my left hand clasped the strap of the carry-on bag slung over the assailant's head. I hung onto the strap and pulled with all my strength.

The strap clung across his neck and began to squeeze his wind pipe closed. The attacker bucked and pushed from the floor in panic, though I refused to let go. The bathroom unit began to turn and slide on the forks.

Then it went wrong. The entire room began to rock. The operator struggled in a frenzy to gain control, yet the room sat too high. It shook and swayed on the forks. His struggle to contain the room didn't have a chance. The violent movement of the heavy weight latched onto the tall forks could not be stopped. The room bounced into the side of the plane.

Flight attendants screamed with panic as one of the passenger side port windows exploded into the interior. The attacker and I rolled from side to side. My grip remained tight with fear and determination. I knew to let go meant my death.

The forklift operator continued to struggle with the hydraulic controls of the tractor. An instant later he realized he had no hope to keep the room from its fall to earth. He pulled the emergency brake and leapt from the fork lift. He ran at top speed from the tractor. It began to go over.

With a terrible slowness the extended arms with the heavy weight at the end of its forks began to tip. I began to slide, and gripped the shoulder strap even tighter. The man almost blacked out. I saw a bluish tint to his face, as I slid over, and let go of the strap. I reached in desperation over my head. I slid near the sink and blindly grabbed the drainage pipes that led from the sink to the wall where the gray water discharged to a storage tank. I grabbed the pipe with both hands and hung on in desperation.

With a huge crash the unit and forks of the tractor struck the ground. I hung on with a death grip to the pipes. The world opened to a glare of light. I lay dazed. As sirens approached, I stirred to action.

The wall that had hit the tarmac came apart with debris blown on the ground for feet around. My attacker flew into the air and came back to earth with a thud. He lay unconscious in the debris. I couldn't tell if he lived, or not. I didn't care.

One thought coursed through my mind. *Escape. Escape now. Try to get away before police, or airport authorities grab me. Get away, and get away now screamed at me.*

My arms ached. I released the pipe and rolled to my side. I could see ground crew personnel ran in every direction. Sirens approached. No one tried to enter the remains of the bathroom. I crawled across the debris of what previously stood as one wall of the restroom, and rolled onto the asphalt. I lay for a moment motionless. A bag handler on a luggage cart jumped off and ran to me.

"Can you hear me?" he asked. I pointed into the debris pile.

"There's another person there. They need help. I'm fine."

The man yelled for assistance as he ran into the debris.

With what strength I could muster, I slid my one foot underneath me and rose so I could stand with a slight weave from side to side.

No structures or devices of any kind stood nearby to grab a hold of. I flailed with both arms straight out to balance as best I could. I took in the chaos. No one paid me any attention. I looked to find an escape, and spied what I needed. The abandoned luggage cart sat nearby.

I walked with a stagger, but I managed to totter towards the cart. No one tried to stop me. I reached the cart, fell on, disengaged the brake and sped away.

A large maintenance structure stood nearby, abandoned in the chaos. I headed for it. People rushed to the emergency on the tarmac. I drove inside, luggage carts towed behind. I saw what I needed. There sat an airport maintenance truck. The driver side door stood open as the worker must have scampered out.

Space had been left to stop along-side the open driver door and I struggled into the pickup truck and found the keys still hung from the ignition. I started the truck and left as fast as possible. I drove on a dirt access road along the edge of the tarmac away from the scene of emergency lights and chaos. Now I needed to get home to New York.

The road ended at the end of the tarmac. Near the end of the runway I spied what I needed. The access road left the runway and headed into a secondary area where staff parked. I looked for the exit, spotted it and headed towards it in the maintenance truck. I passed a gate, made one right hand turn and flowed with passenger traffic onto a side access road. I left the airport behind, and now needed to find another.

To leave from Los Angeles International no longer presented a viable option. That would be more than difficult. I had traveler's checks left, though they dwindled. I needed another airport.

From previous experience on my travel to southern California I knew the John Wayne Airport would be my best bet. It would take time, but I must get away from the current location. I looked at the gas gauge. Almost three quarters.

Follow the signs, I told himself. I looked at the clock on the dashboard. The time neared four forty. Traffic would be horrible, yet I had no choice. I must bite the bullet, and bear the tedious rush hour snarl.

As I headed away from Los Angeles International Airport, brake lights lit up the freeway. I turned the radio on to catch a traffic report and some sort of clue as to the time I might arrive. So far, luck stayed with me.

Within moments the news broke in with the emergency at the Los Angeles International Airport. At least one, maybe more terminals had been shut down. The airport authority encouraged passengers to check their flights, and investigate other regional airports. With their efficiency, the names, and directions to regional locations were announced. I traveled in the right direction and hoped that soon I would be at the John Wayne Airport. Then on my way home to New York.

The bumper to bumper traffic grew tedious and slow. My exhaustion made it more difficult to move my feet from the accelerator to the brake. Each acceleration or braking presented an exercise. I drove with both feet. Luck stayed with me as I spotted an exit sign for the airport I wanted. I took it, very pleased to leave the chaos behind.

I spotted across from the main departure terminal a two story garage. It sent a quiver into my limbs. Any effort to walk that distance would be a nightmare. I continued past the garage entrance to the public lot and watched the overhead signs. As I cruised past the terminals, I saw what I wanted. Directions to staff parking showed up on an overhead sign. I figured that a maintenance vehicle from another airport would qualify for that courtesy. I approached the gate and found it manned by a uniformed attendant. I pulled forward with my window down.

"Hi. Can I park here for a few minutes? Have a quick appointment." The attendant waved me past without a word. I entered the lot and hunted for a spot to park as close to terminal access as possible. Luck still stuck by my side and I found a spot right at the curb. The area had been encircled with a low cyclone fence, which I would be able to use as a hand hold to reach the nearest crosswalk and cross the street at my slow pace. I looked at the course I laid out, took a big breath and exited the vehicle. I used the fence as a hand hold and made efficient progress to the nearest break at a cross walk. Each shuffle brought me closer to home. I knew my struggles did not end, though believed I had the silver bullet to end the standoff. It came time for me and many others to know the truth once and for all.

Chapter 33

As I entered the terminal, I looked for the nearest wheelchair. One sat abandoned close to the doorway. I observed the airline carriers and spotted the one I wanted. As I pushed the chair to reach the ticket counter a courtesy employee approached.

"Where to sir?" he inquired as he grasped the handles of the chair.

"There please," I responded with a point to a ticket counter we approached. The courtesy employee pushed me to the handicap access clerk.

"I'd like a one way ticket to New York please."

"We have a direct flight that departs in sixty minutes and arrives at JFK at one-thirty AM. We ask passengers to show up at least two hours ahead, but with you in a chair, we'll make an exception. Do you have any bags?"

"No," I replied. My cane had again fallen victim to my travel, left in the debris of the shattered restroom on the tarmac of LAX. I reached for my wallet. "How much do I owe you?"

"Six hundred forty-five," she answered. I counted seven one hundred dollar traveler's checks out, signed them and handed them over. "Identification please," the clerk responded. I hesitated for a moment. I knew they would pick me up. I had no choice. They would know soon enough. *I may as well get it over with.* I would be home. Near the documents that awaited me from New Zealand. I thought with smugness, *within twenty-four hours, I will be at a legal office to get the secret out.*

The end neared. Their attempts of disruption could no longer be a bother to me. *No more.* The time had arrived for the truth to come out.

I pulled my passport from my pocket. As the clerk entered the passport number onto her screen, other computers sounded alarms across the Internet. The clerk handed me back my identification. I hoped they couldn't complicate life any longer. I must maintain my hope.

"We've got him in Santa Ana, California at an airline ticket counter. He purchased a ticket for JFK. Plane arrives at one-thirty." Word was transferred to Eric immediately. He dialed the Congressman.

"Can you claim that mess at LAX?" the Congressman growled.

"Yes sir." he answered. "We have him in Santa Ana, California. He bought a ticket to New York. He's going home."

"He most likely feels he found the information he needs. Pick him up in New York. Call me on your arrival." The phone line went dead. Eric dialed other operatives in New York.

"Get me the carrier, flight number and arrival gate, of a flight from Santa Ana to New York," he snapped. The information made its way to him. Eric dialed again. "Get to JFK now. Flight arrives at Gate 74, number 1392. Be there. Give me a fax number. A description of the man to observe can be sent to that number." He clicked off. "Get me a flight to New York. First available," he barked as he set the phone down. He flipped the paper over handed to him, and scribbled a phone number down. "Fax a description of him. Here's the number. Get me a ride to the airport." He grabbed his briefcase and headed out. The escapade must be brought to an end.

Eric knew it would be difficult to finish the task in a sanitary fashion. A car waited. He slid in, and they headed toward the Melbourne Airport. It would be good to arrive home, yet the consequences of failure hung over him.

The courtesy employee wheeled me into the passenger boarding area as the call began for departure. At the entryway to the plane he stopped, offered a hand to assist me from the chair onto the plane and turned to depart.

"Hold up." I pulled a five I had stashed away in my shirt pocket and handed the attendant the bill. "Would you do me a favor please?"

"Sure," the attendant replied. I handed the man a second five.

"If someone asks about a man you helped onto any plane bound for New York, would you please forget me?" The man looked at the two fives and agreed.

After the attendant's departure, I made my way onto the plane and settled into my assigned seat as other passengers boarded. I waited for takeoff that would deliver me home.

A few minutes past departure the plane began to taxi. Within minutes the plane went airborne. *What a circle of adventure,* I thought as the plane lifted off. I thought of Isabelle. I would call the hospital upon arrival. I thought of my daughter. *How has she been?* I would call from home. *What would I tell the legal counsel the papers needed to be turned over to?* I would review the papers before they left my hands, and also make a copy and deliver a set to an attorney, and keep a backup set for myself. *Perhaps the UPS store could make a copy?*

What should I ask of the attorneys? Where would they make their money? Should I go to the ACLU? Though the American

Civil Liberties Union carried a liberal label and sometimes went off the reservation, their purpose could be defined as the defense of civil liberties. The people who opposed me violated my rights. I had been denied my right to pursue medical freedom. I hoped the ACLU would look at the documents and if they believed it warranted, would take the information public. I considered my options and liked the ACLU best.

My funds had been exhausted. A legal firm would want some sort of cash retainer up front. The publicity would be invaluable, though the cash reserves of any firm that handled the case would not be fattened.

My decision made, I planned my initial steps on arrival. I would go to my apartment, sleep, then schedule an appointment with the ACLU, pick-up the documents from the UPS store, make copies and store a backup, review the documents at home, and prepare my synopsis for an ACLU representative. I liked the plan. I lay my head back and fell asleep. At my next stop, I would be home.

Sleep claimed me for the duration of the flight. A flight attendant awakened me to move my seat to a full upright position. I did and looked at the lights that defined the profile of New York City.

What surprises awaited me, I could only imagine. *I considered my options and decided on maximum visibility and to always be surrounded by others.*

As a flight attendant hurried past I stopped her and asked if a wheelchair could be made available for me. She let me know arrangements would be made as she rushed away.

The plane landed and taxied to the arrival gate. I needed to buy a new cane. As the plane came to a final stop at the gate, passengers stood and made their way from the craft.

A chair attendant waited. I rose from my seat, cramped and excited, and made my way to the chair.

As my attendant and I proceeded through the terminal, I spotted my shadow right away. The departure area stood empty. The man was alone, bundled up to fight off the elements. His face looked hard. His stare even harder. He looked at me in attempted intimidation, a gaze filled with the coldness of no more than that given to the examination of a fish on ice at the market.

He made no attempt to hide. The attendant who pushed me served as my bodyguard. I rotated my head and asked if he could please stop at a gift shop so I could buy a cane. The attendant agreed and pushed me onward.

At that hour I knew a few of the gift stores would be open. The airport operated on a twenty-four hour basis and that would keep me surrounded with people to escape that cold stare.

We came to a gift shop and the attendant pushed the chair to the entrance.

I stopped him and explained I could wheel myself into the store. I found a canister of canes, and a good sturdy one. I never knew what the instrument might be used for, and smiled to myself as I paid for the purchase, and wheeled from the shop.

The tail stood across the hallway, a cell phone pressed to his ear. *I felt like a wave,* but refrained. The chair attendant materialized and began to push me to the exit where taxi cabs waited. I balanced the cane on my lap.

The blast of cold hit me as the attendant pushed me out a handicap door.

Certain constants never changed and the winter weather in New York was one of them. A van pulled up to the curb.

I struggled from my chair and pulled myself into the van. The driver slid the door shut, hurried to the driver's door, jumped in and asked where to. I gave him my home address, a place I hadn't been for some time, though a place I relished to return to.

The drive into the city proved uneventful. Night lights shimmered on the streets. Traffic moved at a busy pace. The city held few secrets, although the one I carried would soon set it on its ear.

The cab pulled to the curb before my apartment. I unloaded with the help of the driver, and looked around. No one walked the street nearby at that hour. I plodded to the front doors with the help of my new cane.

The night watchman held the door for me. We talked for a few minutes about how long I had been away, the weather and other assorted small talk. With a polite escape I headed to the elevator. It whisked me to my floor and with great deliberateness I stepped into familiar digs. I had arrived home at last.

My routine to reach the bedroom began. As I passed by the thermostat I pushed it forward so a gust of warm air flowed from the floor vents. I reached for the bed and fell onto it, kicked off my shoes, pulled the quilt over me and went into a deep sleep for the first time in days that didn't feel as if it might be my last. I should have considered with more care.

At first light I woke. Energy coursed through my veins as I headed for the shower. I realized today would move closer to an end. I would call Isabelle and Brenda, get to the UPS store. That thought brought me up short.

My followers posed a bothersome issue. Avoidance would prove critical. I ambled to the kitchen to nibble on what food remained. I had tea bags stashed in a coffee canister and I turned the burner on beneath the teapot. I took English muffins from their package. My normal indiscriminate purchases had been neglected. My cupboard stood empty.

The land line and my home most likely had been bugged. I wanted to keep my final plans quiet, but knew that would not be possible. Right at nine I picked up my cell phone and dialed information for the ACLU.

The front desk attendant answered cheerily when I called. "Good morning. This is the American Civil Liberties Union."

"Hello. I would like to speak to one of your attorneys about the denial of my civil rights at a time when I sought medical attention. I have a handicap and I have been denied fair treatment." I paused and waited for a response. Another receptionist's voice came on the line.

"Jacob Peter's office, may I help you?" I had considered my response and wanted a nonchalant and professional answer.

"Mr. Peters please." The regular litany of questions ensued.

"Can I have your name please? Have you spoken with Mr. Peters before? Do you have an appointment to see Mr. Peters?"

"Mr. Peters and I have not spoken before. I do not have an appointment to see him. No one referred me. My civil rights have been trampled. I have a case that will grab international attention. I would like to speak to Mr. Peters now." Silence enveloped the line. I feared she hung up. Several moments later she responded.

"One moment please."

A voice boomed back in the receiver held close to my ear.

"Jacob Peters. What can I help you with?" I took a deep

breath, and started. My wait for the moment to arrive had seemed like an eternity.

"Mr. Peters, I have just returned from a world-wide journey that started here in New York to pursue stem cell research procedures. I have multiple sclerosis. I practice my professional trade as a research technician. My research on stem cell regeneration uncovered evidence of successful stem cell implantation procedures that have been stopped from proceeding." A deep inhalation could be heard on the phone. No more.

"What's your name?"

"James Armstrong. I'm in New York. You'll get further information at our first get together." Again, silence.

"What proof do you have?" Mr. Peters at last asked.

"I have documentation from a research team out of Australia. They have been killed. I traveled with a doctor from Italy who specializes in stem cell regeneration. As we departed a ship in Australia, she was shot. She's now at a hospital in Melbourne." As I spoke the words, I realized how outlandish it was.

"What's the doctor's name who got shot, where did it happen and what's her condition?" Peters asked.

"Isabelle Giovantti, in Melbourne and she is in guarded condition."

"Do you have the documents?" Mr. Peters asked.

"Documents have been sent via express to New York. They are here now. I want to make copies and have them sent to you when you commit."

"All right, James" Peters responded. "Give me your cell line. I will check on your Dr. Giovantti. If the information supports what you have said we'll talk in two days. Call me at the same time. How do I get a hold of you?" I rattled off my cell number. Peters hung up. I made a fist and struck the table in glee.

If my phone line and apartment had been bugged they now knew my direction, though I wondered if they would interfere with an attorney, or even worse, attack one. I now had a chance to break through. I had a lot to do in the next two days. I stood from the table, and teetered from the kitchen into the front room, and spied my spare wheelchair. Today I would use my chair to get around.

A few moments later, I pushed into the hallway towards the elevator. My mood threatened to suffocate me. Energy coursed through my veins. I pushed the chair with ease. I reached the lobby with such speed, it surprised me. I hit the sidewalk and rolled to the corner and began to flag cabs. My attitude must have showed. A cab pulled over. I opened the rear door.

"UPS store in Manhattan." The driver called in the destination, with the address called back, and he jumped from the car and made quick time to me. I already stood with the assistance of the door and lowered myself into the back. The driver folded my chair and hoisted it into the trunk. I waited for the next part of my journey in excitement.

As the cab made its way into traffic, I began to think of the document transfer. I decided to make two sets of copies at the store. One I would send to Mr. Peters and one I would have sent to myself. The originals I would pay to keep at the store location.

My arrival at the UPS store seemed anti-climactic, though at the same time, I had become ecstatic. I didn't know what to expect, yet some sort of fanfare seemed appropriate. I exited the car waiting for my wheelchair. The driver brought my chair to me. I paid and tipped, and rolled to the doors, pulled them open to enter and rolled to the counter, where I identified myself, showed my identification and asked for my documents.

The carrier last seen at the New Zealand store was brought to me. I opened the luggage and looked at the three to four hundred pages of documents. In my excitement, I knew I would review the pages in rapid progression. I didn't know about Peters, but had to assume a review by him would take a bit longer.

I fought off the urge to rip the rubber bands that bound the pages and begin my review where I was. I waved for a counter attendant and gave my orders. I requested two copies. One delivered to Peter's address, the other to my home address as I wrote them on labels for shipment. I asked if the originals could be stored at that location. They indicated there would be a minimal fee that would hold the documents for thirty days. I pulled the fee from my pocket, comfortable in the knowledge the documents would be safe, and left the store invigorated.

Tomorrow the documents would be in my hands. The secrets of their contents revealed. I became a jumble of nervous anxiety. Christmas arrived early. I couldn't wait to open my present.

I flagged a cab. The driver delivered me back to my apartment, as my tension began to ebb. As I entered the apartment, I thought of a journey to the corner grocery, decided to relax and finish whatever food remained.

I made a call to my ex-wife's number first. No one answered. I left a message for my daughter.

After I checked my watch and did a quick calculation of the time difference, I made the call to Isabelle. I would reach her the next day, Australia time. I dialed the number with a rush of excitement. The hospital receptionist answered on the first ring.

"Isabelle Giovantti's room please."

"This is Isabelle Giovantti's room. Who's on the line please?" a male voice answered. I hung up, with no idea who answered the phone, though I did not want to take any unnecessary chances.

The phone call started a myriad of activity.

"We believe he just made an attempt to make contact" the technician stated. Eric waited in a Los Angeles terminal for departure. The flight from Australia wore on his body. Eric knew James had arrived back home. The man proved industrious. He managed to get past them and sneak documents into the country. Eric knew the risks increased. He saw the e-mail broadcast to all fellow spooks. He received a copy. It had a simple and straight forward message. The intent could not be lost on anyone. "Eliminate threat. Post haste." He knew where it originated. It had been sent from Washington D.C.

Chapter 34

Consciousness returned with a start after I fell asleep to some cheesy horror flick on television. Twilight ebbed through the window. I visited the kitchen to view my dismal food supplies. Not much, but a can of soup for dinner.

The thought of w*ho had I upset to lose my job* passed through my head? My bank accounts neared the zero mark. The time to find a job had arrived. Tomorrow would be the day to begin the process of an employment search.

The package arrived at ten-twenty the next day. The doorman called me to announce its arrival. I flew into my chair, out the door, to the elevator and rolled into the lobby so fast the doorman turned in surprise.

"Hope you received good news," he announced as he handed me the large box to sit on my lap.

"The news could be no better." The rest of the afternoon I reviewed each page in sequential order. As dusk fell, page two hundred forty had been completed. It excited me, though like so many technical documents, could also be a bore. Much of the discussion stayed technical and well above my head. The information Candice first sent had been no more than a synopsis. The meat and potatoes came out here.

Isabelle could help with the process. I hoped to make quick work of it, but continued to read as night fell.

Soup wouldn't do it for dinner. I placed a call for pizza delivery. The document excited me. I wanted to continue the review with as few interruptions as possible. Though the tedious portion of the document explained the outcomes of the research and the expectations of trials, the last pages contained many references to the energy as it grew within the lab in their final days. Notations explained the harassment of fellow lab mates. The material startled me.

Threats had been made, bribes offered, intimidation aimed at relatives and friends. As Candice indicated, young children were used as tools. The notes spoke of the threat of sanctions against Dr. Thimes. Letters received by mail, via e-mail and left on voice mails carried the same message.

The document didn't let on to who might be behind the scare tactics. A list of suspects had been compiled, though they lacked the proof to incriminate.

The pages explained the success of the program. The process could be defined as brilliant.

First, success had been achieved in mice. Then it crossed to chimpanzees. Then man. No wonder the lab staff became thrilled. The manuscript went on to tell how Doctor Thimes continued the program as the scare tactics and attempts to shut him down escalated. In later pages, the manuscript spoke of specific parties. The pharmaceutical interests and the evangelicals merited a mention. The medical industry showed up, though they had been overjoyed by the find. The last group discussed was defined as different. Not pushy. Not outraged.

Defined as professional, cool, calm, and collected, no suspected category had been assigned them. They spoke in clear English with no accents and offered a huge amount of money for the research. I assumed these folks could be associated with political interests.

The manuscript addressed how the Coalition for Life grew angry due to what they believed was their right to buy the amoral technology. Here the research paper turned into more of a personal journal. Details addressed the necessary changes in security, the addition of armed guards on a twenty four-seven basis, several attempts at break-in, harassment of researchers at home and the worst of all, the fear that these tactics brought to the human recipients used in trials. It described their opponent's tactics as archaic.

With the document resting on the floor, I considered, *not too different than the same tactics Isabelle and I faced on our journey.* It began to make sense now.

The Religious right groups scared the researchers into a near morbid fear. They had been defined as the ones with the fewest dollars to gain, yet fiercest belief in their right to defeat the threat. They believed divine power existed on their side. Who could argue with that? As long as they continued their campaign of fear, they garnered attention.

Isabelle and I had labeled the evangelicals as angry souls who fought for what they believed. Not much different than me. I struggled for my right to walk again and assist my daughter. I made no attempt to rise to the level of champion for the oppressed. *That drove Isabelle away.* My pursuit was for selfish benefit.

The pharmaceutical representatives entered my mind. Their goal could not be concealed. Defeat a competitor that threatened their claim on drugs peddled across the globe. Successful presentation of stem cell therapies could make their stock value drop like a rock, until they had secured ownership of the new technology. Up to that time, they played a delay game. As Isabelle let on, their offer to me had been a setup, to track how close the new development would come to fruition before their ready stage was reached.

And then there stood the political front. They played on the very conservative organizations as their vocal champion. They milked the pharmaceutical industry for support, so they could maintain the 'not on my watch' role. The money they spent to hold the battle line assured them they would stay in power and benefit when the ultimate player came to be.

A knock on the door startled me. I flinched, and pushed papers from my lap to the floor, and ambled towards the front. I had no peep hole, so I asked through the closed door, "Who's there?"

Silence held the moment and then came the answer.

"Pizza has arrived."

I undid the two dead bolts and pulled the door open. My pizza waited. It smelled delicious. My wallet came from my pocket, money was exchanged, the door closed and re-latched and I carried the pie to the kitchen table. As the first piece started to come out of the box, the doorbell rang. *What now?* The front door seemed a mile away, and the smell pushed me faster to the front room so I could return and satisfy my hunger.

As I opened the door, I found a monster of a man standing there. His jaw appeared rock solid. He looked like a caricature from a military recruitment advertisement. He stood with hands in pockets. I didn't recognize him, but knew why he stood there.

"May I come in?" he asked.

"Not like I can stop you." The man laughed as he stepped inside, turning slightly so he did not bump the wall as he entered.

"Well, from what I understand you did a pretty good number on the shins of a guy in Italy and the throat of another in Malaysia," he said. I watched him with care as my mind raced. The finish sat so close, and now I wondered if I would ever get there. Escape didn't cross my mind as a realistic option. To run or scream seemed ridiculous. The man could snap my neck like a twig.

"May I sit?" he asked with a point towards the couch.

"Yes." The big man took a seat.

"I saw the pizza delivery man leave. I won't stay long." I stared at him.

"Who sent you?"

"I'm Austin Chambers," he stated. "My people asked me to keep an eye on you. I did pick you up yesterday on your arrival back home. I went to Malaysia to find you. A Malay agent tracked you first. You made his acquaintance." I thought back to that horrid event.

"Does he live?"

"Yes. He won't speak for some time. He received some pretty bad burns on his face from the hot water. You and your girlfriend did a number on him." Silence filled the room.

"She's not my girlfriend. She's a doctor."

"Yes, I know," Austin responded as he pulled a small notepad from an inner pocket of his coat.

"Doctor Isabelle Giovantti. She received her Bachelor's degree from the University of Wisconsin, then her medical degree from University of Southern California. Her credentials are very impressive. You're also impressive, James." He recited the information without the need of his notebook. "You received your Bachelor's degree from New York State University, than went on to get your Master's in Business Management. You took a position as a business analyst with a Wall Street firm, moved into a programmer position, and from there transferred to a financial research desk where you made trade recommendations. Your diagnosis of Multiple Sclerosis occurred while still at work. You started to use a cane and then a wheelchair one year ago and were dismissed for unknown reasons. You are divorced and have one child.

Parents live in Buffalo. Brother and sister in New York," he finished.

"You are very thorough. What's the purpose?"

"James, you have become a threat. Word came down to stop you at all costs. My own life is in danger now. This assignment started for me with no idea what it meant. It didn't matter to me. I work for a private security firm. As I followed you to Southeast Asia and back here to the States, I discovered things about you. Not just your habits, but what you wanted, why you were a danger."

He leaned back on the couch, and stretched his huge arms. I spied the holster. A shiny gun shimmered there, and I wondered if I would survive, and resigned myself to listen.

Austin started again. "I began to take a special interest in you pursuits. My mother has begun to suffer the first symptoms of Alterior Lateral Sclerosis, better known as Lou Gehrig's disease. As you most likely know, her long term prognosis is not good. Your search for successful stem cell utilization somewhere in the world may be her only hope." I knew the disease well. It would kill her. "Some days she does well. I'm told she will become crippled and that she will die. It seems that all she has left is hope." Silence filled the room.

"I'm not here to hurt you, or to try to stop you. I'm here to warn you." Relief flooded through me at the news. *Be very careful how you respond, and you just might live. You can make it. Be smart.*

Austin appeared forlorn and drawn, even lost.

"I'm sorry for your mother. I have some news that may help her."

"Keep it to yourself. If you don't tell me then I don't need to lie, or be broken, and let the information out." I understood with an appreciation for those words. "James, I know you must have found some great news. That's why the order came down all the way from the top. You must be careful the next few days. I'm here to warn you. That's all. I'll need to leave, and lose myself somewhere, though you must keep on until the end."

"How much will you tell me?"

"Try me" he said.

"Who do you work for?"

"As I told you, I work for a private security firm. A past client hired us, known as the Coalition for Life."

"Who shot Isabelle?"

Austin sighed. "Don't know for sure. If it came from our side, it came from higher up than I ever knew. Based on your chance acquaintance on board, we think the order came from the pharmaceuticals. We did not attack you on board the ship. I would guess the drug pushers. We did follow you to Italy. After the failure at the airport to grab your documents and find out what you knew we made another attempt at the doctor's clinic to grab your briefcase, not to hurt you or the doctor. The incident could be called a mistake. An attempt to get your briefcase, that's all, then the doctor walked in. We didn't have orders to hurt you until recently. Our job was to convince you not to proceed, but not to harm. I don't know for certain who burnt the clinic in London. It could have been the drug companies, maybe Alpha since they make their home in Europe. It could have been our people. I don't know. They tried to prevent you and Dr. Giovantti from making any progress. When that didn't work, they may have stepped up their program. I have to tell you the Malay incident got out of control. Our agent had been directed to scare you, not hurt you. The tails on the plane did not belong to us. Good trick with the restroom on the plane, by the way." He stopped, and looked at me. "My presence here has put me in jeopardy."

"It's all about the money isn't it?" Austin didn't answer.

"That's up to you to figure out." Austin started to rise.

"Wait. Who started this?" He shook his head.

"It's up to you to find the answers James. I can't help you anymore." I sat back with a long sigh. My guest appeared uncomfortable.

"I'll help a little and then I need to leave. We think most of the jobs, the drug companies can claim. Your encounter on board ship can be defined as a simple accident. We didn't pull the trigger. We think the order came from the drug conglomerate. The agreement you made, carried no weight. The evangelicals found out. Money flow dried up."

"Wait. So, your salary was paid by evangelicals, who were paid by the drug manufacture's conglomerate?"

Austin leaned forward looking at the floor. He looked up at me with a sad look. "The religious right paid my salary. I would guess the money originated from elsewhere. Start with the Coalition for Life. Go from there, yet know many others are involved."

So, the truth had made it to the light of day. The antagonists had been identified. Isabelle's attacker in Italy, and my attacker in Malaysia.

Part of it made sense. If I could be stopped, the pro-life stance would be preserved. Money spent by the pharmaceuticals on politicians would be redirected back to the moral outcry to preserve life. Drug companies would maintain their position of dealers to the millions. Status quo would be maintained.

Austin interrupted my thoughts.

"They thought wrong about you James. They all did. Go

higher."

He continued to talk as I sat on the edge of my chair.

"The good doctor in Australia we knew about. We tried to track Mr. Winston. We think he served as the agent that brought Dr. Thimes' plane down. We're pretty sure that the invitation to the good doctor in Australia was a phony to get Dr. Thimes and the research team to Perth. We did not issue that invitation. Remember, you are dealing with multinational corporations. Isabelle's attack can be defined as a deliberate act, though not by us. We think the order came from the drug companies.

We believe you were the actual target not Isabelle, and their plans went awry. Danger follows you now. You have scared the pharmaceutical conglomerate, though even worse, you have scared very powerful players in the political world. The drug companies have re-grouped as we talk. They will survive. The government may not. They seem very scared right now. I have been ordered to take you out, as a favor to the political world, but also for our benefit. I don't know what plans you have. I don't want to know. Be careful."

The big man stood to leave.

"Good luck, James. Help my Mom." He stepped to the door, pulled it open and walked out. I would never see him again.

So it all had been real. I must leave my apartment. I stuffed the manuscript back into the UPS box. I wall walked to the bedroom, grabbed an overnight bag, threw necessary goods in, grabbed my wheelchair and sat. I gathered the box and my bag, and headed to the front room. The pizza sat on the table untouched.

The short conversation just finished stirred activity not three blocks away. The man with the earphones on had not been a field agent, just a snooper who listened. He thought of the conversation just heard as he picked up his cell phone and dialed the number committed to memory.

"He's on the run. Been tipped off," he announced.

"Can you get there?"

"Negative. Three city blocks away." A series of harsh comments followed.

"Why hadn't he been dealt with earlier?"

The man with the headphones on answered with care. "We have been in observation mode. The order for the hit just occurred. The agent assigned the task tipped him off." Tirades filled his ear.

"Find both of them. Call in another agent and another team of two members. Go after two targets. I will go after primary target with solo agent. Arrange everyone to meet at principal location." Simon slammed the phone down. Incredible! It had blown. The snooper dialed new numbers.

"Project has moved to code green. Repeat again, two targets now defined. The locations are unknown. Both suspects are now a top priority. Respond to principal location." He ended the connection to pack equipment. The hunt intensified. *Where would their targets go?* Their primary target would go to a motel. It would be local. Simon and the new agent would have that job. The principal location had been identified as a coffee shop around the corner from the listening spot. He could use a strong coffee about now.

James hailed a taxi, and asked for a hotel not far from the ACLU office address to show up to meet with Mr. Peters the next day. A phone conversation would do little and it could be tapped. Plus, Mr. Peters needed to know of my recent visitor. The players had become nervous. Yes, they already struck at me and Isabelle, yet now they must be panicked.

The information found on board the 'Angel' must be passed on. The political contributions reported on the paper work in my possession would make sense to Peters. All of it together would prove invaluable. To prove my civil rights had been infringed upon had become an easy task.

The cab dropped me at a hotel within a two block wheelchair roll of the ACLU office. I pushed the chair forward with the box and overnight bag on my lap into the hotel lobby, new cane between my knees. The check-in clerk assigned me a room near an elevator on the third floor.

Before I retired that night, I completed my review of the final pages of the manuscript, after which I called room service and ordered breakfast for dinner. The time neared two by the time the manuscript re-entered the box.

My thoughts turned to the last pages. No new revelations stood out. There had been more attempts by outside parties to acquire the technology. The requests had been met with the same refusal. The excitement with the invitation to present at Perth became palatable and then it ended. The author and other researchers died. The manuscript came to a close. There would be no conclusion. There could be no expressions of gratitude. It just ended. As I slipped into sleep, I hoped the new day did not end the same for me.

The next day found me energized. My conclusion had reached a greater definition even though my mind refused to believe it. The culmination of my efforts neared. I had no conclusion just yet, although the final scene approached.

That day a tie and sweater came out of my overnight case. I pushed the knot on the tie to my neck and pulled the sweater on, checked my watch, aware I would be early. As I opened the door, I knew that day, the eight hundred pound gorilla would come off my back. The moment had arrived.

I swung the door wide and rolled out to start the final scene of my adventure.

The responsibility to release the secrets uncovered now rested with me. It had become my duty. I thought of the secret that would be revealed to the world and whether I had the strength to turn it loose. Arrangements had begun. The appointment must be kept that day to push the wheels forward. It must occur. The secret and the horrific manner in which it had been kept must be revealed. My sense of moral decency begged for revelation. My obligation cried out for exposure of the truth. Isabelle taught me that.

My journey started with no foreknowledge of the arduous trail I would encounter. The huge responsibility it turned into seemed beyond my ability. The difficulties threatened to overwhelm me, but now they had been accepted, and rested on my shoulders.

My life had experienced formidable challenges. The challenge before me carried more weight. No room existed to compromise. That could not be allowed to happen.

Final exposure of the cover up was within my grasp. The corruption, together with the sacrilegious abuse of power, must be revealed. It would be up to the social conscience of society to determine the ultimate punishment.

My journey began with selfish motivation, which I had admitted to myself. Now my destiny would be to see it to its conclusion no matter the personal sacrifices. The importance of the crusade could change the lives of so many. It turned tragic that it generated such intense fear from so few. Those few wanted control on their terms. There could be no negotiation that would repair the tears in the structure of society between us. The wretched gap had opened too wide.

I wheeled myself that morning ever closer to my final

destination, the ACLU's office. Determination kept me focused. At last, I found the office building. The offices of the ACLU stood within that structure. I made it and would unleash my own retribution. Isabelle and so many more deserved it.

The silent chambers of the ACLU office seemed like a different planet. The conference room stood walled in silence. I waited with patience for Mr. Peters, and drummed my fingers on the large conference room table. My thoughts turned to the documents, and how I had been warned the night before. I waited and considered the steps needed for the ultimate revelation.

The door to the conference room burst open. Mr. Peters powered into the room. He headed straight to me.

"Jacob Peters," he said as he took my hand with a strong grip. "My assistants follow. Any problem with them in here?" he asked. I shook my head and remained silent.

"I received the documents yesterday. Reviewed them last night and finished earlier. Good material. How do these documents infringe on your civil rights?" Mr. Peters asked.

"The documents do not. The people who want to bury the results do." Jacob sat back, hands folded.

"Do you have proof?"

"Do you have a laptop?" Mr. Peters turned to one of the three people who followed him into the room and extended a hand. A small light-weight laptop fell into his hand. He flipped it open, turned it on and pushed it to me. *Wireless technology,* I thought.

Within moments I logged in to my Internet server and with a few quick keystrokes accessed files found on board the 'Angel.' I turned the screen to Mr. Peters, who leaned forward and began to review the financial data.

"So?" Mr. Peters said. "Tell me what I see here."

"You see lots of different monetary transfers."

Jacob Peters knew enough to realize that what he looked at showed foreign accounts that moved large amounts of money into and out of financial accounts. He knew enough people to recognize the names of those who received the transfers.

"So, what you've got here show parties that shovel lots of money to foreign accounts that in turn shovel it to political action committees." Mr. Peters went silent for a moment. His associates in the room didn't move. I sat still.

"My God," Peters exclaimed. "Do you mean to say that the money bought favors at the administration level and has been used to bury the work in the papers you sent me?" An incredulous display of shock came over him, the complexion of his skin scarlet in color. "What's with the large transfer from the Bank of Canada? Where did it go? What did it buy?"

"It went to several representatives reelection campaigns."

Jacob's mouth dropped open. "Run by US Congress representative Belfay," Jacob stuttered.

Jacob Peters began to bark orders. The three gentlemen who followed him into the room scurried in rapid procession. As the men left, Mr. Peters spun to look at me. He surveyed the wheelchair.

"Do you recognize the implications?" he asked.

"Mr. Peters, people have been killed. A doctor I traveled with from Italy survived an assassination attempt meat for me. A man showed up at my door last night and warned me that I have become a target. I understand the implications. The information must be brought forth."

Peters looked hard at me. "What do you want from us?"

he asked.

"I want your expertise to put the pieces together. I can help. My legs may not be too good, though my mind is. I can help your staff build a story so full of the devilish details that these parties can be stopped and that stem cell research successes such as those you read of can be released to the world. You asked how my rights have been violated. Well, Mr. Peters I can tell you how the rights of millions of diseased sufferers have been violated. People around the world who could benefit from stem cell regeneration have been prevented from treatment. Their rights have been denied. My rights have been."

Chapter 35

The team that accompanied Mr. Peters into the conference room would be assigned verification. They spent the day with me. At four that afternoon Jacob Peters reentered the conference room. All three of his cohorts jumped to their feet. The gentleman that served as the superior of the team briefed Peters, on the interview, with raised eyebrows to let him know they had covered serious information. Mr. Peters addressed me.

"I've hired a private security firm to provide bodyguards for you. A new hotel has been booked. You will be escorted there. A guard will watch your door on a 24-7 basis. You will work with my staff for the next few days. I have an expert in stem cell research coming in from Cornell. He will confirm your testimony, and the manuscript. Can you work here?" he asked.

"Yes. Mr. Peters, a few points if I may. The woman colleague I mentioned who traveled with me from Italy. Can you also get security for her?" Peters agreed.

"Next. The man who wrote the notes went down in Australia. If the stem cell technology that he defined can be moved along to clinical practice, his wife asked that college funds be established for her three children."

Mr. Peters listened. He picked up the phone.

"Get me the Washington office. Call the security company you phoned earlier. Tell them to send two additional security guards to the office. I want a guard at every door twenty-four-seven until further notice." He clicked the handset down.

Questions continued until seven that night. Two security guards dispatched to the conference room escorted me out.

They walked on either side of me to sandwich me within a protective glove. The guards escorted me to the rear doors, loaded me into a van, and sped away. The two big men squeezed me between them as they escorted me into the hotel lobby and whisked me into the bowels of the structure where they locked me down. I marveled at the efficiency of the firm that took control. Perhaps, the nightmare would come to end.

For three days I told my story, interviewed by many, a stem cell research expert included. As the interview proceeded, the expert's hands began to shake as he listened to the story of Isabelle's program, the team's direction from Australia, the moment Isabelle fell and the financial web of deceit. He asked questions and listened. He had read the manuscript with care, I could tell, as many of the questions came from the notations that Wayne made.

Other attorneys scurried to review the case, and included labor law experts about my former job, financial brokers, lobbyists, and dozens of specialists. Mr. Peters convinced me that if we did not cover every aspect of the story, our opponents would berate us as nay-sayers. He refused to accept that. He planned to go public soon. The damage the information posed couldn't be estimated.

Late on the third day, Mr. Peters called me into his office. It neared eight at night. I knocked, pushed the door open, and entered the office. Jacob sat behind an imposing desk, nose buried in a file.

"James, come in," he waved with no more than a glance. Jacob closed the file to look at me across the top of the pages he read. I figured Jacob neared fifty years old. No family pictures adorned the desk, or credenza. No wife and no children. No doubt, work drove him and little else. He worked for the people.

"We're ready to go public," he stated. "You need to know some news."

"Go ahead."

"You did an excellent job. We do not doubt you for a moment, though we can't get the top dog."

"That doesn't make sense," I stammered out.

"We can address the evangelical conservatives. We'll chase some of the pharmaceutical companies for obstruction, yet we do not know who hired the goons that followed you, or that have tried to kill you. We think the drug industry tried to kill you on board ship and are responsible for the shot that caught Isabelle, but we have no proof. I'm sorry James. It's the best we can do."

"So they will go free?" I asked.

"I'm afraid so, unless someone rolls over to save their own skin."

"At what point do we go public?"

"Saturday," Jacob answered. "That way, we'll get it on the Sunday talk programs. It will hit the national news stories that night and again on Monday."

"What of Isabelle?" I asked.

"US Marines have shown up at her door as we speak. One of the connections I have. She will be here tomorrow. She'll be back for the announcement.

James, there's more." Jacob said. "We want you to make the announcement. We'll be there as backdrops and to provide any legalese."

Of course, Jacob did not say it would be more believable if it came from a disease-stricken patient, though I figured that one out. "We've prepared a few talking points you may want to address, but we would like you to have editorial freedom,"

Jacob said as he handed me a sheet of paper. I took it and looked at the notes. They had scribbled the usual diatribe of platitudes for the appropriate parties, a discussion of the great potentials for stem cell usage and other statements of gratitude. The points deserved review, though I knew I would write my own.

"What's wrong, James?" Jacob asked. "I thought you would be overjoyed." My response came very deliberately.

"Don't get me wrong, Jacob. I appreciate what you and your co-workers have done. I can't help but feel that the big fish got away. We will get what we wanted, yet for how long have we been locked in our chairs, or worse, with the key available for use so long ago?"

Jacob shrugged. "I understand James, though you need to move past your frustration. You must be at your best. You must be able to deflect criticism. The piranhas will try to eat you alive. We have prepared numerous indictments of various parties that we will announce. You did it, James. You have brought down some of the biggest fish in the pond. You have changed history. " I looked with sadness at the man across from me. He spoke the truth, though he sounded like any other bureaucrat with empty words. An internal voice told me to be happy, yet all I could feel at that time was exhaustion. I still sat in a wheelchair, and my daughter still fought the battle.

Jacob didn't understand. He didn't know. He could play the poor pity parade, though he would never understand. I wished Isabelle could be here. She would help control the frustration that welled inside me. She would understand.

I believed my ethics and integrity had been sacrificed. Maybe, I could get no closer to my pursuit of 'normalcy.' It had become too large an onion to peel.

My time to depart arrived. There were no other options. I turned and began my wheel toward the door. Jacob stopped. Two aides stepped forward to offer me assistance with the door. I shook my head with a smile.

"James," Jacob called. "We're not done yet" he said in a low tone. I turned and looked at him.

"Yes, it's time to call it a night. Thank you for all your energy. I'll be there on Saturday." Obvious disappointment filled Jacob's face. My hand held the door handle. I turned back and faced Jacob.

"It will be fine, Jacob. I cherish your advice and appreciate all your work, yet I have to do this for myself. I've digested the words and heard it all, but this time that is not enough. As a young man, I had it beaten into my head I would never win the battle." I hung my head and shook it in sadness, then said near a shout, "The cover-up must be stopped! Not just for me, but for my daughter. No more, Jacob. No more." Jacob looked at me in sadness.

"Of course, James," he said. "I trust your judgment."

My bodyguards fell in with me at the door as I left Jacob's office. I had many ideas I wanted to share at the news conference. My shadows fell in behind. We didn't exchange words.

We entered the van, and headed for the hotel. They were quiet, professional and adept. I knew they would stay at my side if needed.

That night, my room beckoned early. I missed Isabelle and longed to speak with her. Though the folks at the attorney's office had been great, no close friendships had been built. The new toy interested them for a short time only.

They did their job. It now became a matter not if it could be done, but how it could be done. Investigators still searched the smallest of leads to pinpoint the responsible parties behind the attacks. Jacob indicated it might be months or years, if ever to catch them. It discouraged me, though the real purpose had always been to advance the technology, not to seek revenge. I considered ways to suck the shadows out. Now, I would have my opportunity to do so. The time arrived. I could win and prove my father wrong at last.

Friday night crept up. Within twelve hours I would address a room of journalists, members of the public and other guests invited together to hear monumental news. I had yet to prepare my summary.

The laptop on the desk of my room became my new friend. I sat and wrote the outline, then filled in the details. It flowed with ease. The story I lived filled my notes. I was ready. The time for my quest to come to an end arrived.

Chapter 36

The next day broke clear and brisk. My rest came fast when my mental exercise had been completed. The moment arrived. Thoughts of the crowd filled my head. I felt no fear or nerves. The time to expose the cruelties fostered for so long waited. The preparation came fast last night. My final conclusion seemed impossible. I wondered if it could make sense, and of course knew it could. It had become the tale of my journey. It was the discovery of truth and restoration of hope. My wait had come to an end.

As I left my room, the bodyguards joined me. I appreciated the security, yet looked forward to the chance to have my life back.

We exited together and entered the vehicle for transport to the press conference, setup at a local hotel known more for its luxury than a place to release such monumental news. The scene had been set. My sense of satisfaction swelled.

Our arrival did not go unnoticed. A man stood outside with a hot cup of coffee in his hands. He sipped it with care as he watched the wheelchair unloaded from the vehicle.

Eric watched the entourage enter. The man who stood next to him watched attentively. He leaned closer, and asked, "I assume, there rests our man?" Eric nodded yes. Without a word the well-dressed man headed for the hotel.

As he stepped past Eric, a phone appeared from Eric's pocket.

"We are moving now. Alert all personnel. We are on the move. Attention, all check points. Close now." The cinch began to tighten. The well-dressed man on the move could feel it.

Entry into the foyer of the hotel occurred without fanfare. One of Jacob's research associates approached with a smile on his face and greeted me. He pointed in the direction of the conference room, and we headed there with the two security guards behind. I rolled my chair. At certain moments I accepted assistance to get from place to place. Today would not be one of them.

We entered a small room that adjoined the conference center where I would speak. Jacob sat there as did several new faces. Introductions quickly circled about the room. Several dignitaries, and to my surprise a few reporters had gathered together.

Jacob explained that the reporters were invited. Each had been promised an exclusive so they could hit the ground on the run. I agreed and glanced at my watch. Two hours to go. The questions would serve as a good warm-up.

The questioning began. As questions intensified, my mood became abrupt and the answers filled with more passion. Three reporters stayed in the room. They showed more interest in the research and what I found than the particulars of the events that surrounded the trip. They were not interested in the dates, names, places and events, but more the discoveries. They appeared surprised, even shocked with some of my replies, though they maintained their professionalism.

One of the investigative reporters from the 'Times' displayed interest in the groups that chased the Australian research. The reporter identified himself as Nick Targenesis. He asked questions that probed the delicate balance between professionalism and respect for the deceased. Each question attempted to prod answers from me I did not know. Jacob interceded on more than one occasion.

"Can we revisit the group that you identified as 'professional, thorough and polite'?" the reporter asked.

"I did not define them that way, the notes identified them that way," I answered with a sense of impatience.

"Who do you think these people represent?" Nick asked.

"I have no idea."

"Oh, come on James. You say you have been chased across the globe, almost killed on more than one occasion, your comrade shot and you can't hazard a guess as to who these people are. Who can they be?" Nick asked. Jacob stepped forward and slammed the table.

"Look! You have been invited here as a courtesy, not to harass our client. The interview can now be considered over." I pushed away from the table, and rose from my chair.

"No, Jacob. Mr. Targenesis, you want me to implicate someone. Fine, I'll tell you what I think. I believe the party that visited the Australian research lab and caused the ultimate demise of the research team represented the group with the most to lose. They collected the most money. They control the strings." I glared at the reporters.

"I believe the party that collected more illicit money and lied and destined so many to suffer for so long can be defined as the top money makers of the political party in power, and that includes direct Congressional manipulation by Congressman Samuel Belfay. These steps must have happened at the highest levels to protect their party's ideology, and the money that flows to them." Nick didn't respond. He wrote notes as did the other two reporters. Jacob approached me and rested a hand on my shoulder.

"Gentlemen, this interview is considered closed. You can take additional notes at the conference next door."

Mr. Targenesis continued to scribble. He stopped, stood and extended a hand across the table. I became lost in my concentration, and didn't realize a hand had been extended. Jacob brought the moment to a close.

As the reporters left, some of the others stepped forward and congratulated me on my demeanor and accomplishment. I met the National Chairman of the ACLU, the lead lobbyist for the Coalition to Advance Stem Cell Research and the head of the American Board of Research Scientists. All congratulated me. I met them and shook hands, yet the feeling of loneliness could not be lost.

"It's time. Let's go," Jacob stated. I pushed up from my chair and looked at the door to the conference room. I took a step with the aid of my cane towards my new destiny. Today, I wouldn't use any other aide.

Chapter 37

Jacob gave me the please be patient hand signal.

"Are you ready?" I looked at Jacob's nervous face.

As I entered the conference room, it exploded with flashes. My hand moved to shield my eyes. As the flashes receded, the sea of faces began to come into focus. Cameras on tripods stood by the dozens. Reporters filled the room. Many stood pressed to side walls. Jacob directed me to my seat. Dignitaries entered the room. It grew hot from the burst of light energy. The room had been oversized, even though now it was filled to its maximum capacity.

My eyes began to re-focus as I peered into the crowd. I saw no familiar faces. Jacob sat to my immediate left. The Chairman of the ACLU stood at the microphone arranged on a podium near the middle of the stage. He held up a hand and the room trembled to silence.

"Ladies, and gentlemen," he began. "Today we do not come here for the ACLU. It's a day for all mankind. Our New York office was recently approached by a man you will hear from today with a story of amazement. The story smacks at our very civil rights. It reflects an unbelievable complexity so incredible that our local association director at first did not believe it, though with tedious research, our local representative did come to believe. He presented the facts to me. I reviewed them with our national staff, and though aghast at the consequences of the release of this information, we have come to the conclusion the data must be released for the preservation of all human rights. I introduce Mr. Jacob Peters, our City of New York Director."

Jacob stood, and moved to the podium. The room went silent with anticipation of the first bit of news.

"Thank you for your attendance at this important moment" Jacob began. "We have come here to learn of some remarkable breakthroughs in the medical world. Many of you may ask yourselves why the ACLU became involved in the medical community. The answer very simply can be defined as the preservation of our civil rights. We found not just a violation, but a morbid lack of respect for all our rights."

A low murmur rippled through the room.

"We have reviewed data presented to us and verified its authenticity. We have studied these breakthroughs and examined some of the incredible efforts that different parties pursued to seal the information and keep it from the American public and the world." The crowd murmured louder. Jacob held up a hand for silence again.

"We believe based on information presented to us, that the civil rights of millions of Americans have been violated from the deliberate denial that the information ever existed." A loud murmur now grew more intense. Some reporters raised their hands with questions. Jacob played it cool. He asked for silence. He held both hands aloft for almost a minute while he waited for the crowd to quiet. As order returned, he continued.

"We do not claim to be medical professionals. However, the documents presented to us have been examined by medical experts. The man who unraveled this mystery will answer your questions. I would like to introduce Mr. James Armstrong."

With slow deliberateness, I stood from my position at the table with the assistance of my cane, and approached the microphone. The room fell silent as the gathered crowd stared with upturned faces of anticipation. No one spoke. A mist curled from the gutters on the street. A mystical mood hung in the room. The stares and quizzical looks mesmerized me for an instant.

My speech flowed, not from notes, just ad libbed now committed to memory prepared the night before. Jacob's people exchanged nervous looks, yet shrugged their shoulders. The heart of my presentation began.

"My name is James Armstrong. I have multiple sclerosis, hence my partner, my cane." Light chuckles spread through the crowd. "My training has been as a research analyst." My respiration slowed. "Initial diagnosis set me on a path of discovery. You see, folks my plans include a walk in the park, without the use of my friend in the not too distant future." The laughter now seemed more robust. Jacob was pleased with the response and settled back as he dismissed the nervous looks of his associates.

"Like many people diagnosed with a lifelong disease, my diagnosis sent me to the research files. My research began online and led to papers buried in libraries, phone interviews with notable professionals on both sides of the pond, exploration of medical practices that might restore my mobility and an examination of a number of worldwide practices.

After tedious research, I determined that my best hope to walk again came from a breakthrough achieved in stem cell regeneration." A murmur began to oscillate in the room. "And so, my research continued geared towards stem cell utilization. I found a source that had luck with regeneration practices outside of the country. I pursued the practice and found a much larger path of deceit, greed, and uncompassionate behavior, that it sent terror into my soul and will send shock waves through you today." Their attention intensified as the heads of the crowd began to move forward. The mood of the room changed.

Everyone waited and hung on the next word. "I found that the rights of persons all over the globe have been violated. We, the patients, and you the perspective patients, have been denied our right to pursue health and I found this convoluted, corrupt morality involved one horrid philosophy. It all came down to greed." Hands arose everywhere within the room. Jacob rose. He stepped to my position and grabbed the microphone.

"People, people, people," he pleaded. Reporters began to find their seats again, although the cascade of questions continued. "Ladies and gentlemen," Jacob yelled. "Please take your seats. James will field your questions, but let him finish first," Jacob pleaded. The room quieted. Jacob handed the microphone back to me and with a gentle push, encouraged me to continue.

"On my journey, my colleague and I were attacked more than once. My colleague, a doctor from Italy, has been shot. Several people have been killed." The murmurs grew louder. A woman reporter stood and shouted with a demand to know who had been killed. The woman quickly re-took her seat when waved back by fellow reporters.

"Before she went down from a bullet, my colleague and I found several items of significance. These included, the discovery that the first successful use of stem cells to reverse disease occurred in 1995." The room erupted. No one would sit. Jacob jumped forward and grabbed the microphone. Shouts for quiet went unheeded. He held a hand up and begged for control. I took the microphone back.

"Ladies, and gentlemen, please I have more to report."

People sat. "The father of the science can be tracked to Dr. Paul Moulter a former director of research at a multi-national American based pharmaceutical company. He suffered an early death from a hit and run accident in 1998 after he wrote a critical piece on the F.D.A., where he had just resigned.

Last year a team of scientists from Australia developed a stem cell healing technique that allowed the treatment and cure of diseases. Let me finish please. Patients from Australia and the Far East now live disease-free today. The five researchers and one doctor who perfected this treatment died in a plane crash when invited under false pretenses to present the results of their work at an International Symposium." The crowd grew restless again. "I have been able to return to the States with copies of the data used to perfect that treatment. As Mr. Peters mentioned, that data has been reviewed by medical professionals and substantiated as true. Trials are now underway at undisclosed locations here in the States to verify the results of that data.

The most important bit of information I have uncovered proves that these results posed such a threat to several parties here in the United States whose efforts included murder to hide these results from the world. There have been three principal parties involved in this deceit, and cover up. However," James stopped. The room went silent. "However," he began anew, "the leader of the conspiracy, those who control the fate of this direction and those who receive illicit money, those with the power to control final decisions on stem cell therapy represent leaders of their political party, led by Congressman Samuel Belfay."

The room erupted into commotion. Digital cameras worked over-time. Reporters jumped to their feet as they jockeyed for position. My gaze roamed the room. Jacob stood by my side, with a firm grip on my elbow. He leaned forward and shouted above the commotion. With calm returned, I stepped back to the microphone, and stared at the room that had erupted into pandemonium.

Through it all a face had caught my attention. I knew him and struggled to focus. It had disappeared in the madness that enveloped the room. Jacob stood by my side. He still held both hands up. No one sat.

Jacob turned to the rabid crowd and pointed to a female reporter. A microphone quickly found her.

"Can you identify your travel colleague? What of her condition?" I took a deep breath and plunged ahead.

"My colleague became more than a colleague to me. Doctor Isabelle Giovantti was educated here in the States. She started a medical practice in Italy. She fell in Australia from a gunshot as we departed a cruise ship from Malaysia. She honored me with her presence. I understand her recovery in Melbourne proceeds ahead of schedule and her transport here to the States occurs soon."

As I finished my answer the room erupted with more yells and shouts of questions. Jacob tried to deflect the barrage with little success. He stepped forward and pointed at a gentleman in the second row.

"Let me." Jacob turned and looked at me with little knowledge of the direction I would go in. He acquiesced and stepped away.

I stared over the heads of the crowd. My sight fell on the person I looked for. He leaned against the back wall. A man with a cold expression stood next to him and stared at me, as I lifted my arm and pointed straight at the man.

"Mr. Congressman, do you have a question for me?" I had found a picture of him in an earlier published evangelical newsletter. Congressman Samuel Belfay stared back. Members of the crowd turned and looked where I pointed. The Congressman pushed away from the wall and stepped forward to grab the microphone from the attendant's hand that approached him.

"You make a very strong accusation Mr. Armstrong. Do you recognize you have just committed slander?" The crowd fell silent.

My stare stayed leveled on the Congressman. "Mr. Congressman, how many appointees have you recommended for seats on the Food and Drug Administration board?"

No response came to the question.

"Mr. Belfay, can you tell me why you head the committee to oversee all stem cell research at domestic clinics, and why the National Security Agency became involved in a desperate attempt to follow and thwart the activities of a citizen from the country of Italy? Mr. Belfay, can you tell me how much in re-election contributions you have accepted from the pharmaceutical conglomerate led by Sheldon and Ashton pharmaceuticals? Though defined as public information, I would like to hear it from you, Mr. Belfay. Can you explain your reason for the appointment of a representative from the Coalition for Life as your campaign manager?"

The room fell silent. No one dared move. I hadn't finished. The Congressman stared back at me. Eric stood aligned to the Congressman, hatred clear on his face and body posture. The Congressman responded first.

"You sir, have just slandered yourself and I will sue you," he stated in a loud, yet unsteady voice.

"You, Mr. Congressman, dare to deny the rights of medical treatment to so many? You want to sue me for slander, sir?" I spat out. "I want to sue you, Mr. Congressman. I want to sue you for murder."

My hand grew sore from my grip on the podium. No one raised their hand to ask another question. Mr. Belfay's voice boomed in the room.

"You sir, do not believe. With power we can lead. I have the power to lead. Not you!"

No one dared budge, or utter a word. My heart pounded. I stared at the Congressman dressed in his immaculate suit and tie, and fashioned my response.

"No, Mr. Congressman. The power to lead cannot be bought and sold. It can only be earned, and you sir, have not earned it."

The room stayed still. No one dared move. Anger entered my voice. "Perhaps, Mr. Congressman, you could explain to these good people, how your party, who you represent as its chief fundraiser, collected some three hundred and fifty million dollars in the past 12 months for evangelical groups you have been photographed with for years and why those funds never made it to them. Perhaps Mr. Congressman, you could explain to these good people the transfer of funds to offshore accounts and the transfer back to the States for deposits made to your political action committees. Perhaps sir, you could explain why you have elected to keep me and thousands more handicapped at a time you knew that the technology existed so that I might walk again someday? Mr. Congressman, you should be ashamed of yourself. I know I am."

Jacob stepped forward and placed a hand on my wrist.

"Ladies and gentlemen, in a moment, Mr. Jacob Peters will begin to unravel a very slithery path of money movement to foreign banks, international financiers, back to re-election committees that have aided the Congressman and many party insiders while they and the pharmaceutical industry kept a rein on your lives. Mr. Peters will go into more detail of those charges in just a moment, though first, I want to complete my response. It came to me last night. I forgot to follow the money. I considered it before, even figured it would lead me to the responsible party, but then I forgot it until last night. I went back to follow the money, and when I did, it led me on a convoluted path. The path the Congressman and friends built to enrich themselves, their party, and their largest contributors. In my research and investigation of the powers that tried to beat me down, I followed hundreds of millions dollars from the largest pharmaceutical manufacturers in the world to the political base that wished to maintain their power.

That money bypassed organizations in the country it should have gone to, and instead found its way to political re-election campaigns, the Congressman's included. I have watched legislation that may improve the lives of so many fought with money intended for public benefit. It all represents a dismal break from the reality of how government for the people should be run. The government failed to run the government for the people. Today, our elected officials run our government for the biggest buck, and not the people. Mr. Congressman, you have some questions to answer."

The room went silent, filled with tension. I raised the mike once again.

"You and your colleagues, Mr. Congressman, betrayed our trust. An elected official, a so called protector of the people, betrayed the hope so many of us hold so close. You should be ashamed of yourself. You tried to destroy our belief in the integrity of the system. Our pride, our honor, our very belief in goodness, though to those of you that tried to take our thirst for a chance to return to as normal as possible, you failed. We still stand here and soon you won't."

With a flippant toss, of the microphone to Jacob, I headed to my seat. With the backs of chairs along the table, I began to stride back to my spot. No one dared breathe, or move. No one raised their hand to shout a question. My statement had been made. The words flowed freely. They flowed like water. They could not be turned back. To capture them again would be useless. For better or worse, the words were spilled.

Jacob broke the silence. He stepped forward and placed the microphone in its stand.

"Ladies and gentlemen," he began. "Through the research of Mr. Armstrong, Dr. Isabelle Giovantti and the diligent efforts of our staff here at the offices of the ACLU, we have prepared subpoenas of various persons, organizations and institutions that we will serve on Monday. A story of incredible deceit, denial and disrespect will come to the surface in the courtrooms in the days ahead. As enticement for those of you interested, please be advised." Reporter's pens went to their pads, cameras re-focused and silence filled the room. Jacob rattled away a list of organizations, companies and individuals that would be served subpoenas to testify before grand juries. They included the Congressman and staff, Malcolm Prentiss from the Coalition for Life and representatives of Sheldon and Ashton Pharmaceutical.

Jacob stopped. Several New York City peace officers entered the room. They began to walk towards Congressman Belfay. Heads rotated to the rear. The man now recognized as Congressman Belfay, one of the most outspoken critics of stem cell research in the House and an ardent supporter of the rights of evangelical fundamentalists, squirmed.

"And, oh by the way, civil lawsuits will be filed against five of the largest pharmaceutical manufacturers in the country for interference with the development of the technology. Our conference can now be closed."

As he stood next to the Congressman, Eric heard enough. With a scream of rage he pushed the female reporter who stood next to him with an anguished cry of fury. She flew into the man next to her with an abruptness that sent them both to the ground. Eric threw his long overcoat back and pulled a revolver from a holster he wore. He pulled the gun and pointed it at me while the crowd screamed and dived to the floor. Eric cocked the gun back his face twisted and set in a terrible grimace. I stared at the man, yet did not move. I had no desire to die, but refused to let go of the moment of announcement to the world. The wait had already been too long and hard.

The room exploded in gun shots. One, two, three shots echoed through the room. I stood at the head table, with a stare at the man that fell to the floor.

No bullets struck me. In fact the man who pointed the gun never had a chance to pull the trigger, as he crumpled to the floor, eyes sightless as he fell. He died as his forehead struck the ground. The Congressman fell to the floor. The staff around him and secret service agents buried him with bodies as the shots rang out. Police officers from NYPD converged on the scene, guns drawn. They began to pull at bodies that covered the Congressman, as did Secret Service agents assigned to his security detail. As they pulled the Congressman from the pile, he began to shout as peace officers still held their guns drawn.

"I didn't do it! It didn't do it!" the Congressman screamed. An officer grabbed a wrist and held it plastered against the window.

"No!" the Congressman bellowed. "He did it!" he screamed. The Congressman tried to point at the man on the floor. "The evangelicals forced us! They attacked in Malaysia! The pharmaceuticals on board ship! The evangelicals shot Dr. Giovantti. They burned the publishing house in Australia, they brought down the plane! They did it!"

Simon stood quietly as a member of the crowd in the room. He listened to the Congressman spill his guts. It disgusted him. They would never prove it. The government would take the blame. Malcolm Prentiss had nothing to worry about. He was in the clear.

I stood behind a chair at the front table. The scene had unfolded with cold brutality. I did not flinch, or hide. My tormentor had now been faced, my fears overcome. *Would my father be proud?* It didn't matter. I used the back of my chair to steady myself, swung to the seat and plopped down. My head hung low and my breath came with exertion. Jacob stood next to me.

"You did it James. They identified themselves. She's here for you."

To follow Jacob's gaze proved an emotional experience. She stepped away from a side door. My heart beat faster. In that moment of terror, I managed a smile. As I pushed myself up, I scanned the room. My bodyguards stood on opposite sides of the room. Both stood with handguns still drawn. Police officers bent near the crumpled body on the floor. People rose from the floor and headed for exits. The Congressman had been quickly ushered from the room.

My movements took me towards the stairs from the floor to the stage, and I made it to the end of the presenters table and leaned into the handrail. I extended one hand to Isabelle as she stood at the bottom of the stairs her left arm slung close to her chest. She reached for my hand and stepped to me. I wrapped an arm around her waist and pulled her to me. We kissed with passion.

"Nice to see you," I whispered.

"Nice presentation. You even got some fireworks. I'm jealous. No crowd I ever addressed became so excited with my presentation." She laughed that beautiful laugh of hers. I leaned back and smiled at her in warmth.

Epilogue

Quiet permeated the closed conference room. No notes of any kind would be taken or any digital tapes or videos made. Simon completed the summary report of the past 90 days, which included the wild press conference one week earlier.

"You can assure me, we cannot be tied to the events of last week?"

"No chance of that," he replied.

"Can the contract be reinitiated?" the questioner asked another man.

"Fund reallocations by the conglomerate move forward as we speak."

"What about a political friend?"

"Wheels continue to roll. Another candidate has been called upon and will be in place in 30 days."

"That news couldn't be better. We kick off a protest next week here in Atlanta. Do we have any other matters?"

"What of Armstrong and his doctor friend?"

"Let them be for now. By tomorrow, they will be old news."

The man at the head of the table buzzed to the outer office.

"Could you send the minister in please?"

The door opened for a man to enter.

"Please join hands and let us pray," he stated.

www.ingramcontent.com/pod-product-compliance
Lightning Source LLC
Chambersburg PA
CBHW051616010526
44107CB00042B/1490/J